String Bands in the
North Carolina Piedmont

String Bands in the North Carolina Piedmont

BOB CARLIN

with a foreword by Steve Terrill

McFarland & Company, Inc., Publishers

Jefferson, North Carolina, and London

LIBRARY OF CONGRESS CATALOGUING-IN-PUBLICATION DATA

Carlin, Bob.
String bands in the North Carolina
Piedmont / Bob Carlin
With a foreword by Steve Terrill.
p.   cm.
Includes bibliographical references and index.

ISBN 0-7864-1826-5 (softcover : 50# alkaline paper)

1. String band music — North Carolina — History.
2. String bands — North Carolina.   I. Title.
ML3520.C37   2004   784.7'09756'5 — dc22   2004012124

British Library cataloguing data are available

Cover photograph: The Hill Billy Pals;
background ©2004 PhotoDisc.

Manufactured in the United States of America

*McFarland & Company, Inc., Publishers
Box 611, Jefferson, North Carolina 28640
www.mcfarlandpub.com*

For Rachel and Benjamin,
who tolerate (barely) all this,
and for my brother, Richard Carlin,
master editor and best friend.

Contents

Foreword
by Steve Terrill

I remember one of my first contacts with Bob Carlin. It was somewhere around 1995. My string band had made it into the finals at Harper Van Hoy's Fiddler's Grove fiddlers' convention. Since we immediately preceded a special intermission performance by the John Hartford group, we both were practicing backstage. Hartford and his companions were all decked out in black and muted gray ties, vests, suspenders, pressed white shirts and bowler hats. They looked like 19th century riverboat men on their way to a captain's funeral. That is, all of them but one. Bob wore his usual attire: khaki pants, a Hawaiian shirt with at least eight colors, a straw fedora with a multicolored band, a pair of the classic saddle bred shoes from his extensive retro shoe collection and trademark hot pink prescription sunglasses. That evening, Bob floated like a fluorescent buoy above the Hartford band's pool of simulated authenticity.

It is fitting that Bob Carlin would be the person to tell the story of string music in North Carolina's Piedmont. In all he says and does, Carlin embraces an eclecticism that is found in most of American traditional music. The history of Piedmont string bands cannot be told in blacks and grays. Perhaps the multicolored Hawaiian shirt is a more adequate parallel.

As Bob makes clear several times in this book, the fiddle and banjo music of the South is closely associated with the mountains. In fact, the terms "mountain music" and "old-time music" are still used interchangeably. String band music from somewhere other than the North Carolina Mountains is considered less than authentic. As a result of this stigma, the musicians of the North Carolina Piedmont have not received the attention of their mountain counterparts. This book rights that wrong.

Bob has told me of his admiration for works that are long on research and short on analysis. Instead of pages of theories based on a few tidbits of information, Carlin has chosen to dig, dig, and dig and unearth a variety of source materials on his subject. Years of slogging through un-indexed newspapers, scattered files in county courthouses and hours of cassette tape interviews have resulted in a narrative rich in detail and deep in fact.

This book embraces the complex web of influences that created the varied string band music of the Piedmont, allowing readers to draw their own conclusions. If you are prepared to put aside your need for blacks and grays and ready to embrace the colorful diversity of the Piedmont's musical traditions, this book will prove a fun ride. Enjoy!

Preface

My interest in the history of old-time string band music grew out of an obses-
sion with playing and performing this music. Ray Alden provided my first extended
contact with traditional North Carolina culture, taking me along on a visit to the
state in 1975. Once I had entered into the world of the banjo and the fiddle, many
scholars provided the impetus for me to begin my own research. Two in particular
have served as my mentors. The late Guthrie T. Meade taught me about the use of
public documents to trace the movements of musical figures operating outside of
mainstream channels. Meade also showed me how a researcher is rewarded through
a tenaciousness and dedication to his subject. From Dr. Charles Wolfe, author of
many books focusing on the commercial side of early country music, came the inspiration to write and publish the results of my inquiry in a (somewhat) timely fashion.

Special thanks is due those who advised and aided the *Musical Change in the
Western Piedmont Project*: Davidson County Community College staff, including
Kitty Montgomery, Nancy Potts, Bette Newsome, John Thomas, Dee Best and Mike
Anthony; Dr. Glenn Hinson at the University of North Carolina-Chapel Hill; Pamela
Grundy; Mike Casey of the Southern Folklife Collection; Paul Brown, WFDD-FM;
Catherine Hoffman of the Davidson County Historical Museum; Judge Peter Hair-
ston; the Historical Society of Davidson County; and Jeanette Wilson and the geneal-
ogists at the Davidson County Public Library.

Wayne Martin, head of the Folklife section of the North Carolina Arts Council,
has generously supported my efforts by issuing contracts to underwrite fieldwork
and championing parts of this project to countless grant panels.

Larry Davis provided many leads and introductions through the Piedmont.
Davis, the son of banjoist Glenn Davis, seemed to intuitively understand the value
in preserving and publishing this information (fiddler Nolan Johnson is another
member of this select club). Larry seems to know the whereabouts of every musician between Statesville and Raleigh, and is either personally acquainted with or
related to them. Thanks to Larry for accompanying me on many of the journeys that
led to this book.

My webmaster Steve Terrill gave me the "heads up" on many useful bits and pieces of information located in obscure corners of the Internet. Steve's insightful comments were also helpful in providing an alternative view to some of this information.

Regional repositories I utilized included the local history departments of the High Point, Greensboro, Winston-Salem, Salisbury, Charlotte, Kannapolis, Statesville, Asheboro, Yadkinville, Siler City and Mocksville libraries. Much of my newspaper research was conducted at the Southern Historical Collection of the University of North Carolina-Chapel Hill.

Jim Scancarelli helped with information about the Union Grove Fiddlers' Convention, George Pegram and WBT-Charlotte. Robert Winans very graciously shared the results of his 1981 North Carolina fieldwork into banjo styles as a Smithsonian fellow with me. Frank Mare provided taped copies of Frank Wilson's known commercial recordings. *Bluegrass Unlimited*, the "bible" for bluegrass musicians, provided much information on bluegrass in North Carolina. Genealogical information was gathered from familysearch.org and ancestry.com.

Raw materials for the section on Ernest Thompson, previously published in *The Country Music Foundation Quarterly* ("Forgotten Pioneer," Vol. 18, No. 1.), was from surviving Thompson family descendants, and from Charles K. Wolfe, Nora Poisella, Matthew Neiburger, Frank Mare, Rick Kennedy, Kinney Rorrer, Dave Freeman, Mark Wingate, Mary Barnes, Barbara Natanson, Bill Mansfield, and David Sheppard. Special thanks to Kirk and Lisa Sutphin, and to Kevin Donleavy, for information collected for Kirk's article on Thompson.

The High Point Museum organized an exhibit to honor WMFR's first fifty years on the air. Both the staffs of the museum and WMFR were extremely helpful in sharing the information gathered for the exhibit.

Some of the information in this book was first published in the booklets of recordings I produced for Rounder Records, including *George Pegram, Marvin Gaster: Uncle Henry's Favorites, Joe Thompson: Family Tradition* and *The North Carolina Banjo Collection*. Other essays were printed in the music magazines *The Old Time Herald* ("Down in Old Hollow: Sutphin Family Music," Vol. 6, No. 4., May-July 1998), *Bluegrass Unlimited* ("L.W. Lambert: True Banjo Picker" and "Dwight Barker," Vol. 33, No. 9, March 1999 as well as "Mother Songs Are Not Dead" Vol. 31, No. 2., August 1996), and in notes for the recording *Nolan Johnson: Old Aunt Katie, Won't You Come Out Tonight?*

My choices for the chapter on bluegrass relied on my own prejudices and experiences. I apologize to all those that I have slighted by leaving them out of this story. It was my decision to focus on one musician and his compatriots to tell the story of all the Piedmont's post–World War II bluegrass players.

Extra special thanks goes to all those who agreed to be interviewed and who are cited within these pages. Ultimately, this is your story. Without your help, this project would not exist. All quotes and information are from interviews conducted during the research for this book and listed in the bibliography, except as noted.

Bob Carlin
Lexington, North Carolina
2004

Introduction

"It paid for the strings."
— Lester Porter

I have loved the music of North Carolina ever since I heard my first recording of banjo and fiddle music thirty-some odd years ago. Initially, I visited the mountain areas and played the tunes found there. As I learned more about the regional distinctions within the state, I began to study the history of Piedmont music. After moving there in 1989, I formed relationships with musical families that I will treasure for the rest of my life. I started to document the music of the Piedmont region, and examined other investigations into this area's banjo and fiddle styles. "Why hasn't more been done in this area," I wondered, "and why isn't a stronger case being made for Piedmont music as a distinct genre from that of the Blue Ridge Mountains?"

Identifying the Piedmont

North Carolina has been a popular locale for movie making, due in part to the variety of terrain within its borders. There are mountains in the west and north, and islands and beaches in the east. There are cities and stretches of country, farms and factories, woods and lakes, ancient structures and modern developments. The state's midsection is commonly known as the Piedmont region. The Piedmont contains the largest tract within North Carolina, enclosing the majority of its industry, cities and population, and is characterized by its red clay soil, rolling hills with pine forests, and rivers.

The Piedmont runs from Statesville in the west to Raleigh in the east, is bordered on the north by a line running from King through Reidsville and Roxboro, and is bordered on the south by Charlotte and Sanford. All or part of the counties of Forsyth, Guilford, Alamance, Orange, Durham, Wake, Lee, Chatham, Randolph, Davidson, Davie, Rowan, Cabarrus, Stanly, Iredell, Yadkin, Mecklenburg, Montgomery,

Unknown musicians who lived outside Oak Ridge, Guilford County, circa 1890-1910. Courtesy Jim White.

Moore, Harnett, Hoke, Stokes, Rockingham, Caswell and Person are included in this area.

Notions of Authenticity

August 30, 1918, should have been a red-letter day for the traditional music of North Carolina's Piedmont. On that date, noted English folklorist Cecil Sharp and his assistant Maud Karpeles arrived in the newly amalgamated western Piedmont city of Winston-Salem. For two years previously, the pair had been traveling the mountain south, collecting over 1,500 ballads in the process. However, upon reaching Winston-Salem, all Sharp could think of was leaving the Piedmont. As he wrote in his diary:

> We smelt Winston-Salem about 8 miles away — tobacco and molasses. I had an attack of asthma on getting off the train…. It is clear we shall not have much rest here. Winston-Salem is a dull, ugly sort of place with a square in the middle of which stands the Town Hall, quite the ugliest building I have ever seen ["Cecil Sharp in America"].

Folklorists of Sharp's time (and probably of all times) had a strong notion of musical "purity." Looking back on that trip from fifty years later, Karpeles explained:

Olin Berrier outside of his backyard automobile repair shop in Welcome, Davidson County. Instruments are (left to right) tenor banjo, mandolin, plectrum banjo, and two guitars with mandolin in front, fiddle, five-string banjo, partially hidden banjo and string bass. Note that Berrier is holding a violin and a screwdriver instead of a violin bow, reflecting the title of a contemporary newspaper story about him, "He Mixes Music With Motors." June 1958. Courtesy Jeanne Beck.

> Owing to their isolation, the mountain people had been preserved from commercialized music and the songs they had inherited from their forefathers had been evolved according to the taste of the singers themselves without any extraneous influences ["Cecil Sharp in America;" this section on Sharp and Karpeles is based on the unpublished writings of Steve Terrill].

These notions of authenticity, and the Piedmont's lack of it, have continued to plague its culture into the present times. Stereotypical definitions are still used in labeling southern string band music as "mountain" or "Appalachian."

Much exploration has been done into the music of the North Carolina Mountains. The verification of fiddle and banjo styles within upland communities is due to a combination of variables. These include outside recognition for this music, a local historical perspective that acknowledges folk music traditions, and the inclusion of old time music and dance in economic plans by government agencies encouraging tourism within the region. This combination of factors has gone far in promoting the documentation and publication of writings and recordings preserving and promoting highland traditions.

However, string band music was just as abundant in the Piedmont area as in the northern or western mountains of the state, albeit with some different influences and stylistic conventions. Outside of haphazard fieldwork, primarily by affiliates of the University of North Carolina Folklore Program, and a few narrowly focused studies on aspects of flatland culture, no scholar or project has thoroughly documented the whole Piedmont region. And no one book completely traces the development of Piedmont string music vis-à-vis the history and culture of the area. In this book, my goal is to document and analyze the musical changes in string band music within the traditional communities of Piedmont North Carolina.

Possibly the reason that people underappreciate Piedmont music is because players were never afraid to incorporate outside musical compositions and styles into the string music of the region. Piedmont musicians embraced minstrelsy throughout its history and the popular classic banjo method of the late nineteenth and early twentieth century. The same desire to incorporate new sounds into the old has also encouraged musicians to learn more modern music. Larry Davis, the son of banjoist Glenn Davis, started out playing with his father, then played in modern country bands, and eventually, after formal musical study, played in area jazz groups. Howard Hudson, a finger style banjoist, learned the piano by ear and afterwards joined a big band.

Another reason for the undervaluation of Piedmont music has been the rejection of the traditional culture by the region's residents. Standing in a food line at the Lexington Barbecue Festival, I struck up a conversation with an older woman, who told me, "I grew up cooking on a woodstove and living the old time way. And I wouldn't trade it for anything, but I don't want to go back. I like my central heat and air, and cooking on a modern stove." Old times are equated with hard times; old music was left behind with the old ways.

The Piedmont is also the site for the largest and most populated of North Carolina's cities, which are also home to its industries. Folklorists such as Sharp and Karpeles considered such factories as antithetical to authenticity. The Piedmont was never quite rural (or genuine) enough for folklorists to consider the music of the region valid and so, like Cecil Sharp, they fled to the mountains as quickly as possible.

Music in the Barbecue State

Music is the universal language of North Carolina's culture. Within the Piedmont region, musicians were commonplace and omnipotent as barbecue in all communities. Mildred Council, known nationally for her Dip's restaurant in Chapel Hill and for her *Mama Dip's Kitchen* cookbook, grew up in an African American community of the Eastern Piedmont. Will Johnson, one of the founders of Lexington-style barbecue in the Western Piedmont, was from an Anglo-American community located in southern Davidson County. Both grew up with fathers who were string musicians: Council's father made and played banjos; Mr. Johnson's father played the fiddle and was a banjoist himself.

The fiddle and banjo styles of the Piedmont have their roots in the melodies of

Europe and the rhythms of Africa. Europeans brought the violin and their dance tunes to North Carolina's Piedmont and Africans brought the ancestors of the American banjo, along with its playing style and rhythmic patterns. In the nineteenth century, Anglo and African styles mixed with the songs of the American popular stage to form a uniquely American blend of these traditions. Called minstrelsy, it was probably the biggest and first truly American musical phenomena, and it had a great effect on Southern folk music. The parlor songs of the late nineteenth century were the next ingredient to be added, and seasoned with the banjo style known nationally as "classic" or "guitar" style. Piedmont banjoists of the new generation switched at the turn of the twentieth century from the older African-derived down-picking style to the newer up-picking of the city banjoists.

Although the guitar had been in the Piedmont since the 1850s, it didn't enter the picture as a part of the string bands until early in the twentieth century. With the guitar's addition, the archetypal old time North Carolina Piedmont sound was completed: long bow fiddling combined with cascading banjo runs and strong guitar bass lines used in support of popular songs and dance tunes. However, as a broader national country music style was formed, it too was emulated at the local level and combined in the Piedmont with the older instruments and repertoire. Amplifiers and steel guitars made playing in larger venues possible; microphones and radio encouraged a softer vocal sound. Interestingly enough, audiences and musicians in the state that produced Earl Scruggs, who gave bluegrass music its distinctive banjo sound, initially preferred the smoother country of a Lefty Frizzell to Scruggs' and Bill Monroe's hyper string band stylings.

This music was an integral part of Piedmont North Carolina culture. When curing tobacco with wood, the days of tedium tending the fire was passed with a fiddle or banjo in hand. Both Preston Fulp and Joe Thompson, a couple of African Americans, remember being able to hear from far away the music drifting from one tobacco barn or another. Musical instruments were present at the conclusion of other agricultural endeavors. Whether it was a corn shucking, a barn raising, or the like, a house dance accompanied by live music ended the day. Public schools as well enjoyed the sounds of string bands. The old unconsolidated country schools used string music as a part of commencement exercises, while the newer and larger ones held fiddlers' contests as fundraisers. For the life of the Piedmont, private parties and public occasions all held the prospect of string band music. But not all musicians were associated with the agrarian life. Area string bands drew their members from all professions. There were fiddling politicians, postal workers, and barbers, banjoists who ran stores and restaurants, and guitarists who worked in the furniture factories and mills.

Back when fiddlers and banjoists were common around Piedmont North Carolina, there was no country music industry. And while a few local virtuosos dominated community events, most musicians were not much more than adequate. Often, the best players somehow found time to continue music even after familial obligations were added into their already busy lives. However, most people set instruments aside when raising children, for the demands were just too great. Later, when one could earn a meager living from string music, many serious pickers would again give up the pursuit of a career when married with children.

Colin Escott, a well-known writer on country music, comments in his biography of Hank Williams how poorly documented country music was by the contemporary media, resulting in the loss of much valuable information:

> Hillbilly music was a cottage industry in the late '40s, only recently elevated from folk music played in the small community centers of the rural South. As such, the day-to-day routine of its performers scarcely warranted a mention anywhere. Newspapers, even in southern towns, tended to concentrate on the goings-on among society's grandees.... Trade paper coverage was a random affair edited out of New York or Chicago, often with more than a touch of condescension. Radio stations programmed country music in the early morning hours before the network feeds were picked up [xi].

Because information about Piedmont music was ignored, much has been lost for researchers and historians today.

This is a story that needs telling. This narrative is based on words and images generated by the participants themselves, collected over fifteen years. Sadly, many of the tellers have since passed away. Hopefully, the compelling nature of their tales will once again bring them alive for generations to come.

ONE

True Believers

"[The inheritor] is to have no fiddling and dancing and card playing nor parties, if he does, he forfeits all his claims on the lands."

— December 13, 1908: *Mt Airy News*

The first European arrivals in the New World landed in the 1600s and early 1700s on the eastern shore of what is now the United States. After that period of initial settlement, and as the lands closest to the ocean were spoken for, immigrants began to drift inland, looking for new acreage and opportunities. In such a manner, Scottish settlers moved up the Cape Fear River valley to homestead in the sand hills of southeastern Piedmont North Carolina. The original English and Scottish settlers of the eastern Piedmont were joined between the 1740s and the 1760s by pioneers from Pennsylvania, New York, and New Jersey. These groups came down the Shenandoah Valley into the western Piedmont, as did the so-called "Pennsylvania Dutch" Germans. Germans, Scotch-Irish (in 1737), and English were the first to settle the western part of the Piedmont, displacing the native dwellers.

Upon arriving in their new home, émigrés would gravitate toward those sharing their ethnic or religious persuasion. The Scotch-Irish Jerseyites banded together in the Granville District of the Yadkin River Valley; and English, Irish, and Germans set up housekeeping in and around the Abbotts Creek area of the Western Piedmont. Moravians settled in the extreme northern part of Davidson County and, most notably, founded the Salem community in what is now Forsyth County. English Quaker meetings dotted the landscape in a band across the midsection of the state, stretching from Davie County north to Guilford College and then zigzagging east through parts of Randolph and Chatham Counties. There may have been a variety of languages and customs practiced within each of these distinct communities, but there was one thing upon which they all agreed: Each member of the "true believers" (those sects with strong religious convictions) frowned upon fiddling and dancing.

11

Fiddler John Calvin Bray (1859–1929) with an unknown pipe-smoking friend, in Cedar Falls, Randolph County, circa 1885. Courtesy John Bray.

In an 1821 depiction of a dance in Randolph County, Brantley York tells of the reinstallation of a community's spiritual beliefs:

> The Athenians in the days of St. Paul were not perhaps more fully devoted to the worship of idols, than were the young people of this neighborhood to the worship of the god of pleasure; for they held weekly two dance frolics on Wednesday and Saturday nights,... But a change came, and the cause of that change was not a little remarkable. Some minister preached on Sunday previous to the Wednesday night dance, and Miss Ester Morgan who was an expert in dancing was convicted....

The Wednesday night dance came on, when several young men called at Mr. Morgan's to gallant the girls to the frolic. Miss Ester however manifested an unwillingness to go; but being importuned and pressed, she consented and went.

The party having assembled, and ready to commence, the young men began to select their partners, but Miss Ester refused to dance with any. This doubtless was surprising to all; but when they commenced their exercise and the music began, she dropped upon her knees and began praying aloud. This was to the party as a clap of thunder in a clear sky, and perhaps if an earthquake had shaken the house, the alarm would not have been greater, for a greater part of them left the house and fled as for life. The fiddler fled for home and some two or three with him, and one that was with him made the following statement to me: "We went over fences and through corn fields, taking the nearest way for home, and as I heard the blades of corn cracking behind me, I felt certain that the Devil was right after me, and on reaching the door of the house we didn't waited [sic] for any one to open, but broke down the door and jumped into bed and covered up head and ears without pulling shoes, hat, coat, or a rag [of] clothes off, and were almost afraid to breathe, lest the Devil should hear us in our concealment." Only a few had courage enough to stand their ground. These sent for the young lady's father and some other members of the church and so the dance frolic was turned into a prayer-meeting, and just before day the young lady was converted. So dance frolics ended and prayer-meetings began. A revival of religion spread all over that community, and nearly all the young people of both sexes professed religion and joined the church [19, 20].

However, by the end of the nineteenth century, religious fervor had diminished enough for there to be no effect by prayer on a dance:

On Thursday night, Christmas eve, the young gentlemen of Lexington gave a social party in Finch's Hall, complimentary to the young ladies of the town. A large number of the young people attended it.... The managers had secured music for the occasion, and dancing was permitted. Those who chose to trip the light fantastic did so, while others did not, their action being entirely of their own volition.

Scotch Rambles were danced, and in the midst of the first set the participants were astounded to see Rev. C. W. Maxwell, pastor of the Presbyterian church here, walk into their midst. Their astonishment and amazement increased when the minister ordered the music stopped, and asked that the dancing quit. He then asked those present to listen to him for a few minutes, when he spoke to them for half an hour, and was very strong in his condemnation of the dance. He then prayed for ten minutes, after which he requested all who were Christians to leave the hall at once; but those who were present before his coming, remained, and the balance of the evening was spent as it first began [*Dispatch*, January 8, 1892: 3].

William Claude Winslow (April 26, 1877–December 9, 1937) was the son of practicing Quakers William C. Winslow (January 3, 1846–January 22, 1933) and Sarah E. Wilson (December 11, 1834–March 13, 1924). The elder William's family had come to North Carolina from Pennsylvania at the end of the eighteenth century. Claude Winslow's mother had been born in Indiana, but was a resident of Randolph County by the time of her marriage in 1876. When he was about twenty years old, as Claude's son Worth Winslow relates, William Claude's father sent him to Philadelphia for college, "to become a Quaker preacher." (I assume this meant to receive serious religious training as, traditionally, there are no preachers within the Quaker faith.) As Worth tells it:

He didn't like the preaching. He come back as a musician. He learned how to play a violin rather than preach.

He boarded with a family, and that fellow liked him and he bought him a fiddle and he taught him how to play the fiddle and then they give him the fiddle. And he brought it back when he come back and rather than bring it into the house, he left it at a neighbor's because he knew his daddy wouldn't like it.... The way I understood it, that he didn't mind hearing religious songs, but the kind that [wasn't] supposed to be played, he didn't like it.

Well, he didn't keep it over — maybe a year. But he'd go up there and play it. He just kept talking to his daddy about letting him bring it home. And finally, he let him bring it home. So, he just played like he didn't even know how to play, you know — he said he was learning. And then one day there, he just struck off on a pretty piece. And you know how the Quakers talks, thee and ... [his father] said, "Thee's picked up that music mighty fast!"

With the coming of Claude Winslow's generation, the attitudes of the Quakers, as well of those of other religious groups, began to change. By the 1920s, when William Lewis Allen (born May 10, 1908) was growing up as a part of a Quaker family in an area of Alamance County brimming with Friends, musicians were common. Allen's grandfather had been part of the Quaker migration from Pennsylvania to North Carolina. Bill's father, George Washington Allen (October 30, 1858–December 24, 1924), was born in Snow Camp. "Them Quakers," commented Allen, "all liked string music" even though "they wouldn't have an organ in a church or a piano." Rather than looking down upon music and dance, the conflict between religion and entertainment had been settled. As Kermit Brady stated to me about his area of Randolph County, "It was understood that there was a time and place for everything."

This didn't prohibit the occasional yielding of musicians to the demands of religion and vice versa. A 1908 fiddling event in Wadesboro had to be postponed when residents chose to attend an event at the Baptist church instead. (*Ansonian*, February 11, 1908: 3 and February 25, 1908: 2)

The Introduction of the Fiddle and the Banjo

Even though many residents were restricted in their actions by religious beliefs (or the disapproval of others holding those beliefs), fiddling and dancing were practiced in the Piedmont from the time of the earliest settlements. Researcher Mac Whatley has found mentions of fiddles and violins in estate inventories and other documents in Randolph County dating to the period of 1836–1848. This points to the existence of stringed instruments in the area during the late eighteenth century. Another early but unfortunately undated reference is to a fiddling stage driver "who was killed when his fresh team of horses ran away with the stagecoach and threw him from the drivers seat.... The driver was a good fiddler in demand at social functions and some say he can still be heard playing his fiddle near the old persimmon tree where he was killed when thrown from the coach" [Neese, 11].

Calvin Henderson Wiley wrote of Alamance County, describing life around the Revolutionary War. He witnessed multiple instances of fiddling (although Wiley did not note the race or ethnicity of the musicians), which caused him to observe, "I found they were a nation of fiddlers, and every village and hamlet was kept awake by an everlasting scraping of cat gut" (Wiley 57–60).

Other eighteenth and nineteenth century documentation — newspapers, travel accounts, histories–are lacking in mentions of string band music. We only have anecdotal evidence for the existence of Anglo-American fiddlers during the period before the Civil War, and, even then, only four European Americans who could have possibly been playing have been identified (see Chapter Two for references to African American fiddlers during this time). And none of this group was born before 1835.

The string band music of the Piedmont reflects the interaction between settler and slave groups in the inclusion of musical style and instruments from each group. The Germans and Scotch-Irish contributed a fiddle tradition and the melodies from songs and instrumental pieces. The African Americans brought their highly developed sense of rhythm to the table, along with the banjo (see Chapter Two). Although this instrument was new to Anglo-Americans, they quickly adopted and adapted the banjo for use in their string band music.

Early Banjoists

The earliest known Anglo-American banjoist in the Piedmont of North Carolina was Manly Reece. The son of George (possibly Washington) and Jane Moffit Reece, Adam Manly Reece was born in 1830. Around 1849, utilizing blacksmithing skills learned from his father, Manly built a banjo, which survives to this day. This instrument definitely exhibits knowledge of manufactured banjos from the period. Where and when he saw other banjos is unknown.

Reece's biographer, Andy Cahan, feels that Manly was playing while still residing in Piedmont North Carolina, basing his opinion upon a statement by Manly's sister Julia. If so, Manly either was taught by one of the area's few banjoists of color (as the district's Quakers did not hold slaves), a local player with African American contacts, or by a traveling black face (white) minstrel. Unfortunately, the best we can do is speculate about Reece's musical influences. Manly left behind no solid evidence as to how and from whom he learned to play.

Contrary to the great myth of the South's cultural isolation, touring entertainers were crisscrossing the region as early as the second quarter of the nineteenth century. Minstrel banjoists— white musicians wearing burnt cork makeup in order to portray black characters on stage — began performing in North Carolina as early as 1841, when Dan Emmett, later known as the author of "Dixie," appeared with the Cincinnati Circus in Raleigh and Fayetteville (*Raleigh Register and NC Gazette*, August 20, August 24, August 27 and August 31, 1841: 1, 3; *Fayetteville Observer*, August 25, 1841: 3 and September 1, 1841: 4; Thayer, 290). Banjoist Joel Walker Sweeney, one of the only Southerners to appear in early minstrelsy, came to the Piedmont a number of times during the 1840s and 1850s (*Raleigh Register*, November 1, 1848: 3; *Carolina Watchman*, November 11, 1849: 3 and April 21, 1857: 3; *Western Democrat/NC Whig*, April 12, 1857: 3).

The Civil War, in which Manly Reece fought and lost his life, had an injurious

Banjoist Manly Reece, originally from Randolph County, holding the instrument he made. Location unknown, circa 1860. Courtesy Andy Cahan.

effect on the South as a whole, disrupting and rerouting the cultural life of the region. In North Carolina, 40,000 soldiers were killed fighting for the state. Surprisingly, touring shows continued almost unabated, often bringing banjoists along with them as a part of the entertainment. The postwar version of the minstrel show, as well as the vaudeville and stage shows that sprang from minstrel roots, replaced the older, African derived "stroke" method of banjo playing. Instead, the newer "guitar" style for banjo was featured, with performers only utilizing the older method when portraying old-time blacks. This "up-picking" method of playing the instrument was adopted, along with the rest of the country, by Piedmont banjoists by the end of the nineteenth century.

Troupes presenting the banjo to Piedmont audiences included the Union Minstrels, who appeared in Greensboro around 1870, aided by Messrs. Garrison and Courtney in a "banjo duett." Ironically, this show also explicitly advertised that there was to be "No Admittance of Negroes," the very Americans who helped introduce the banjo into Southern life (Broadsides). Within the next fifteen years, Statesville saw at least two minstrel shows, including Ish Anderson's New York Minstrels. Charles Brown, appearing at Stockton Hall as a part of Anderson's show, played a "Banjo

Solo" and participated with Lou B. Davenport in the skit "Taking Banjo Lessons" (Broadsides).

Paradoxically, probably the best-known Southern banjoist of the late nineteenth century used the older down-picking style he had learned from slaves. Monologist Polk Miller, who accompanied his stories about "the characteristics of the old plantation negro [*sic*]" with the banjo, toured the Old North State many times during the last decade of the nineteenth and the first two decades of the twentieth centuries (Polk Miller scrapbook, 88–89; *Winston Salem Journal*, May 10, 1904: 6 and May 12, 1904: 4; *Stanly Enterprizes*, February 28, 1907: 3 and March 7, 1907: 3; *Sanford Express*, March 6, 1908: 5; *Asheboro Courier*, February 17, 1910: 5).

After the turn of the twentieth century, more and more banjoists were abandoning black face and leaving the confines of the minstrel show. In the mountains, the old down stroke style (referred to as "frailing," "knocking," "rapping," or "clawhammer") continued into the first half of the twentieth century, often coexisting beside the newer guitar-derived style. Possibly this is why clawhammer became associated in the national mind with old-style country music. In the Piedmont, the old banjo style was replaced by finger picking, which quickly and thoroughly moved into string band music in the late 1800s. Although there were some pockets of frailers, most young banjoists wanted to be associated with the newer method of playing. Not until the picking of Earl Scruggs, which used his own spin on city-bred banjo, began to be heard over the Grand Ole Opry at the end of 1945, did a banjo method again so totally take over with such speed and completeness.

However, the techniques behind this picking approach, which originated in urban areas far away from most musicians' normal sphere of travel, was not always readily available to the Piedmont musician. Oral sources such as records and radio broadcasts, and brushes with traveling performers gave only a partial knowledge of the secrets to this new way of playing. So, youngsters with banjos had to rely on other sources for knowledge and inspiration. Some musicians, like Glenn Davis and Price Saunders, turned to local guitarists for the basics of finger picking, transferring the related guitar playing style to the banjo. Many others practiced a version of telephone, using bits and pieces from others who had assembled their own version of playing. A lucky few, like Kelly Sears, took lessons from an accomplished Piedmont musician. Piedmont players turned this disadvantage into an attribute. The lack of access to information about this new instrumental method was the reason behind the many wonderful variations on the three-finger banjo picking style found throughout the South.

Others had to leave the region entirely to learn about the banjo, including Hubert Daniel Lohr (April 30, 1903–November 7, 1975). Hubert's son Jack tells the story of how his father learned to play:

> It's kind of funny. None of [Hubert's] parents played and none of his brothers, and the way he got started, when they were young, they had a uncle that lived in Youngstown, Ohio, his father's brother David Lohr. And Charlie, daddy's brother, and daddy, they went up there [about 1920]. And Charlie just loved the banjo, and I think he bought one. He was left-handed and he couldn't do a thing in the world. And Daddy came along and just picked it up and went right on with it, you know.

> And he took lessons from William Baxter. Now, I don't know where William Baxter is from, [but] he must have been a good banjo player. But daddy could play by sheet music — he could put a music stand up here and sit there and play that thing just like a piano player can read sheet music. And I don't think there's any around [here] that ever could do it.

Hubert learned the three-finger, up-picking style from Baxter using a thumb pick and two finger picks. William Baxter also taught Lohr to read music, which resulted in Hubert's brothers nicknaming him "Doc," short for "Doctor of Music." Lohr thought so much of Baxter that he named one of his sons William Baxter. This naming practice continued with Hubert's youngest son, Garland Berrier Lohr (born 1945), who was named for Hubert's friend, Olin Berrier.

Tar Heel Hawaiians

As with the outside influences on banjo styles, the Piedmont was susceptible to another national craze for Hawaiian music. Touring bands such as Vierra's Hawaiians played Lexington's Lyric Theater, and appeared at a Lyceum course meant to introduce this exotic music to Davidson County (*Dispatch*, February 19, 1919: 5). Combined with the influence of phonograph records and sheet music, Hawaiian music soon captivated the hearts and minds of many North Carolina guitarists. From Bynum in the East, where Frank Durham led a band, to the Lamb brothers Paul and Coy outside of Randleman, to the trio of Stamper, Dunnagan, and Dunnagan who entertained at local picnics in the Western Piedmont, Tar Heel Hawaiians sprang up everywhere.

If one lived in the High Point area, lessons could be had in person from William Alonzo Payne (September 22, 1889–March 6, 1956). Payne was born in Georgia, and had come to North Carolina from Washington, D.C., in 1925. A barber by day, William Payne taught music above his shop at night (High Point City Directories).

Gurney Calvon Peace (born July 8, 1909) was one of Payne's star pupils. The son of Earl Lee Peace (June 9, 1878–August 28, 1965) and Nannie Cornelia Spencer Peace (September 9, 1876–December 30, 1967), Gurney's father had played a bit on the banjo before the birth of his last child. But, by the time Gurney had come along, Earl Peace had been injured and could not work. The family didn't have the resources to send Gurney to music school as he desired. Instead, Payne was enlisted to give the boy weekly instruction, in no small part because the barber was willing to take Nannie's homemade butter in trade! Gurney Peace gained further skills by playing with William Payne at local fiddlers' conventions, as well as over the radio on WBIG-Greensboro. Payne helped the younger man obtain a Gibson instrument, an upgrade from the Stella guitar Peace had been using. "Owning a Gibson was like getting a Rolls-Royce back then," says Gurney, using a simile that reflected his later career as an auto mechanic.

Peace remembers Hawaiian music becoming really popular around the High Point area during the late 1920s. By 1930, he had assembled a group to play at some

Carl Weevil (standing) and Lawrence Hill (seated), two "Hawaiians from High Point," show off their proficiency with brand new National brand instruments. These metal-bodied guitars were made with both a standard guitar neck for noting with the left hand (like Weevil's instrument) and a square neck with raised action for noting with a metal bar in the slide "Hawaiian" style. National utilized an acoustic speaker mounted in the body to produce the volume necessary in the days before sophisticated sound systems. Guitars made by National cost four times the amount of a decent Gibson brand guitar, and would have taken a big bite out of the salary earned by a mill or factory worker during that time. Circa 1930. Courtesy Leroy Hill.

of the area's tonier locales, such as the Colonial Country Club. Variously called the Three Southern Accents, Ginger Snaps, Southern Jacks, Carolina Melody Boys, and Carolina Tarheels, Peace's band included the Lohr Brothers, who had worked with Gurney playing square dances, as well as their sister Eleanor Lohr, Gib Young on piano, and Lawrence Odell Hill (September 20, 1913–November 22, 1972) on steel guitar (Lawrence Hill scrapbook).

Like Peace, Hill had come up playing at fiddlers' conventions, as well as for upscale movie theaters such as the Paramount and Broadhurst on North Main Street in High Point (at a salary of $15 for the whole band!). Lawrence's National brand Hawaiian guitar cost more than $100 and was possibly purchased through a jewelry store in High Point. His father, Hal I. Hill (December 9, 1889–March 13, 1949), bought the guitar on time, making payments from his salary as a woodcarver at various furniture companies. Hal was born in Randolph County, and played the Hawaiian guitar as well. In addition to Gurney Peace and his compatriots, Lawrence Hill assembled groups featuring his first cousin Dillard E. Webb, a weaver by trade, textile worker Rome E. Sale, Jr. (September 3, 1913–February 15, 1936), a guitar student of Hill's, and Robert Carlton Weavil (August 5, 1910–January 1, 1987) born in the Davidson County community of Wallburg. Wilma Virginia Hayworth (July 10, 1915–July 19, 1972), who by 1933 was married to Lawrence, danced the hula at the band's performances (High Point City Directories).

Lawrence Hill went professional in the mid–1930s, unlike the majority of musicians I interviewed who played this variety of string music, and worked at nightclubs up and down the east coast. This was in sharp contrast to his friend Gurney Peace, who never left the area, never made his living exclusively from performing, and made a point never to work where alcohol was being served.

String Music Down on the Farm

In spite of all the influence from outside music and groups, the most popular ensembles for grass roots community events continued to be the fiddle and banjo led string bands. These groups had such popularity and longevity due in part to the flexibility of the form. String bands musicians were open to new compositions and playing methods, molding and shaping outside influences to fit the limitations of their instrumentation. One is tempted to credit Piedmont players with a more open-minded attitude than their counterparts elsewhere. However, it is hard to make any particular assessment as all rural string musicians drew from outside sources.

When it came to entertainment, not all Piedmont dwellers had a choice in the matter. Before the existence of television and widespread daily use of phonographs and radios, and with theater attendance only a special occasion, people had to make their own fun. Many smaller settlements and organizations could not afford to hire an outside group to entertain at events, or, at least, could not manage to support the needs of a professional band.

Area newspapers reported that string bands were present for a variety of local functions from 1885 on up to World War II. Throughout the Piedmont, at churches, picnics, parades, schools, reunions, holiday celebrations, birthday parties and in homes, at meetings of the Farmers' Union, the Tobacco Growers' Co-operative and the P.O.S.A. (Patriotic Order Sons of America, a fraternal insurance organization), aggregations named for locales like Longford, New Hope, Cool Springs, Muddy Creek, North Winston, King, Lexington, Mooresville, and Shiloh provided music to make the day gladder and the occasion seem more important. Golf courses featured string music at their clubhouses and local grocery chains sponsored their own bands. String bands even played over the telephone when that device was first introduced.

Out in the country, before the noise of motor vehicles, high tension wires, tractors, and the like had penetrated the region, sound would carry from far away. This was especially so at night, when one could sit out in the yard and listen to the baying of foxhounds and the playing of stringed instruments. Joe Thompson, an African American musician who grew up on the Orange and Alamance County line, remembers being able to hear music made from a distance of one or two miles: "Johnny Wade ... used to sit by the tobacco barn every night. He'd be curing tobacco and sit out there and you could hear him [playing the banjo] clean across the country" (Conway, *African Banjo Echoes*, 17). Charles Cheek, from Randolph County, spoke of being able to hear his neighbors George and Harvey Moore playing banjo on their porch a half-mile away.

There were two occasions where music served a central function for the agrarian culture: tobacco curings and corn shuckings. The Lexington *Dispatch* mentions the existence of corn shuckings and tobacco curings as early as 1891 (October 22, 1891: 3), although they were a part of local life at least by the post-bellum period. The tobacco harvest came first, as remembered by Piedmont residents. Tobacco began to replace cotton as the cash crop for the region in the 1850s. Sometime in February or early March, wood "chopping time" signaled the end of winter.

Then the tobacco was "cured" or dried using a wood fire that needed three days or more of attention. This description of tobacco curing in the late 1920s and early 1930s from Davidson County comes from a number of residents: Leonard Berrier and Jeanne Beck, the children of Olin Berrier, described curings at brothers John and Arthur Tussey's, musical cousins to Olin who lived in the Arnold area; Ray Walker talked of curings in the Whitehart community of Davidson County:

> [The tobacco curing] was from the last of July to in September. It takes about three days to cure a barn of tobacco, four, five or six days. You have to yellow it and then you cure it, and then if you're curing it with wood, you have to stay there and fire it all the time and maintain a certain temperature within that barn. And they'd always have a little shanty sitting out in front of it, and it'd be full of straw. And, of course, they would sleep in those shanties. Someone had to sit up with them all night so they wouldn't catch fire. We would go to those places and play music so it wouldn't get so boring. You know, we would sit out in a little circle outside, around the barn and the women would make chicken stew in a big old pot. And the women would make pies and we would have pumpkin pie and all these things, and we would play music and then eat. And play some more music. Most of the time they was curing the last barn when they had the big frolics. Families would get together and neighbors. Pitch horseshoe, play music. Most of the time it would be on the weekend ... on Saturday night or Friday night, something like that.

Music was a good way to pass the time, and also served as an accompaniment for dancing as a reward when the curing was finished. Tobacco curing, with its long lapses between chores, was also a good time to pass along musical skills from one generation to the next. Leonard Berrier recalls:

> I would play [mandolin] with 'em and I was a kid and I would just get so sleepy and [my father]'d say, "All right. Lay it down, get in and go to sleep." And I'd crawl up in the shanty and sleep until it was ready to go home. We'd play [until] midnight, sometimes after midnight. I know that it was a trying time for kids, you know, to be up that late. Of course, you know, kids get sleepy at eight, nine o'clock at night, and I did, too. But I would play or attempt to.

As with any occasion, humorous stories were remembered about the music making. Charlie Buchner (born circa 1900), a fiddler who lived between Brown's Store and Bennett south of Siler City, came to play at a tobacco barn, but forgot to bring his bow. When he arrived, Buchner whittled on a tobacco stick with a piece of glass to fashion a crude violin bow, rosined it, and proceeded to play for those gathered around the barn.

In some parts of the Piedmont, one would go each night of the week to a different home until all the neighbors' corn was shucked. At dusk, all hands would start shucking until sometimes as late as 10 P.M. or midnight. Only then, after all the corn was shucked, would there be food and music. One year, Worth Winslow remembers attending forty shuckings at neighborhood farms! One early account comes from a former slave, who recalled that

> Following tobacco curing was the time for gathering and shucking the corn for storage. Beginning with the first Saturday in September, corn shuckings ran until Christmas. At a corn shucking during the Civil War, on Dr. Fab Haywood's plantation in Wake County, Tanner Spikes recalled, "Dey kisses when dey fin' a red year 'an atter dat dey pops some popcorn an' dey dances ter de music of de banjo which Uncle Jed am a-playin'; Dey dances all night de best I can 'member'" [Federal Writers Project, *Slave Narratives*, 309–310].

Micki Berrier Smith, born in 1923, recollects the shuckings of her childhood:

> When we had corn shuckings in the fall, all the tables were set up you see, and you had all sorts of pies and cakes, and maybe a hot dog occasionally. They would invite all these people to come, and everybody would sit and shuck corn. If you found a red ear, that was good luck. After they got through eating the pies, and the corn was all shucked and they had their refreshments, so to speak, why then my dad would have the instruments in the back of the car.

As Smith remembers, the music would only start after all the work was concluded. Her sister, Jeanne, concurs, adding a description of the dancing that accompanied the music: "You know, you had a fiddler and a banjo picker and after you had finished [shucking corn] then you'd have a little square dance in the living room and places like that. They'd move all the furniture back and it was something you don't forget like that."

Corn shucking time signaled the launch of the harvest celebration terminating with Christmas. As farm chores wound down, residents could relax and observe the end of their daily labors. Corn shuckings ended sometime in the late 1930s or early 1940s when farming methods changed.

At the end of the yearly growing cycle, families would often make a trip to purchase new clothes, shoes, foodstuffs like sugar and coffee, and possibly a special item like a musical instrument. Once the tobacco was cured, the corn shucked and stored, and all farm work was over for the winter, farmers would bring their tobacco crop into town. There, during the first months of the year the harvest was placed in warehouses, where auctioneers sold it to the companies that processed the crop for market (this method of selling is almost extinct; the growers having moved to direct contract sales with the tobacco companies). And when the farmer and his family emerged from the warehouse with cash in hand, musicians busking on the street competed for his earnings with the supplies a farm family could not grow or make.

Kermit Brady, a Randolph County native, would often accompany his father on these yearly trips to the tobacco markets in the city of Winston-Salem. Brady recalls as a small boy between 1920 and 1930 leaving the farm for a day or two to market the crop. Among those contending for their tobacco money was a medicine show that would rent an empty storefront near the market. One of Brady's favorite features of the show was the string musicians. Medicine shows were a common sight in the Piedmont during that era, usually setting up shop in a town for three or four days. The one remembered in Cooleemee utilized local musicians.

Sometimes, the growers themselves used music to show their appreciation for the Warehouse owners. In 1888

> A string band from Davidson county, drawn by four fine horses, came into [High Point] Monday and serenaded our popular warehouseman, Mr. T.A. Wiles. This was ... showing their appreciation of Mr. Wiles untiring efforts to sell their tobacco to the best advantage. ... they carried a banner which bore this significant device: "Davidson county for fine tobacco and the Anchor Warehouse the place to sell it" [*High Point Enterprise*, April 6, 1888: 3].

The trip to town in order to sell the tobacco crop brought rural musicians in contact with outside influences. Another way tobacco aided in the exposure to outside musical influences was the migration that occurred as modern farming methods opened up new areas for growing. In the 1930s, Lee County experienced an influx of musicians from the mountain communities in Surry and Yadkin counties.

From the Farm to the Factories: Down from the Mountains

The lack of extraneous noise to compete with the music being made around the tobacco barn and at corn husking time contrasted sharply with the noise of the railroad, the textile mill, and the furniture factory. Although cotton mills existed at least fifteen to twenty years before the Civil War, textiles didn't become a major industry in North Carolina until the period following the war. Primarily through the efforts of the Holt family, mills opened throughout the Piedmont. When that family got into financial trouble during the twentieth century, ownership of the cotton mills transferred to the Holt's northern retailers and wholesalers.

Often, where the mill was synonymous with the town, owners would sponsor local brass bands. In 1889, the Randleman Mills bought musical instruments and paid a teacher to organize the first mill brass band in North Carolina.

Throughout their history, the mills recruited from off of the farms. Circa 1890, for a six-day workweek of twelve-hour days, a cotton mill worker could expect an average wage of $5.95. By 1932, with ten-hour days, that wage had risen to about $20 a week. The average textile worker's wage by 1946 was $35 per week (*Wennonah Story: 75th Anniversary, 1886–1961*, 15, 27, 35; *Wennonah Story: 100th Anniversary, 1886–1986*). Laborers would leave rural Piedmont and mountain communities during the slow time in winter, and migrate temporarily to mill centers. When family land grew scarce through subdivision over the generations, millwork became permanent, and many traveled from mill village to mill village in search of a livelihood.

The mills were a treacherous place for musicians. Machinery threatened the appendages needed to note and pick strings, dust clogged the lungs used to raise a voice in song, and the sheer volume of noise took away the hearing employed to learn and reproduce tunes. And the attitudes of mill owners toward music varied from place to place. So, although mill workers were sometimes musicians, mills were not necessarily breeding grounds for string music.

John Vestal Prevette (August 4, 1913–July 15, 1992) was a fiddler, banjoist, and guitarist who ended up working at the Erlanger Cotton Mill (now Parkdale) in Lexington. John was born in the Surry County community of Mountain Park, nestled in the mountains in the northwestern part of the State. Prevette's musical family included his grandfathers, John Prevette (1867–1971) and Gid Franklin Moncus (April 16, 1854–February 20, 1943), as well as his father, fiddler Andy Melvin Prevette (March 1, 1891–November 26, 1962). John Vestal's mother Millie Elizabeth "Bessie" Moncus (July 27, 1896–February 26, 1972), and her brother Levi (June 17, 1901–January 28, 1989) both played the banjo.

After John was born, the three generations of the Prevette-Moncus family moved in search of better acreage, working in cotton mills when farming didn't pan out. They moved to Draper on the North Carolina and Virginia border around 1918, then south to Madison in about 1925, to the Stokes County community of Walnut Cove in 1929, and, the following year, to High Point in Guilford County. Gid and Levi Moncus had split from the rest of the family and relocated to Lexington as early as 1925, where they worked in the Erlanger Mill. It is possible that Gid and Levi were at the Davidson County textile mill in the late teens or early twenties, as Hilda Reid remembers her father Clay Everhart playing with Moncuses who lived in the Erlanger mill village during that time period.

John Vestal started playing the banjo at the age of 7 or 8, remembering the "first tune I ever played was 'Old Reuban.' My mother learnt me how to play that." He started on the fiddle soon after. In 1931, when John was 18 years of age, the Prevettes and Moncuses moved to Welcome and joined Gid and Levi Moncus working at

Levi Moncus with banjo, Andy Melvin Prevette standing next to his brother-in-law and Andy's son John Vestal Prevette sitting in front. This photograph was made in the mill town of Draper near the North Carolina and Virginia border. The Prevette and Moncus family's search for textile jobs took them from their Surry County home to the Leakesville, Spray and Draper area and finally to Lexington in Davidson County. Circa 1918. Courtesy Andy Prevette.

Erlanger. John played music with fellow Erlanger employee and banjoist Dewey Hyatt (April 28, 1907–November 1974), and guitarist Floyd Morrison (born February 25, 1923) (Lexington City Directories).

Sometimes, company-sponsored events included string band music. Erlanger, the mill where John Prevette worked, began holding a gathering for its employees sometime around World War II. "They used to have what they called an 'Erlanger Day,'" remembered John's son Andy. He went on to say that

> It was a big picnic, they had it, [and] I believe it was in August. Usually on Saturday mornings so you could feed everybody and they'd have maybe a star attraction, music coming in and then you'd have your locals. And 9 times out of 10, your local musicians, whenever they wanted to, could show 'em up. The last one I guess was mid–70s.

The bosses at Erlanger once showed John Prevette's friend Floyd Morrison a rare example of altruism. Morrison needed time off to go play an engagement. His boss told him, "Sure, you'll be paid right on," meaning that he could take the time off with pay. Another musical employee, Phil Hege, had a similar experience:

> I remember my fourth grade teacher played violin. And she called the [Erlanger] plant, and she said, "I'd like to have Phil to go to Raleigh with me to play the violin for a square dance." "I'm sorry, ma'am," said — whoever she was talking to, "We can't let him off." And she kept messin' around there and called him back and by golly, the bossman walked out there and said, "You go when you get ready and give yourself time to change clothes and go," and I went down there and did the job and he didn't deduct me for the hours I was off that evening.

The Dulcimer

The string band music of North Carolina sometimes featured a strange instrument that shows up within a small area in the central Piedmont. Part piano and part percussion instrument, this trapezoidal-shaped box is named the hammered dulcimer. A member of the zither family, the dulcimer is stretched with strings that are struck with wooden (sometimes padded) hammers. The hammered dulcimer probably came to the United States from Britain during Colonial times, and survived in isolated but strongly concentrated pockets throughout the country. Mail-order catalogue companies, such as Sears and Montgomery Ward, offered the instruments around the turn of the twentieth century, along with method and tune books.

Within the Piedmont, dulcimers and dulcimer players have been identified in two areas of Randolph County. One area stretches from Asheboro in the middle of the county northeast through Central and Cedar Falls, then to Ramseur and Staley. The other encompasses the border area of the extreme southern part of Randolph, northern part of Montgomery County and southwestern section of Chatham County. Instruments and players have also been located in Forsyth and Guilford counties.

Most of the dulcimer players documented by researchers are known by little

Standing (left to right) are guitarists "Pee Wee" and Lois Carter and kneeling are fiddler "Shorty" Cruise and mandolin player Floyd Morrison. This band of workers at the Erlanger Cotton Mill performed at local square dances around Lexington, in Davidson County. Circa 1943. Courtesy Floyd Morrison.

more than their names. Of this group of eighteen players, five were women. Additionally, dulcimer researcher Ed Babel lists two dulcimer builders: a Mr. Kennedy in Montgomery County, and an unnamed nineteenth century maker located in Friedberg.

THOMAS VIRGIL CRAVEN

The most famous Randolph County dulcimer practitioner was Thomas Virgil Craven (November 23, 1902–December 11, 1980). During the 1970s, a steady stream of folklore students from the University of North Carolina like Tom Carter, musicians like David Holt and record producers such as Barry Poss, came to Virgil's home in Cedar Falls. In the later days of his life, Virgil was likely to have his band around him, an informal aggregation of Glenn Glass on banjo, Fred Olson on guitar and, later, Lachlin Shaw (February 11, 1912–April 30, 2000) on fiddle. This group knew Craven's tunes well, and provided apt support for old pieces like "Cedar Falls Breakdown," "Darling Chloe," and "The Italian Waltz."

Virgil Craven's grandfather, James Prior Reynold Craven (November 29, 1849–February 18, 1911), played the dulcimer, as did Virgil's father Walter Lee (February 6, 1867–November 4, 1934). Virgil learned the instrument from his father when just a boy (Babel, 26). At that time, Walter Craven played at community functions such house dances and school exhibitions. His group included Charlie Glass on the banjo and Ben Gray playing the fiddle (Craven and Carter).

Benjamin Franklin Gray (April 1871–May 7, 1942) was just one of a large group of musicians that lived between Cedar Falls and Grays Chapel in northeastern Randolph County and is remembered as being one of the top bow pullers in Randolph County. Gray was often in the company of fiddler Francis Marion Trogdon (December 2, 1863–June 29, 1936). Trogdon's grandson Vernon remembered that Marion could read music and always made the other musicians "put all the grace notes in." The Gray-Trogdon group was rounded out by guitarist (and sometime fiddler and mandolinist) George Wesley "Bub" Pugh (January 6, 1875–February 13, 1962) from Gray's Chapel. Bub Pugh learned music as a teenager attending school in Ramseur, solo guitar pieces popular in those times like "Sebastopol" or "Star Waltz." The trio of Gray, Trogdon and Pugh was a familiar sight at area fiddlers' conventions back in the first quarter of the twentieth century. Pugh even ran a contest at the Grays Chapel School in 1930.

Virgil Craven was inspired by his father to play music. Unfortunately, a bout of religion put a stop to Walter's music making. As Virgil told Tom Carter: "I couldn't exactly watch my father play because he had quit playing by the time I really got started. I got a few pieces directly from him but when I was about 12 years old he sold his dulcimer when he joined the church (Craven and Carter).

Even though Walter Craven had given up music by the mid–1920s, there were plenty of opportunities in the area to pick up tunes and technique. Virgil stuck close to Ben Gray and Marion Trogdon, and learned many of his pieces from them. Even though he followed his father into music, he decided that Walter's trade of carpentry was not for him. When he was big enough, Craven followed many of his peers into the town's cotton mill.

Left to right, Virgil Craven with his hammered dulcimer and Glenn Glass with his homemade banjo during one of their regular rehearsals at Virgil's home in Cedar Falls, Randolph County, 1977. Photograph by Ed Babel.

As he came of age, Virgil Craven formed a band with his brothers in which he primarily fiddled. Craven told Tom Carter where they played:

> At political speakings, I was hired to [play the dulcimer], to play a tune or two after speeches were over. I'd go to fiddler's conventions but always played the fiddle. Never played much alone, we had the Craven Family Band. My oldest brother Gurney [February 26, 1893–November 2, 1941] played the Autoharp. Next oldest, Roland [born February 1897], played the guitar and Russell [December 23, 1909?–October 20, 1956] and I played the fiddle…. [The conventions were held] at the courthouse in Asheboro, others at Franklin, Pleasant Grove … there were a lot of them. I used to play square dances at the bottom of the hill, in the schoolhouse down there. Schoolteachers liked it, had one almost every Friday night [Carter and Craven interview].

The Craven Brothers string band became the band to beat at area fiddlers' conventions. Despite Virgil's recollections to the contrary, Walter Craven did occasionally appear with his sons.

Eventually, life's responsibilities and changes within the community precipitated the break up of the Craven family band. Virgil continued to fiddle at home, and hooked up with Fred Olson in the late 1950s. When folklorists and musicians alike started searching for tunes and musicians in the late 1960s, Virgil became one of their stars. The Craven band of recent times became a familiar site at folk festivals and concerts in North Carolina and many recordings were made of Virgil's dulcimer playing by young musicians eager to learn his style.

TWO

African Americans and
String Band Music

*"'Bout twict a year we had a sociable when de niggers
from de neighborin' plantations 'ud be invited an' dey'd
come wid deir banjos an' fiddles an' we'd dance, all o'
us, an have a swell time."*

— Julius Nelson, born around 1860
in Anson County, Federal Writers
Project, *Slave Narratives: Volume
14, Part 2,* 143, 144 and 146

This chapter deals with the contributions of African American musicians to
Piedmont string band styles. Although string music is the product of the interaction
between whites and blacks, the latter's influence has often been ignored by both
scholars and the public.

Many assume that the earliest African American music was the blues. This is
due in no small part to stereotypes throughout both Anglo and African American
society.

One determinant of the image of rural music has been the record companies.
During their nascent days in the 1920s, the American record industry made a star-
tling discovery. Rural dwellers, both black and white, would buy local music (or a
commercialized version of it) if offered on the then-standard 78-rpm discs. This
sparked a wave of recording for southern and rural music. Musicians were brought
to northern studios or had portable studios carried to them. Inadvertently, representatives of the business, by deciding what to record and how to market the resulting discs, aided in shaping the way Americans saw their own music. By and large,
African American string band music was ignored in favor of the more modern Black
blues. Along with the rising popularity of the guitar, the cultural changes brought
by World War II and the final death toll by rock and roll, the record labels helped in
the extinction of the fiddle and banjo among African American musicians. Since that

time, the banjo and the fiddle have been thought of as white country instruments, losing their association with Africa and African Americans.

The difficulty I had in assembling this chapter stems from the lack of period reportage about string music within the black community. Because African Americans have often been marginalized, the few bits and pieces that have come down to us in print are mostly from a white point of view. This viewpoint is often derogatory, from the standpoint of an outsider looking in on events. For example, in 1892, the *Lexington Dispatch* reported on a black banjoist, but only because he used his instrument as a weapon in a dispute with another man (January 8, 1892: 3). This makes all the more precious the stories in this chapter.

The banjo's ancestors were brought from West Africa, with African Americans the original purveyors of the instrument. Slaves and later free black fiddlers were common dance musicians for both blacks and whites throughout the nineteenth and early twentieth centuries. This led to a shared dance band repertoire between Anglo and African Americans, with only stylistic differences separating each race's interpretations. It is easy to characterize black fiddling and banjo playing as rougher and more rhythmic than the fiddling and banjo playing of their white American counterparts. One must be careful, though, not to draw too drastic a distinction between musical styles, for all African American, like all Anglo-American, musicians do not sound the same.

Certainly, North Carolina was not one of the states with a large slave population. Within the Piedmont, only 22 percent of white residents owned slaves. Most slaveholders held four or five, barely 7 percent owning 20 or more slaves. The Hairston family, one of the largest slave owners in the state, was an exception. Their plantation, Cooleemee, boasted 300 slaves in 1860.

The size of the African American population didn't necessarily define the number of black musicians, nor the influence by blacks on white repertoire and style. It is hard to tell if the Piedmont's smaller black settlements encouraged musical interaction with their white neighbors. Conversely, larger groupings of African Americans didn't necessarily discourage the mingling of the races. Some areas with large concentrations of slaves, like the Cooleemee Plantation, had very few documented string musicians. Other areas with a large black population, such as Iredell County, were overrun with fiddlers.

Folklorist Kip Lornell suggests that the equality of social position and occupation within some Piedmont communities encouraged a positive musical exchange between the races. Lornell also explained "white and black communities [in the North Carolina Piedmont] are not quite as stratified as in, for example, Mississippi.... There was generally more interaction between white and black, especially among musicians" ("Pre-Blues," 27).

The Beginnings of African American String Music

In the early history of the United States there was an effort made within North Carolina to control the slave population by banning music and dancing. In 1794, the

General Assembly passed an act forbidding slave owners to permit slaves or free Negroes to gather "for the purpose of drinking and dancing" (James Howard Brewer, 160). The law further stated that

> It was unlawful for a person to permit the slaves of others to dance and drink on his premises without the written permission of their owners, but the law not always was observed rigidly and the Negroes, both slave and free, sometimes danced to the music of the banjo until a late hour. In 1822, for instance, a correspondent of the *Raleigh Register* complained of the house of a certain free Negro where slaves danced and frolicked without restriction [*Raleigh Register*, July 19, 1822: 3].

When government wouldn't enforce its own statutes, members of the populace took matters into their own hands. In 1815, a group of Raleigh residents formed the "Raleigh Association for the suppression of vice and for the promotion of morality and good order." Their main object was to inhibit "Negro dances and frolicks" (*Raleigh Register*, February 10, 1815: 3; and Battle quoted in Johnson). Ultimately, these efforts were unsuccessful, as shown by the survival of "Negro dances and frolicks" into the mid-twentieth century.

While it is hard to trace white musicians in the first half of the nineteenth century (see Chapter One), strangely, there are an abundance of accounts featuring black fiddlers. Slaves with musical talent were often trained to accompany the white dances of their masters. (See for example Sensbach, Jon. F., *A Separate Canaan*, Chapel Hill: UNC Press, 1998, 240–2.) Not surprisingly, their musical talent and training gave these slaves an increased value. Owners frequently advertised for the return of runaway slaves, and the fact that one Mecklenburg County master mentioned that Jacob, about fifty years of age was a "fidler," shows how important that attribute was (*Western Carolinian*, October 19, 1821: 1).

So it is not surprising that the earliest references to African American fiddlers in the Piedmont have them performing for Anglo-American gatherings. In approximately 1830, a house dance was held in the Chinquapin district (later Clarksville Township). The northwest corner of what is now Davie County was, at that time, inhabited by hunters and fishermen. The dance was held by Mr. Swab, described in the account as a "Dutchman" (probably a Pennsylvania Dutch German), and it lasted into the small hours of the next morning:

> There was an old negro [*sic*] fiddler sitting in the corner of the room patting his foot and wagging his head squeezing out the "Mississippi Sawyer," the "Arkansas Traveler," "Leather Breeches" and other tunes fashionable in those days. The dancers were cutting the pigeon wing, running the double shuffle and the three-step high-step with great vigor [*Local History from the Lexington Dispatch*, 35–37].

By the 1890s, the elite of the Rowan County town of Salisbury practiced a more refined style of dance, but still utilized the skills of African American musicians. "Eli's Band" included "Jimmy Wrenn's talented Eli, playing the first violin, and another colored man named Locke, who wrangled a good alto or tenor from the second violin, while a little fellow called Son manipulated a bass violen [*sic*], much larger than himself" (McCorkle). The practice continued into the twentieth century. The Big Five string band, five "colored" musicians from Chester, South Carolina, accompanied a dance at Statesville's armory hall in the spring of 1908 (*Landmark*, April 30, 1908: 5). And the Cedar Grove musicians (see below) remember playing for white dances as much as for those within their own African American community.

Other blacks in the Piedmont were a part of traveling shows. J.M. McCorkle writes of a time in Salisbury, around 1880, when a one-horse medicine show came to town. The "doctor's" black helper sang and played a banjo (McCorkle). African American musicians were based in urban areas as well. A blind black fiddler, reports Johnny Ham, performed on Winston-Salem streets around World War II.

Black Banjo

African American musicians provided the accompaniment for black dances as well as white dances. The WPA's *Slave Narratives* features many mentions of black dances during late antebellum times. Richard C. Moring (born around 1854) of Apex recalled, "When dere wus a weddin' ... De ban' which wus banjoes, an' fiddles 'ud play an' de neighborin' folks 'ud come" (*Slave Narratives*, Federal Writers Project 139). Bryan Tyson told another story from the same period:

> The past summer, a year ago, I was at a friend's house in Chatham county, North Carolina, who owned a good many servants. It was in time of wheat harvest. About dusk the hands came in from their laborious work. It would seem that all might have been tired enough without seeking farther exercise in diversions, but not so. After supper the banjo was brought forth, and preparations made for a social dance. They soon struck up in high glee [12–13].

Black banjo styles survived into the late nineteenth and early twentieth century as well. Both references I have to banjo players in the Western Piedmont are in settlements that are offshoots from Hairston Plantations. Anglo-Americans in this area were playing the banjo in the 1890s; my earliest references to African American banjoists date to the same period. Banjoist Charles Davis, now deceased, lived in Petersville. Formerly called Upper or High Buncombe, Petersville is three miles west of Route 150 on the Yadkin River in southern Davidson County. Petersville is descended from the slave settlement Low Buncombe, established when Cooleemee was founded in the early 1800s. Joseph Fulp (ca. 1875–1965) lived in Walnut Cove, on the Stokes and Forsyth County line. Joe "knocked down" on the banjo and sang, using the instrument to pass the time while curing tobacco. Some of Joe's pieces were "Georgia Buck," "Rockingham Cindy," "The Fox Chase," "Careless Love," "Don't Let Your Deal Go Down," and possibly "Black Eyed Daisy." His marriage to Ressie Allen (ca. 1885–1950s) yielded eleven children. Sons Preston Sylvester (November 1, 1915–October 16, 1993), Robert (deceased) and Clifton (deceased) all played guitar. Clifton also played the banjo.

Preston Fulp stands in the carport of his home in the Walnut Cove section of Stokes County just over the Forsyth County line. Note the guitar capo (pitch raising device), which is homemade with a pencil and rubber band. December 1990.

Will Gales was from Swann Station in southeastern Lee County, along the Harnett County line, and was a neighbor of Marvin Gaster's family. Marvin repeats how the older generation describes Gales' music:

> Will Gales had, no doubt in mind, been a slave, although there is no way I could document it, because my granddaddy said as far back as he could remember his hair was "just like a ball of cotton." But, he was a terrific banjo player and he had a big old robust voice. As Granddaddy used to put, he would "rare" back in his chair. And Will Gales was the one that talked his way through "Catfish" and said all that stuff. Of course, [my] Uncle Henry and Aunt Alice sang "Catfish." I knew [Gales] played that one and I knew he played the one we called "Nigger Holler," and he would sing it, you know:
>
> > Way up yonder 'neath the setting sun
> > Lives a great big nigger with a forked tongue
> > Yonder comes a pateroller with his gun
> > Hear the nigger holler
> > See the nigger run
> > Yonder comes a pateroller
> > I bet 'cha he's got his gun.

Chatham and Orange counties in the Eastern Piedmont were also hotbeds for black banjo playing. These included Elizabeth Cotten (January 1895–January 29, 1987) and James Phillips "Dink" Roberts (born around 1895) of Haw River, both who came from musical families.

Cece Conway writes of Chatham County banjoist John Snipes (ca. 1906–1981), who got his first pieces in the old down picking style from "Uncle" Dave Alston (ca. 1835–1910). These included "Long Tail Blue" and "Ain't Gonna Rain No More" (Conway, Dissertation, preface). Snipes also learned from Duke Mason of Durham, (Bastin, *Orange County Special*, 4) but, primarily acquired his knowledge of the banjo from Will Baldwin (1870–1940), who is remembered as being the finest banjoist in Orange County of any race. Baldwin played for white dances held by mill workers on Saturday evenings (Lornell, "Pre-Blues Banjo and Fiddle" and Conway and Thompson, "Talking Banjo," 63).

Jamie Alston, grandson of Dave Alston, played banjo with two white musicians, Cary Lloyd on fiddle, and Tom Bradshaw on banjo, in the 1930s. It was unusual, but not unheard of, for musicians of both races to band together, if only for private white events (I've found no examples of white musicians playing for black occurrences) (Lornell, "Pre-Blues Banjo and Fiddle").

Willie Trice (February 10, 1910), was raised out in the country just west of Durham. He remembers his Uncle Luther (died 1933) who, in a variation on a common learning superstition for guitarists, tried to improve on his playing skills by making a deal with the dark side:

> Luther ... he ... played banjo. He was good.... Played "Coo Coo was a fine bird," "Old Black Annie," "Reuban," "John Henry." He heard he could go to the crossroads for nine mornings, and you could learn how to play.... Send yourself to the devil, y'know. So he went over there Sunday morning right early, got up on the

dogwood limb and started playing…. After a while, the wind got to blowin' a little bit and something came up there. He didn't pay it too much mind, kept on playing. After a while, it got to dancing, kicking leaves everywhere and balls of fire coming out of his mouth and his eyes bright red. He said, he jumped out of that tree. It came towards him, too. He ran a solid mile acrost [*sic*] that hill and ran back over here [Bastin, *Willie Trice: Orange County Special*, p4; *Blue and Rag'd*; Bastin, "The Devil's Goin' to Get You," *North Carolina Folklore* 21: 190].

Communities of African American Fiddlers

Communities of African Americans existed throughout the Piedmont. These were often offshoots of former slave settlements, and many times contained their own musicians. It was in a small settlement between Coleridge and Siler City in extreme southwestern Randolph County where white musician Glenn Davis learned to play guitar from an African American. Davis also knew of Marion ("Jordan" or "Trogdon") (died 1950), a left-handed fiddler whose band included two sons on guitar.

Another group of African Americans lived outside of Randleman in northern Randolph County. Salem was originally a Quaker community and the birthplace of fiddler Marshall Davis. It was not unusual that Davis played for white functions, but he was unique in that he worked with white musicians at public dances.

Marshall Fred Davis was born in November of 1884, on a farm rented by his father. Marshall's father, Elkanah "Caine" (born 1842), had come from South Carolina. By 1913, Marshall was living in High Point, where he worked as a "fireman," which meant he tended waste furnaces for various private concerns like Slane Hosiery Mills and Thomas Mills, as well as for the City of High Point (Census; High Point City Directories; *High Point Enterprise*, August 15, 1948: 14A).

Sometime in the late 1930s, Marshall Davis became acquainted with local guitarist Gurney Peace (see Chapter One). *"He was about as good a fiddle player as I ever heard,"* Gurney said of Davis. Gurney, who was white, persuaded Davis to work with Peace's group at local public dances. There association continued into the 1930s, and even included performing for a postal convention. Gurney Peace, looking back on events from another time, commented on the unusualness and difficulties of working with an integrated band: "Back then, segregation wasn't like it is now. And I'd always have to pick where I'd take him, and see if it was alright. I couldn't take him everywhere to play…. But he was about as good a fiddle player as I ever heard."

There were two areas of African Americans in the Piedmont that "cropped out" fiddlers. One existed around Orange County and extended its influence into the later part of the twentieth century. The other was outside Statesville in Iredell County, and was considerable enough to support its own highly unusual fiddlers' convention.

Homer Keever, in his history of Iredell County, writes of a "colored" fire company in the town of Statesville. Organized in 1878, "The Defiance Volunteer Company [was] composed of Negroes [and] remained in existence for years…" (Keever,

324 and 385). To support such a venture, there must have been a substantial African American population. The Company would have been one of the social cornerstones for the black community, and a source of great pride. In fact, at least one fund-raiser was held in honor of the firefighters, anchored by an African American fiddlers' convention. As reported by the local newspaper, the *Statesville Landmark*, "A Meeting of Old-Time Colored Fiddlers" took place on Easter Monday, 1909:

> Old-time fiddlers of the colored race will dispense old-time music at the opera house Easter Monday [April 12, 1909] afternoon and evening. The old fiddlers' convention is for the benefit of the colored fire company and J. W. Byers, Lee O. Martin and John H. Gray are the committee of arrangements. Such famous old-time fiddlers as Baldy Gaither, Albert Gray, the Bailey brothers, Pink Keaton, Jo. Sallie and others will perform and prizes will be given the three best performers. A dance will be the feature of the afternoon and the old fiddlers will perform at night.

What made this event even less common was the integrated audience, which was assisted by ushers of both races. Attendance was good, and the event well received (*Statesville Landmark*, April 9, 1909: 1, 5 and April 13, 1909: 5).

It is hard to describe how unusual was this fiddlers' convention just for black players. There were other communities with enough African American musicians to stage such an evening (see the information in this chapter on Cedar Grove). They, however, didn't sponsor fiddlers' conventions. African American musicians, at the very least, were known and played for events held by the Anglo-American population in other Piedmont areas. But black fiddlers from other communities didn't appear in the white contests.

Here again, Statesville was different. At the white convention held in the year prior to the "colored" meet in Iredell County, one of the African American musicians mentioned above was present:

> About the conclusion [of the Statesville Fiddlers Convention] there were many calls for Baldy Gaither, an old-time colored fiddler from north Iredell, who, after the regular program was finished, appeared and gave some of the old tunes with a vim that pleased everybody. As the audience went out, Baldy, who is 78 years old, gave an exhibition of his proficiency as a dancer [*Western Sentinel*, January 21, 1908: 5].

By all known evidence, these were two highly unusual events, even for Statesville. I've found no evidence of either convention recurring. More could be learned about these events from the stories of their participants. Unfortunately, biographies for the majority of these contestants are non-existent. The few facts that I have been able to assemble are incomplete and based to some degree on conjuncture.

The original Keatons were slaves in New Hope Township (*Iredell County Landmarks*, 71). Pinkning Keaton (born August 1840) is listed by the census as farming in Sharpesburg or Bethany Township, and as being illiterate. His wife Martha (born January 1840) had borne around eight children by 1900. Even though the couple was living in slavery as man and wife and had children, Pink and Martha were only wed after the Civil War because slaves could not legally marry (Census).

If Baldy Gaither was close to 78 years old when he appeared at the 1908 fiddlers' convention, then he was just one of two namesakes that played music. The first Baldy was born into slavery, in June 1838. During the time of the newspaper accounts, Baldy was a farmer who owned his land in Eagle Mill Township. Harvey (born June 1884), the youngest son of Baldy Gaither, was also known as "Baldy," and, like his father, was a fiddler (Census). Harvey Gaither was the first black musician to appear at the Union Grove Fiddlers' Convention (See Chapter Six). Harper Van Hoy, the son of the convention's founder, was inspired to fiddle after watching the older player. As Harper told Roy Thompson:

> Harve Gaither, a black fiddler, lit the fire under [me]. Gaither was a novelty in northern Iredell County, a fiddling black man who played "Pop Goes the Weasel" in an unforgettable way:
> "He would end up playing while lying on his back jumping up from flat on his back and land on his feet ... still playing "Pop Goes The Weasel" [Thompson, 4].

Gaither last seems to have appeared in public sometime in the mid–1960s or early 1970s.

Cedar Grove was one of the centers of black population within Orange County. Black-owned farms almost equaled white-owned operations, at around 250. Folklorist Kip Lornell, who has spent much time in Cedar Grove, explains why it was a place with good interactions between the races and a large musical community:

> Although it is nearly impossible to believe that race relations were relaxed anywhere in the South during the depression, evidence suggests that in Cedar Grove blacks and whites lived together in relative harmony.... Cedar Grove was also a self-contained settlement.... The town's population was quite homogeneous. Whether white or black, the Cedar Grove adult male was typically a tobacco-growing farmer ["Banjos and Blues," 227].

We can say with certainty that the African American string band tradition was widespread throughout area communities. Unfortunately, even the scantiest of documentation is lacking about older men such as fiddlers Emp (Imp) Wright, Rufe Atwater and Bruin Moses, and banjo players Bill Britton, Mathew Hackney, Bal Satterfield, Johnny Wade, Willie Crisp and Jimmy Nicholas of Hurdle Mills, and Dick Bratcher/Dink Bradshaw and Minnick Poteat of Carwell (Lornell, *A Study of the Sociological Reasons* 31 and 41; Bastin, *Orange County Special*, 4; Conway, *African Banjo Echoes*, 6).

Joe Thompson is among the last African American fiddlers from the Cedar Grove community still active in the American South. Family tradition traces string playing back to Thompson's grandfather Robert (born March 1849), supposedly a fiddler. Oral history places Bob Thompson's family as slaves on a large plantation located in Person County, where they gained the sur-name "Thompson." As Joe told me, "A man called Walter Thompson had so many slaves.... And he had so much land, he gave

Fiddler Joe Thompson (left) and banjoist Odell Thompson stand on Odell's porch in northern Alamance County. These musical cousins were coaxed out of retirement in the 1970s and since have taken their family's brand of African American string music throughout the United States, to Carnegie Hall in New York City and to Australia. April 1988. Photograph by Alice Gerrard.

them all a place up the road and right now it's called Thompson Road down there [in Person County]."

Robert came into adulthood after freedom came, married Catie (born August 1858) and settled in the county's Brushy Fork Township. Their sons John Arch (April 15, 1879–October 28, 1968, who was Joe's father), Jacob A. (born May 1876) and Walter Eugene (born January 1882) all became fine musicians. When Walter married, two more banjoists joined the family — his brother-in-law Elder Crisp and sister-in-law Flossie Crisp Byrd.

By 1900, the Bob Thompson family had relocated to Cedar Grove Township in neighboring Orange County. John Arch and his brothers played fiddles and banjos, and, along with their friend Charley White, were the musicians of choice for both white (called "square dances") and black (called "frolics") house dances in the earlier part of the twentieth century. Actually, Bob Thompson spoke of attending set dances as a young man, so the tradition probably extends back to his generation as well. Although African and Anglo-Americans had different names for the occasions, tells Joe, there was no difference in the music or the figures. At that time, the custom was to clear a room or two of furniture in a private residence to make way for the dancers. Musicians more often than not were given the space in-between rooms so that all those assembled could hear them. The tune selection was fairly stable as, in this insular community, older musicians uniformly trained the younger ones. Set callers in the black community included Prez Evans, Jim Love, Fred Thompson (no relation), Pete Vincent and Joe's eldest brother Chesly. Christmas was an especially popular time for dancing, and Joe remembers that "somebody was bound to have a dance nearly every night," between December 25 and New Year's Day. The dances held in Cedar Grove were especially popular, and participants would often come from a distance. After the holidays, the music and dancing would continue until spring, when farm work would once again command the community's attention (Lornell, *A Study of the Sociological Reasons*, 32–5).

These events were fun times, but had their serious side as well. Joe relates the story of when his father and Uncle Jake accidentally played on Sunday, although Bob Thompson had warned his sons against it: "[My daddy] said they used to play for the white folks every Saturday night. And he said he played one Sunday morning until three o'clock, him and Jake…. And the ashes and coals came out of the fireplace by themselves. And Jake said, 'John, it's time for us to go home.'"

The Thompsons interacted with local white players as well. Fletch Pittard and Alec Tinnin, two men for whom they sharecropped, influenced their technique and repertoire. From a distance of 70 to a 130 years later, it is hard to reconstruct the flow of fiddle tunes, banjo pieces and songs between whites and blacks in North Carolina's Piedmont. Many of Joe's pieces—"Georgia Buck," "Molly Put the Kettle On," "Black Eyed Daisy," "Old Corn Liquor," "Soldier's Joy," and "Old Joe Clark"—are staples of both African and Anglo-American string bands throughout the Piedmont. "Goin' Downtown" and "Pumpkin Pie" can be traced back to the earliest days of minstrelsy, although it is hard to follow them back farther. At the very least, the passage went both ways, with some melodies coming from African Americans, some from Anglo-Americans, and some from outside sources.

Joe Thompson grew up on the family farm, surrounded by music making. As a baby, Joe would "just listen" to his father play, naturally absorbing all of John Arch's tunes. When Joe was five, his brother Nate (1916–1997) was taught to clawhammer a banjo by their father. Thompson, who always imitated his older brother, decided he would learn to play the fiddle. However, John Arch forbade Joe to touch their only violin. And, although Joe made a few attempts when his father was not around to punish him, this did not satisfy Thompson. Joe remembers:

> My father said, "He just too little to play my fiddle…." And, so, I kept on giving him a problem…. Finally, my mama's first cousin came over [Jimmy Wagstaff]…. Jimmy said, "I got the thing for him." Back in those days, you could sell seeds and get a premium. He sold 48 packs of seeds for the garden, garden spot seeds, and got that little fiddle … for the premium…. He had broke these first two strings off of it…. He said, "Tell him to come on and get this fiddle and see what he gonna do." And so, when I come [home] from school that day, mama give me a 48 pound flower sack, stuck it in my pocket and went on over there about four miles and a half. And got that fiddle and walked back home…. This brother of mine … said, "Well, you ain't got no strings on it!" I said, "Well, I['ll] get papa to get me some." He said,

"Hah, hah, he ain't gonna get you no strings!" That's back when times was tight. I says to him, "Well, I'll tell you what, you just come on and go with me." So we went out to the truck and tractor shed, and I slide in-'tween the door there and got me a pair of pliers. Come back to the house, and got me two strands out of the bottom of that screen door. But, mama didn't see that! And I put them two screen door strands on there. In two hours or less, I was playin' "Hook and a' Line." When my daddy come home that night, my mama said, "Well, you wouldn't let him play your fiddle, won't you listen at him now!" So, he come on in there and me and my brother played it for him, played it good, too! He said, "I believe that boy gwinna play that thing! Well, maybe he *can* have mine." I wanted to tell him, "No, I got one now, you keep yours." But, I didn't tell him that [because you didn't talk back to your parents then].

Joe and Nate Thompson replaced the older generation at local house parties and frolics. The brothers were quite the sight, both still children whose feet didn't even reach the floor when sitting in those old-fashioned straight back chairs! On some occasions, their cousin Walter Odell (Walter's son, August 9, 1911–April 28, 1994) would fiddle or play the guitar as well.

The Thompsons music making ended after World War II, when rock and roll and other diversions took people away from square dancing. Joe served in Europe during the war, followed by marriage and a job working at White Furniture Company to keep him busy.

In the early 1970s, folklorist Christopher "Kip" Lornell encouraged Joe and Odell to take up the fiddle and the banjo again. As Joe recalls, "He found my sister and said, 'Do you have a brother that plays a fiddle?' And she brought him over where I was. And that day, that's what got us started back. He didn't turn us loose until he told us we could do it, until he got us going. And he really did bring us through it."

From that time until Odell's death in 1994, the duo toured the United States and Australia. The Thompsons appeared at the National Folk Festival, the Festival of American Fiddle Tunes, the Tennessee Banjo Institute and at Carnegie Hall in New York City, among others. Along with Odell, Joe received both the North Carolina Folk Heritage Award (in 1991) and the Brown-Hudson Award. Since Odell's passing, Joe has continued to travel the country, appearing at Merle Fest, the Augusta Heritage Workshop and the North Carolina Museum of History. A stroke in the fall of 2001 has left Joe's noting hand somewhat paralyzed. But Joe Thompson is nothing if not resilient, soldiering on after the death of both his cousin and brother. Joe is determined to get back his strength, and it shouldn't be long before he's back to fiddling the old family pieces.

THREE

"Anything That I Knew Was Something I Heard Him Play"

"Them old musicianers, they was uneducated, but they could play up a storm, and they'd think of some verse they'd put to it out of just common, cornfield language, that they'd add to it, and they'd come out with the right timin.'"

— Kermit Brady

Anyone who has collected information about rural music making is immediately struck by how pervasive this cultural experience was among nineteenth and early twentieth century Americans. In Piedmont North Carolina, the commonality between fiddlers and banjoists is echoed in the learning stories given in oral histories. After comparing more than a few tales about picking up music, one is struck by a keen sense of déjà vu. I swore that these musicians had been calling each other on the telephone and consulting among themselves on what to tell me, considering how close were their accounts. It is true that these older residents had many years and numerous retellings in order to codify these events into myth. However, it is kind of spooky the way all learning anecdotes followed the same patterns.

Musical Families

If someone came from a well-to-do family, music was a part of their schooling. The offspring of the well-heeled attended local academies, which were one step up from the more common one- and two-room schoolhouses. This was especially true for the young ladies of the community. Instruction on the guitar was a part of the offerings at the Salem Female Academy. The Elizabeth College for Women, in Charlotte, had a "Music Conservatory, With course leading to diploma." In addition to

(Left to right) Jack with fiddle, Ruth with harmonica and Clayton with guitar, the children of banjoist Clay Everhart. Jack and Clayton later joined their father in a family-based band on the radio and for regional appearances in western North Carolina. Welcome, Davidson County. Circa 1930. Courtesy Ruth Everhart Coffey.

the guitar, instruments taught included violin, banjo and mandolin (*Davidson County News*, July 1, 1897: 1,4). There were also instructors plying their trade in the larger towns of the state. During the first quarter of the twentieth century, music teachers set up in Piedmont towns and cities, advertising music lessons on guitar, banjo, violin and mandolin.

But for the most part, string music was learned through osmosis. Musical skills were by and large acquired from the example of an accessible individual or individuals. More often than not, the teacher was a member of the student's family. This

Unknown music class. This mixture of guitarists, violinists, mandolinists, cellists and horn players flank their instructor (standing in front holding rolled up musical score). Liberty, Randolph County, circa 1895.

often led to the appearance of "music running in families," although it is hard to tell whether genetics, proximity, or both contributed to this phenomenon. Banjoist Elmer Dunn boiled it all down to being one of the chosen few. Dunn told me, "I think everybody [that] can play, the Lord give 'em a gift."

Herman Boyd, who was born 1923 in Winston-Salem but grew up outside the city in Forsyth County, had two uncles who played the fiddle. He learned music at a young age. His brother Elgin (born May 11, 1922) picked up the guitar. He said, "They had two or three … neighbors that'd play, and a fella gave me a guitar hanging in his barn…. And I took and put some strings on it, tuned it up and I think, Well, now, I can go around and play some with 'em. And I kept on making chords, you know, … I finally got to playin' with 'em."

Larry Daniel Beam (born August 15, 1935) of Lexington had a grandfather and uncles who played, and a brother with an instrument:

> My brother bought a guitar from my Uncle Troy Beam. So, I'm the one that beat on it all the time after he bought it. I started playing with my Uncle Bob Everhart a lot. He played the fiddle and guitar and I would just sit and play with him. And that's how I got started. I'd probably started doing pretty good when I was about seven, eight or nine.

Larry Beam showing off his guitar and cowboy hat. Lexington, Davidson County, 1940s. Courtesy Larry Beam.

Larry's mother Hilda Reid, a great lover of her father's playing, encouraged her son. "I thought [music] was the greatest thing," Hilda said, "and when Larry taken it up, I thought that was the greatest thing that ever happened to me."

Thomas Roscoe Parker (ca.1886–1955) was from Mechanic in Randolph County. His people came to this area in the 1850s from the mountains of North Carolina and Virginia. Roscoe Parker's son, Raeford Dugan "Tommy" Parker (born January 16, 1925), took up his father's banjo style "since I was big enough to hold it" at the age of ten. "You know if he laid it down and go on," Tommy allows, "then I'd pick it up see what he had done on it."

It appears that female musicians were plentiful during the late nineteenth and early twentieth century. Many came from musical families or had musical siblings that influenced their activities. The Nance sisters, Mattie Rodena (May 26, 1881–September 1941) and Essie (born around 1888), of Salem Church in southwestern Randolph County, played both fiddle and guitar, and had a brother who played the banjo. Janet Marie Miller (May 30, 1898–January 17, 1997) grew up in the South (Yadkin) River community of Rowan County. Her ancestors had been in the area since the 1700s. The youngest of eleven siblings, she began working on the family farm at the age of seven or eight. Miller had a special relationship with her oldest brother, Samuel Reid (born November 12, 1885). Since Reid played the banjo, Janet learned it as well. Another brother, Elbert Woodfin (February 26, 1890–October 6, 1967), played the fiddle. The three siblings appeared together at community functions along with Will

Sisters Mattie (guitar) and Essie (fiddle) Nance formed the core of their family band that also included their brother Carl on the banjo. These young ladies are in their fancy dresses, possibly posing with their mail order instruments outside of their home after church on Sunday circa 1910. Courtesy Glee Arnold.

This rare photograph of a female musician in her prime shows Pearlia McNabb Spivey (see Chapter Four) with her banjo in Lee County, circa 1910. Courtesy Doris Spivey Ashburn.

Safley, a compatriot of the two Miller boys. Janet Miller married at the age of eighteen, and moved away from her family. This concluded her music making because she no longer had anyone with whom to play.

Marriage often meant the end of a woman's playing, unless she was fortunate enough to form a union with a male musician. Adie Lassiter (October 1, 1888–February 7, 1947) played the banjo and piano with her husband, fiddler John Vuncannon (August 1, 1869–February 13, 1948). Even then, women were more likely to play the banjo, guitar, or piano than the fiddle.

Regrettably, I've been able to learn even less about female music makers than about male African American players. Mostly, just their names and instrument of choice survive, such as with Rosie Lamb in Randolph County. Others are known to us only because they started their sons in music, as is the case with the mother of Kelly Sears (1907–1984) from Chatham County, who began her son on the banjo at the age of nine. Ira Rufus Britt (April 16, 1909–July 5, 1965) obtained his first real banjo through a female cousin. His nephew, J.G. Britt, repeats the story told him by his father, who was Ira's brother:

> He said they had a cousin that come by one time, and she picked the old clawhammer style banjo. Her name was Wincie Deaton, she was my dad and Ira's first cousin. She got ready to leave and Ira, he was interested in that banjo, and he asked her, "Would you leave that banjo here, I'd like to learn how to pick a banjo." She said, "Yeah, I'll leave it!" And my dad said, in about a month's time, [Ira] done pickin' out tunes on that thing. So, she listened to him pickin' some, and she said, "I'm goin' to just give you that banjo, you're gonna make a banjo player."

An Instrument of One's Own

Musical instruments, however, were valued commodities, and novice players of a fiddle, banjo, or guitar were not often allowed to use them by adults. William Lihu Voncannon (July 1874–December 1943), from the Pisgah section below Ulah in Randolph County, kept his fiddle in his top dresser drawer. The Voncannon children were told not to mess with it even though they were dying to get at it. Joe Thompson's father always forbade his children from playing his violin. When I quizzed Thompson about his father's intentions when hanging his instrument on the wall where Joe could easily reach it, Thompson agreed that he had always wondered if his father was using reverse psychology in trying to interest his son in music.

Sometimes, concern about an instrument was well founded. Pierce Van Hoy's parents, H.P. and Ada Casey Van Hoy, both played the fiddle. As Roy Thompson wrote:

> Pierce never made it as a fiddler. As he told it later on he "screeched things up so bad" his mother chased him out of the house. Then his father came home one day and found Pierce "dragging his fiddle around the yard like it was a sled." Pierce's brief career as a fiddler was over. Dead as a doornail ... and unmourned [4].

Odell Brown, from a musical family, was given a mandolin from Sears-Roebuck by his father. When Odell had trouble mastering the instrument, he traded it for a baseball mitt!

Some youngsters would begin their training by pretending or "playing" at making music, utilizing sticks for bows, cornstalks for fiddles, and pots for banjos. The

Homemade cigar box banjo (made around 1900) belonging to Levi Johnson. Johnson used a wooden Virginia Cheroots shipping box for the body of his instrument, adding a rough carved wooden neck. Hasty, Davidson County.

aspiring musician might next get a homemade instrument, using materials cast off from other pursuits around the homestead. Wooden cigar boxes became banjos, fiddles, and guitars, with scrap lumber used for the neck and screen wire used for strings. Glenn Davis (March 28, 1909–February 4, 1986), born in Coleridge, began playing at the age of fourteen on a banjo made from a wooden Virginia Cheroots box, with a two by four for the neck and strings made of screen door wire. "It was somethin' the size of a good sized uke. And I made the neck, and cut a hole in that thing and had that for my banjo. I didn't have no frets, so I marked the frets off with a pencil.... I sold it for a dollar and a half (laughs)."

John Herndon, Leonard Eubanks' second cousin, made Leonard a banjo:

> He was about six years older than I was. I wanted to play one and he just made it out of a solid piece, that be the neck and the pegs and the bridge, out of solid cedar. It was pretty, red cedar. Where he got the can I don't know, it was tin, [like a cookie tin] just about so deep, just the size of a banjo. He put that neck in it, and that was just as pretty as you ever seen.

Area artisans would also be called upon to conjure up a banjo or fiddle. In Robbins, a blacksmith named Garner made crude banjos; about four have survived. The one I saw had a single piece of bent oak nailed together for the rim (which might have started life as a cheese hoop), with a fretless, hand-carved neck. The instrument was small, an eight-inch rim with a 22-inch neck. The dowel (a long stick of wood attached to the end of the neck that runs through the inside of the rim, therefore holding the banjo together) was round as opposed to most squared-off dowels on commercial banjos. The few handmade hooks that held the head taut wrapped around the top and bottom of rim.

Instruments could also be earned by saving wrappers or selling seeds. Joe Thompson tells of his cousin getting a half-size fiddle by selling garden seeds (see Chapter Two). Saly Newman's sister played a Stella brand guitar, which she had got-

Banjoist Robert O. "Rom" Phillips sits holding a homemade banjo at the family home in Anson County circa 1910. Courtesy Mary T. Smyrl.

ten by saving Octagon Soap wrappers. In Forsyth County, Herman Boyd sold Rose Bud Salve in order to earn his first violin. If a musician got really lucky, he or she could win a fiddle, banjo, or guitar as a contest prize. C. R. Wilson received a banjo as a premium at the first farm exhibition and fair held in Winston-Salem in 1889. *The Twin City Sentinel* reported that "Mr. Wilson ... used to be known as one of the best pickers in this section" (October 7, 1924: 14). And a guitar valued at $50 was third prize in a contest to sell the most new subscriptions to the Winston-Salem *Union Republican* newspaper.

Finally, if a youngster showed serious intent or became accomplished enough, an instrument passed down in the family might become his or her own. The handing over of a fiddle or banjo by an elder symbolized the passing of the musical mantle from one generation to the next.

Elmer Harrison Dunn (May 16, 1913–April 21, 1998) was given his father's banjo to use. Both Elmer's grandfather Noah Dunn and father William Alexander Dunn (September 19, 1883–November 8, 1966) were farmers as well as fiddlers and banjoists in northern Davie County. Elmer's father loaned his own banjo, a "Rex Professional" brand instrument, to Elmer until he could afford to buy one. Elmer had earned his father's trust by showing how serious he was about playing.

In an interview with me, Gene Britt remembered, "You'd get hold of a Gibson, you thought you'd died and went to heaven." Vernon Lamb snared a similar sentiment. Talking about his father and uncles, he said "If they had had some really good instruments, they could have been Opry material."

Money to purchase a musical instrument was not often easy to come by. And, if a young adult gathered enough to obtain a real, manufactured string instrument, music stores were not plentiful and those that existed were not well stocked with a variety of makes and models. In some places, instruments or money was in such short supply that they had to be shared. The brothers George and Harvey Moore, as well as Harvey's wife Lee, owned one banjo between them and would have to take turns playing.

One way to get an instrument was to trade for or buy a used one. "When I got to doing pretty good" on the banjo, Leonard Eubanks recalled, his father

> bought me one from Rom Eubanks, he had played a little, but he was getting old and he had quit, you know. He was some kin to us. He had this banjo and boy I mean it was a pretty good sounding old banjo.... Papa didn't give over 5 or $6 for the thing or $10 or something like that, you know....

Elgin Boyd tells how he acquired a good instrument, a 1932 Gibson guitar:

> Five or six of us ... we was playin' at a little store ... and this fellar was playin' this guitar, and he'd had it for a year. And I bought it from him.... And I give him $22 for it.... And I didn't have the money. I borrowed the money from a fellar and told him I'd put out a half acre of tobacco. And that come a hail storm and it beat the leaves plum off that tobacco; I didn't get nothin' out of it. So, I worked for him, ten cents a hour ..., a dollar a day and my dinner, diggin' sweet potatoes. And that's how I [worked off that money that I owed him].

In 1912, Thomas Roscoe Parker had to travel to Kansas City, where he was helping his sibling to move, in order to buy a Lyon and Healy brand banjo.

Often, mail order was the only choice for a rural string musician. Many graduated from a homemade banjo, as did Glenn Davis, to a Supertone brand instrument from Sears and Roebuck or to its equivalent from Montgomery Ward. In the 1920s, $7 got Davis his first manufactured banjo. Lester Ray Porter (born July 21, 1933), originally from Erwin, learned on a $25 Harmony brand guitar from Sears. His mother had purchased the instrument around 1942. It eventually passed to two of his brothers for their musical education. Kermit Brady, a resident of Randolph County, commented on how quick and direct the mail-order services were. In 1935, Brady ordered a violin from Sears; it cost $9.98, and only took three days to arrive at the local post-office.

Stores catering to the music trade were in the Piedmont as early as 1890, when the C. B. Ellis Music Company was founded in Burlington. Originally, the shop sold sewing machines, then added pump organs and pianos, and finally stringed instruments. Many shops added musical items to their original specialty as demand dictated, as Ellis had done before becoming a full-fledged music store.

Before World War II, top-quality instruments were out of the reach of most string band musicians. Inexpensive copies of fine violins were made in the hundreds of thousands and readily available to rural fiddlers. Since these are labeled identically to those worth one hundred or one thousand times more, it is hard for the novice to differentiate between inexpensive and pricey violins. Such is the explanation for so many "Stradivarius" instruments in the world. Similarly, guitars and banjos can fool the eye of the beginner. In that case, however, at least several brand names came to be known as the best for string band music. And, as factory work put money in people's hands and their standard of living rose, name brand instruments became affordable to Piedmont musicians.

In the 1920s and 1930s, a Gibson-brand guitar, along the lines of the one purchased for $22 by Elgin Boyd, was considered the best. These were small-bodied guitars and sold new for around $30. By the end of the 1930s, instruments by Martin, which made the most expensive acoustic guitar on the market, began to show up in the area. In 1939, Elmer Holden paid $85 for one of Martin's large bodied guitars, the D-18. Even though it was the least expensive D model (or "dreadnought," as the body style was nicknamed), Holden must have impressed the others in his musical circle with the instrument. And, as late as 1954, the D-18 was not readily available in local shops, and had to be special ordered, often with a wait of six months or more.

When it came to banjos, there was no question in anyone's mind that the Gibson Company made the best. During the 1920s and 1930s, the five-string banjo, preferred by Piedmont string bands, had fallen from favor in the rest of the country. Most banjo production went to the four string tenor (tuned like a violin in fifths) and plectrum (tuned like a banjo without the fifth or "short" string) instruments. All of the remaining five strings that Gibson made in that period seem to have ended up in North Carolina.

But such quality didn't come easily or cheaply to Piedmont players. Glenn Davis had to special order his Gibson banjo from Harvey West Music in Greensboro. Joe Reitzel's father was making good money in the Depression, and was able to spend $125 for an instrument at Resnick's in Winston-Salem. And John Gainey (known as "J.G.") Britt, Jr. (born November 21, 1925) bought a new Gibson banjo for $95 in 1943. "It took a half an acre of tobacco to pay for that banjo," remembers Britt.

Bill Allen is typical of the more serious of the Piedmont's banjoists. He has owned a succession of instruments, most of them purchased through Burlington's local music stores. Allen obtained his first banjo in his early teens through a trade for a flashlight. Real strings were not available, so screen door wire served as a poor substitute. Next, Allen spent $13 at Moore Music in Burlington for a manufactured instrument. When the neck warped, Moore took back the defective banjo and gave him a credit, which allowed Bill to upgrade to a Bruno brand banjo. In 1923 or 1924, Mr. Moore talked Bill into acquiring an Orpheum #2. This high-grade instrument had a price tag of $125, which was way beyond Allen's means. Since he couldn't afford to buy the banjo, Moore allowed him to come into the store and play it whenever he pleased. One day, the dealer made Bill Allen a deal he couldn't turn down. "Take the banjo," said Mr. Moore, "and pay me what you can when you can." Although Bill's mother strongly disapproved, Allen found that the new instrument helped him in procuring engagements. Within six months, Bill had earned enough from his music to pay off the instrument. Bill Allen's success as a musician continued, and, in 1930, he purchased a Gibson Mastertone from Ellis Music for $144.

Two banjos being proudly displayed by their owner, Bill Allen (right) and his nephew, Johnny Maness. Allen holds his Orpheum brand five string, while Maness shows Bill's new Gibson Mastertone model. Alamance County, circa 1930. Courtesy Bill Allen.

Catching the Tune

Because formal lessons, let alone much direction, weren't given by the accomplished musicians of the community, players learned "by ear." This method of learning by imitation in "catching a tune" led to the often-heard claim that "I just picked it up," and the phrase, "being self taught." In reality, since music was all around them, children (as Joe Thompson tells in Chapter Two) could often hum, sing, and, therefore, play the dance pieces and songs of their elders at an early age. Bill Allen summed this up well by commenting, "We heard one, we wanted to play it — it gets in your mind! You get a tune that's on you, why, if you can hum it, you can pick it out."

Elva Jeanne Beck (born September 5, 1926) explains how her father, Olin Berrier, passed along the dance tunes to her:

> I can remember [daddy] playing at night, his banjo or his fiddle and playing for hours, just himself, entertaining himself. But we didn't play at that point because we had strict rules about going to bed early. We heated only the den area and we slept in that room where we all sat, so we would have to go to bed and daddy would sit there and play. And I could never go to sleep. So you see, I would lie there and listen to all these tunes and the next morning I could get up and go play 'em if I wanted to. I could pick 'em out on the piano.

At the age of six, Janet Miller Gillean had heard enough music to be ready to try herself: "My brother was out plowin' beside the house one day and I got his banjo and went out there and I kept pickin' till I picked up the first tune. And it thrilled me to death. He stopped and listen at me, and it wasn't too long till they got another banjo and I'd play the tunes along as they did and just taught myself from hearin' them."

James Kermit Brady (born April 15, 1915) had heard music all of his life. The area around the Kermit's southern Randolph County home was thick with fiddlers and banjoists from the time that his father was a boy in the late nineteenth century. Kermit Brady's father, Alson Brady (April 27, 1882–November or September 1971), fiddled, as did Kermit's first cousin William Colon Brady (August 7, 1906–December 11, 1962), his mother's brother Alpheus L. Brady (1886–1941) and their first cousin George Brady. Kermit took up the fiddle between the ages of ten and twelve years old. Alson would help his son by tuning the instrument, and he and the other member of their musical family would tutor the boy from time to time.

One of the best-known players in southern Randolph was Henry Brady (April 29, 1857–January 16, 1945), a "fiddler from years back." Kermit remembers how the older man offered him encouragement:

> This old man Henry Brady, when I started playin' the fiddle, he could play "Arkansas Traveler" and he was a blacksmith and his fingers made my hands look like a little boy. But, he could come over there and note that fiddle just perfect.... He wanted me to play "Arkansas Traveler" and he sort of showed me. Well, I knew the tune of it and when I sort of got over it, fumbled it of course, but he told me right then, "Boy, you gonna play the fiddle!" Well, that was the best thing I ever heard tell of, he was gonna encourage me to play.

However, some players did read music, a skill picked up from singing schools or music lessons. Musical notation was used more as an adjunct to ear training rather than as a replacement. It seems that reading music depended on the particular player and was somewhat generational. Glee Arnold's father, Carl Nance, says Glee, learned indirectly from music in this novel manner: "[Fiddler] Lee Miller got the music to ["The Italian Waltz"] and he got down on the floor and he could read music enough that he learned it from the music and then Daddy learned it by hearing it."

Once a youngster got the music bug, nothing would get in the way of his or her practice. Olin Berrier talks of playing the harmonica while plowing (see Chapter Four). Mostly, every break from farm chores was utilized in rehearsal. Leonard Eubanks recalls

> I was playing that banjo and boy I could roll on that thing then. I'd go up there and be with a mule plowing corn, well…. I wouldn't dare leave no mule standing out there — he would eat up a half acre of corn. I'd just drive him back up in the barn lot, shut the gate and have the plow still hooked on him and say whoa and then just turn him loose. He would eat grass all around there. I would run down to the house and get me a drink of water, that's what I was going after; but I never went to get me no drink of water what I didn't reach back under the bed and pull the banjo out and cut a loose a little bit on it a time or two and then put it back under and go back and get my old mule and go back to plowing. I'd do that maybe three or four or times a day…. We'd take about an hour for dinner to put the feed in and then throw a bundle of fodder and about seven or eight ears of corn while you's eating. I eat and then I'd play a little and go back to plowing.

Elmer Harold Holden (born June 25, 1921), from Winston-Salem, tells the story of how he learned to play:

> Back when I was small, my grandmother took care of us while mother worked. They had a fireplace there, and I was about one or two years old. Even before I started walkin', they said I'd crawl up to the fireplace there and get the shovel, and turn it around like I's playin' guitar. So, this lady that lived across the street, after I got up eight or ten years old, she'd bring her guitar over there and play it, and she'd lay it down, I couldn't keep my hands of off it. And I guess they saw I was interested in music, and so [my mother] bought me a guitar for my tenth birthday. And there was an old boy [Harry Crouse] that lived across the creek over there from us, he'd show me a chord on that guitar. And I'd go home, practice it. He showed me several different chords, and I started puttin' 'em together. And I started playin' guitar pretty good, you know. And the boys would come by — my daddy, he was a Baptist minister, you know they don't believe in dancin' much. So, the boys would beg daddy to let me go play with 'em at the square dances. I must have been twelve years old. And they finally talked daddy into lettin' me go, and I thought, "boy, this is really somethin', goin' out playin' square dances." And we finally formed a band, back in the '30s.

Recording Machines

In the days before portable and affordable recorders, the only way to hear a tune over and over was to have a musician repeat it in your presence. Cylinder and disc players were available in the Piedmont as early as anywhere else in the country, along with a plethora of recordings featuring opera, military bands, vaudeville singers, and the like. Commercial transcriptions of fiddle tunes and country music became obtainable around 1925. Seventy-eight-rpm records helped to bring instantly repeatable performances to the player as a learning tool.

As Everett Moffitt remembers: "People got a lot better way of learnin' a tune

Label used by the Nelson Teal recording service for the discs made by Teal. Burlington, Alamance County, circa 1940s.

now you know…. I'd walk to Bennett, which was about six mile from where we lived and hear a tune, and then walk home and get my fiddle and play it, not like they done it, but, I had it in my head. And now, you record it and keep playin' it back, it's just a world of difference in how you learn it now. It's a lot better you got it all. If you missed it you can back up and try it again."

Around 1940, the first recorders aimed at the public, albeit an affluent one, became available. They utilized acetate-coated discs into which a groove containing musical information could be etched. Mostly these early recording machines were bought by radio and television repair shops, which would make records of their customers for a price. Nelson Teal, a radio and television repairman in Burlington, learned about these machines in a "CCC" (Civilian Conservation Corp) camp. Teal made discs of local musicians at his shop, and even carried the recorder to local fiddlers' conventions. Glenn Thompson used his discs made by Teal to press commercial 78-rpm records. In Asheboro, Vic Smith, a radio announcer for WGWR, ran a recording service similar to Teal's.

One musician who managed to gather the money to own a disc cutter was Olin

Berrier of Welcome in Davidson County. Berrier's machine was a model 6A10 Wilcox-Gay Recordio. Olin said that he purchased the machine as a musical aid, in order to record his own music, listen back to it, hear the mistakes and improve his playing. Besides using the recorder to analyze his own performances, Olin wanted to capture those by musicians he admired. This was as much to learn the pieces they played as to immortalize their performances. When he visited musicians such as Tom and Dewey Cooper or his neighbor Artis Koontz, Berrier brought along his disc cutter. Of course, since Olin wanted to play as well as record, the task of running the machine fell to his children or those of other musicians. Both Jeanne, Olin's youngest daughter, and Lawrence Cooper, Tom's son, were enlisted in making records. Jeanne recollected, "It seemed impossible this machine could do this."

Olin Berrier realized that others would find recording as amazing as his daughter had. He says,

> I set it right inside of that door there one night and put [my daughter] Jeanne in there with it and [Artis Koontz and I] got out here and got our fiddle and banjo out and I told Jeanne to record it, you know…. We got through. I told Artis, "Jeanne's

Recording machine owned by Olin Berrier. This disc-cutting machine was made for home use by the Wilcox-Gay Company and was among the first truly portable recorders offered to the public. Berrier acquired it in the late 1930s.

got a record in here she wants to play for you." She turned it on, you know, and played it. He said, "Who in the world's that playin' fiddle? That's you pickin' banjo, ain't it?" I said, "Yeah," and he never did recognize hisself playin' the fiddle.

One of the unforeseen byproducts of Olin's recording were the 181 discs he left behind. Contained in their scratchy grooves are echoes of local musicians such as the Coopers, Artis Koontz, Clay Everhart, Odell Smith and of course Olin himself.

Bands of Kids

Many Piedmont musicians began as children, abandoning their music as adult responsibilities commanded their time. Others built the foundation for a life of music making on childhood experiences. When the possibility of a livelihood from music became a reality in this century, only a few ever really "made it" as performers.

Just north of the Deep River, there is a neighborhood in Randleman where some of the youngsters decided to get together and form a band. James Lee Hall, Jr. (born January 29, 1923) had a father who "could saw a fiddle" and also played in the Randleman Brass Band. But the banjo captured James' attention, particularly as played by Henry Claude Lamb (August 1, 1882–September 22, 1960). Claude Lamb was one of the local virtuosos, and Hall used to go sit on his porch just to hear the older man play. In the mid–1930s, James got hold of a banjo, and, in the company of guitarist Paul Holland, started to tinker with music. The next recruits were the Allred brothers; Richard Earl (January 24, 1921–April 18, 1990) played guitar, and his younger brother James Fred (October 13, 1922–July 14, 1996) the mandolin. Last to come on board were Lester Bruce Beane (January 24, 1921–December 16, 1939) on guitar, bringing along the brothers George (born July 9, 1922) on fiddle and Gilbert Harrison Christenberry Jr. (August 30, 1920–September 16, 1944) on guitar.

The boys were originally only a local phenomenon. They would play at each other's homes, or at the local grocery store for sandwiches and ice cream. Their first truly public appearances were at local fiddlers' conventions, where they would often win a prize because of their age. Initially, they were too young to have driver's licenses, so either their friend Robert Hunt or the Christenberry's mother would provide the transportation.

By 1937, sponsored by Holsum Bread, they were one of the first groups to broadcast over WMFR-High Point. The boys were let out of school one day a week for the programs, and their class would listen to them on the radio. The group also appeared on WBIG-Greensboro. The band made some personal appearances in addition to playing on the radio. Perhaps their biggest gig and the pinnacle of their short time as a band was appearing between the moving pictures at Asheboro's two movie palaces. Every Saturday, the boys played three fifteen-minute shows, alternating between the Sunset and the Carolina theaters. For their labors, each made $5.

This all came to an end as the band members grew into adulthood. Gilbert Christenberry went to work at Randolph Lingerie, where he met his wife in 1938. The

Left to right, Richard Allred (guitar), Bruce Beane (guitar), George Christenberry (fiddle), Fred Allred (mandolin), James Hall (banjo) and Gilbert Christenberry (guitar). The boys, although grimly posing in a local photographer's studio, must have been proud of their new cowboy hats and local celebrity acquired through their music. Randleman, Randolph County, late 1930s. Courtesy Mrs. Gilbert Christenberry.

band's fate was sealed when Bruce Beane was killed at the end of 1939. He hitched a ride, and the car he was riding in wrecked. George Christenberry left the area around the same time, but has fond memories of their music making. George told me, "That so-called music that we made kept us out of kids' problems."

Down in Old Hollow: Sutphin Family Music

Head north out of Winston-Salem, North Carolina, on Highway 52. At the airport exit, drive east toward Walkertown. Turn north again and pass the White Rock School, currently a community center and the scene of long-running Friday night jam session. Just ahead lies Old Hollow and the home of the Sutphin family. It was in this area where Sid Sutphin gathered some of the local teenagers into a string band before World War II. But, the roots of this group lay back in time, in the mountains to the north of Forsyth County in Mt. Airy and the Round Peak area of Surry County, and Lambsburg, in Carroll County, Virginia.

The town of Mt. Airy and the legendary Tommy Jarrell loom large over the current practitioners of old-style fiddle and banjo music. Jarrell, born the same year as Sid Sutphin, legitimized the fiddlers' convention in the Granite City for young, city-bred musicians. He helped to convert those players to the musical style from Round

Peak, above Mt. Airy, and to a tune family performed by musical ancestors such as Zach Payne.

"Zachariah 'Zach' Payne (1845–1929) is the furthest one back who played music in my family that I know of," says Kirk Sutphin, Sid's grandson. "He was my great-grandma Sutphin's uncle. Her dad, Wiley Payne [born October 1851], was Zack's brother. The Paynes lived in Lambsburg, Carroll County, Virginia. Wiley Payne's family moved to Round Peak [around 1900]. There, they met the Sutphins."

As of 1880, the Sutphin clan was farming at Round Peak. North Carolinian John Wesley Sutphin(circa 1832–1900) had settled in Georgia after being wounded there during the Civil War. John brought his family — wife Mary (born in 1842) and their children — back from Georgia to Franklin Township in Surry County, where their last son, George, was born. After Wiley Payne's migration, Payne's daughter Irene (or Irena) Margaret (known as "Reenie," February 8, 1882–February 22, 1962) met and married John Wesley's youngest boy. "I remember grandma saying that Reenie would dance and play the harmonica," tells Kirk. "She kept her harmonica in her apron pocket with her snuff box!"

"As far as I know," continues Kirk, "my great-grandfather George Washington Sutphin [May 28, 1880–?August 6, 1966] played two or three instruments. I've never known for sure. I know he played a little bit on the fiddle and the banjo. Cindy [Lucinda, Reenie's youngest sister, November 1894–1992] would say, "Grandpa George played 'Once I had a Fortune' on the fiddle and 'Georgia Buck' on the banjo."

Kirk's grandfather was also a musician. "Sidney John Sutphin (December 13, 1901–September 28, 1977) was the oldest of George and Irene's children. My grandfather was a fiddler and played banjo and guitar somewhat. He played the pump organ, too, but fiddle was his main instrument."

Kirk's uncle, Rupert, remembers Sid's fiddling well: "[Dad] patterned his fiddling after a Lowe [possibly Logan or his brother Charlie Lowe]. He had a real smooth bow. He wanted to play like him, instead of the fast, jerky bow like Tommy Jarrell."

Sidney Sutphin married Trudie Flippin in 1921 and they moved to Eastern Virginia. The couple stayed one year at Amelia Courthouse with Trudie's uncle. The pair then returned to Round Peak, where their first son, Rupert Clinton, was born December 11, 1922. In 1925, like many others of their ilk, the family came to the Piedmont of North Carolina in search of work in the furniture factories of Winston-Salem.

Rupert reports his family frequently changed residences, in search of a better house or of cheaper rent. Mostly, they lived outside of the city limits in Forsyth County, says Wayne, Rupert's brother and Kirk's father. During the depression, Sid only worked one day a week, so the family got by farming, raising a garden and keeping animals.

Rupert tells of walking long distances to hear a neighbor's radio or phonograph. Around 1930, the family would go to Mr. White's home on Davis Road Sunday afternoons and listen to his gramophone. As they sat in a circle in his living room, their host would play recordings by Jimmie Rodgers and the Skillet Lickers, among others. Rupert says, "I remember my dad getting ready on a Saturday night to go play music. His fiddle was on the bed and I plucked a string. My father gave me hell! I wasn't to touch that fiddle." Shortly after that, Sid loaned the fiddle out.

Sidney Sutphin. Round Peak area of Surry County, circa 1920. Photograph by Will Flippin, courtesy Kirk Sutphin.

Kirk has similar memories. He recollects

> He wouldn't normally let nobody touch his fiddle. It was one similar to the one Tommy Jarrell had, with the inlay in the back. And some of his buddies borrowed it and were drunk and were going to a dance. They got stuck in a snow drift and put the fiddle under the T-Model, in the case, to try and pry the wheel. And broke the neck out. They stuck it in a violin repair place, maybe like a pawn shop and went on back to the mountains. And he didn't know it till later on. Grandpa's brother Harv hunted all around Winston until he found it. It was six or eight dollars to get the fiddle back, equal to a week's paycheck. And Grandpa refused, he said that they should pay for it. And Grandma begged him, but he refused to go get it. He just borrowed fiddles to play until the 1950s, when he bought a fiddle off his brother-in-law.

Rupert remembers how he started playing the guitar. A dance was held at their house in 1935, and Dallas Nicholson was there playing the banjo (the Nicholsons were from Wilkes County). Sid Sutphin had borrowed an instrument and was fiddling that evening. The bed had been taken apart in the back bedroom, and "they all crowded in there." A big storm hit that night and because the musicians didn't have cases for their instruments—a fiddle, a banjo and a guitar — they left them at the house. The bed was reassembled and Rupert went to sleep in that room. He says,

> And I was given strict instructions not to bother those instruments. But I watched those musicians and watched the guy playing the guitar and I watched where he put his fingers on the strings. And it just set me on fire. So, that day, when dad

was at work and mom out in the garden, I tried out the guitar. Because, I learned three chords watchin' them.

Next, Rupert's neighbor, Bessie Bell (nee Disher), got a small black Gibson guitar. "I taught her how to chord the guitar in order to get to play it myself," Rupert relates. Since he had also heard musicians like Jimmie Davis and programs like the Grand Ole Opry on the radio (the family acquired one around 1939), Rupert had progressed past the three chords he had initially learned. However, Rupert never advanced to the fiddle. "I didn't have a fiddle and so stayed with what I started with."

Sid Sutphin also provided music for community events. "Seems like it was Willie Walker that'd come and get Dad to play at a square dance on a Saturday in the neighborhood," recollects Kirk's father, Wayne. "Mama would get mad cause that Walker feller would never ask her to go. I was about ten or twelve, around 1940, '41. Sid played mostly for square dances up until 1939. Then, he organized all the kids in the neighborhood into a band and they played all over."

Robert Emmett Walker was one of those neighborhood children. Born in 1921, Emmett had three musical brothers. Of those, fellow band members were Virgil Odell, born in 1925, and Gerald Wesley, born in 1927. An older brother, Edward (born around 1915) played mandolin, but not with their aggregation. Emmett's father, Rober Wesley Walker (1890–1960), was a fiddler [from the Oak Summit Community]. "Robe" kept the fiddle in just one tuning, says Emmett, and played "the old breakdowns: 'Arkansas Traveler,' 'Soldier's Joy,' 'Boil Them Cabbage Down,' and 'Home Sweet Home.'" Emmett Walker remembers that "They had a band back in the early '30s that [Robe] played with." Bud Nicholson, "the leader of it," fiddled, his sons Dallas played guitar and Clifton "thumb-picked" the banjo, although he could also play guitar and fiddle. All the Nicholsons were farmers. "That was just a neighborhood band like we were," says Emmett. Robe's youngest brother, Willie, played banjo and autoharp. Another younger brother, Kyle, might have also played the autoharp.

Emmett recollects the occasion in Walkertown when the band was formed. Norman Fry and Rupert Sutphin were also in attendance that evening. "A guy [possibly May Johnson] was playing a washboard. And I though, 'I can play one of those things.'" Norman said he'd get a banjo if Emmett would get a washboard. And, so the Walkertown Washboard Band was born. "The kids band," recalls Wayne Sutphin, "was my brother Rupert on guitar and Emmett Walker on washboard and Norman Fry on tenor banjo and Virgil Walker on mandolin. And Gerald Walker on guitar."

The group started playing at neighbor's houses once a week. Rupert remembers that "all the young people would gather there and [therefore] none of us got into any trouble." Mostly, the youngsters played fiddle tunes like "Chinese Breakdown," "Flop-Eared Mule," "Walkin' in My Sleep," "Bully of the Town" and "Peekaboo Waltz." Mrs. Emmett Walker is from the same neighborhood. "Every time they'd play," she tells, "we'd dance. Our neighborhood was full of teenagers. You didn't have the money to go nowhere. We made our own entertainment, it was clean fun." Emmett relates that he did most of the dance calling. "I'd heard enough on the Grand Ole Opry that we could get by." Enthusiasm more than made up for inexperience. "We walked

The Walkertown Washboard Band. Left to right, Virgil Walker (mandolin), Rupert Sutphin (guitar), Norman Fry (banjo), Gerald Walker (guitar) and Sidney Sutphin (fiddle). Taken Easter Monday, 1940 or 1941. Courtesy Kirk Sutphin.

through the snow onetime," as Emmett tells it. "It didn't matter how cold it was. We'd go to Sid's and play."

With their neighborhood reputation established, the band was summoned by Mt. Pleasant Methodist Church to play between the acts of a theatrical production designed to raise funds for the church. The presentation was toured to all the schools in Forsyth County. One Friday night, the troupe went down to El Dorado to perform at a school. A storm came up and knocked out the lights, so farmers brought lanterns in and placed them on the stage. For all these engagements, the band was not paid, all monies going to the church.

Wayne Sutphin was too young to be a member, but he followed the Washboard Band's progress. He remembers that

> Back in those days, you played school houses. I remember they would play at places like Trinity and different school houses in the outlying counties around Forsyth. They would advertise it and charge people a quarter to get in. Mostly where they played was high schools on weekends. Iredell, Guilford, Rockingham, Davie and Stokes counties.

Rupert relates the story of the Washboard Band attending a talent contest at the state movie theater in Winston-Salem. The band that could play "Comin' 'Round the Mountain" best would win the $25. Unbeknownst to them, Roger Smith and the Swingbillies (not the same band as Dunk Poole's), playing at the time on WSJS (see Chapter Nine), also had decided to enter. The Swingbillies took the stage, wearing their uniform of gray hats, light blue shirts and pants, and won the contest.

Virgil and Gerald continued to play together after Emmett went into the service in 1942. "After the War, we all went our separate ways and that was it," concludes Emmett.

Sid, however, did not stop playing music. "Most of all the playing Sid did during the War was with that bunch on the radio," tells Wayne Sutphin.

> It was a daily through the week morning program, something like six till six-thirty, at WAIR.... Cliff Nicholson, he was the guitar player, just as good as Merle Travis or Chet Atkins, he could play everything they could. His brother Dallas played guitar and their daddy Bud played fiddle. He was really good—his specialty was "Cacklin' Hen." Fiddler Johnny Ham was on those programs. There used to be a guy who was a pretty good singer and nearly every morning, he'd play that tune, "Each Night At Nine." They didn't stay on it very long; it was only a few months. It was one of the hundreds of bands called the Carolina Buddies.

Before entering the air force, Rupert also assembled a band that auditioned for WAIR. The station told them they were too hillbilly, and to get an accordion player!

Paul Johnson was another musician appearing on WAIR at that time. "Dad worked with Paul Johnson," remembers Wayne Sutphin. "He played guitar and his son played guitar. Harvey Hester played tenor guitar with them." Sid and Rupert Sutphin maintained a regular performing schedule with the Johnsons. Every weekend, Paul Johnson packed them into his car, tied the instruments on top, and went to Collin's Garage on Main Street in King for the Friday night jamboree. Paul and his son would dress up like cowboys, with identical Gibson guitars. The stage and mikes were set up in front behind a window with speakers out on the street. "And the street would be so full of people," says Rupert, "that the traffic would have to be detoured. But that was every Friday night for us." This went on until Rupert went into the service in January of 1943.

Music Sessions

Musicians are always looking for opportunities to play. "I can't remember a week that didn't go by that we didn't have the playing of music," Glee Nance Arnold told me. Outside of the organized social situations like dances, fiddlers' conventions, and farm work, there were lots of other times when musicians performed. Who knows when a situation might present itself: lunchtime on the job, at a store when stopping for gas or supplies, at the home of a friend. One never knew who would be visiting, passing through on a trip, or employed by a factory or mill. It always paid to have an instrument close by, in the trunk of a car, stashed in a locker, or stuffed under a desk. These informal, unorganized jam sessions provided an opportunity for honing musical skills, learning new techniques, chords, and styles and for picking up a tune or song. Any free time could turn into an informal get together at the home of a neighbor or relative.

Oberia Walker's family had regular sessions in rural Randolph County. "Once a month," she remembers, we just quit [the farm work] early in the afternoon, and eat supper. My sister, she was two years older than me and my mother would carry one and my daddy one. And [we'd] have the lantern and we'd go across the woods, back of our house, through a cow path, and up to our next neighbor, Jason Hoover, he played the fiddle. And they'd get all of their children together and we would go on then and cross the woods to another neighbor named Monroe Hoover—[he and Jason] were probably first cousins, I believe. And that's where the music took place then. I believe [Monroe] played the fiddle. Or maybe a guitar. I'm not sure. And my dad Joel Addison Ashworth [November 20, 1887–October 12, 1971] played banjo. And these other two families, they had several children, so it was a pretty good gathering once we all got together. And they would play at Monroe Hoover's house till way in the night, probably 10 or 11 o'clock, and then we'd come back with the lantern, back through the woods and go home. [And this would happen] fairly often, mostly in the fall, before the weather got too cold and then occasionally through the winter, it might be at a different neighbor's house. But if it was real cold, well, we didn't, you know, walking that far and all. Even before I stopped going to school at the little country school [around 1928], they had stopped playing then. Most of these families—the Victrolas stopped 'em from playing.

Tommy Parker's family had to wait until farming slowed down to do their music making at neighbor Claude Winslow's:

We traveled by a wagon and mules or walked. It was always in the dead of winter. We were too busy in the summertime. We'd play music all night long if we wanted to. Then we'd walk on back home. It's like a mile and a half away. Then they'd do the same thing and come to our house. Lots of times when I was a small kid, I'd go on to bed and go to sleep and they'd still be playing [*Nuggets*, 50].

Sometimes, certain locales would become *the* gathering place for musicians, such as the home of James Milton Scotten (1869–1938). "Uncle Jim," as he became known, was a harness and shoe maker, who farmed a bit as well as traded horses for a living. In 1891, Scotten married Luzena Miriam Stout, a Quaker school teacher who had some music training at Guilford College. When Luzena died in 1912, James's main interest became fiddling and his home became a community center for string music. Sunday afternoons, he would play on his porch, and was eventually joined by his son Bonney Clay (January 5, 1892–January 14, 1984) on clawhammer banjo, Leondas Wright on autoharp, Tom Cox on the dulcimer, Carson Cox on fiddle, and Glenn Davis on the banjo.

Sometimes, the urge to make music was too great to find a suitable and comfortable location. Elgin and Herman Boyd were two such musicians who carried their instruments in case of the spontaneous session. "Back then, me and my brother," tells Elgin, "we had a car. And we carried a guitar, and he carried his fiddle everywhere we went.... And a bunch of us would get together and we'd meet up here on [Route] 158. We'd get out in the middle of the road, stand there at two o'clock in the mornin' and play till we give out. Wasn't no cars comin'. [If] we'd see one way off ..., we'd get out of the road."

Fiddler Nolan Johnson

A fiddler extraordinary for still playing the tunes popular in the nineteenth century was Nolan Johnson of Davidson County. For the last forty years, a steady stream of traditional music enthusiasts have visited the small shop out in back of the Johnson home. Some came to buy or trade an instrument. Others called to get a favorite violin or clock repaired. Additional guests filled the small back room of the building, or a converted tobacco barn close by, on a Friday or Saturday night. They came to play along with Nolan on the tunes that his grandfather had taught his father, and his father had taught to him. These included "Old Aunt Katie, Won't You Come Out Tonight" (more commonly titled "Buffalo Gals"), "Sally, Will You Marry Me," and "Jackson's March."

Nolan Vestal Johnson was born June 20, 1918, in Davidson County's Hasty Community, the next to youngest child of Levi and Annie Johnson. With the exception of military service during World War II, he lived all his life on the Hasty School Road, first in a house built by his father, and, after marrying, on a corner of his family's property. His grandfather, Joshua Calvin Johnson (October 15, 1835–May 15, 1923), of Scottish descent, had settled on what is now Club Drive just outside of High Point, on the Guilford and Davidson county line. Joshua, a cooper and a Wesleyan Methodist minister, Joshua's brother Frank, and Nolan's father, Levi White Johnson (July 24, 1874–November 11, 1964), were all fiddlers. In fact, the instrument that

Nolan and Dot Johnson, the founders of "Johnson Grass." Hasty, Davidson County, 1995.

Nolan learned on had belonged to his grandfather. "Since grandpa played," said Nolan Johnson,

> I imagine [my father] did somewhat like I did, you know [learned the fiddle from his father]. You see, my dad picked the banjo some [in the clawhammer style] and they'd go [to my grandfather's house] to spend the weekend, why they played music, so my sister said. My uncle David [Linville, my dad's younger brother, born in 1877], he picked the banjo some [as well].

In 1896, Nolan's father moved slightly west to the Hasty community, married several years later and raised his own family. Levi Johnson was a brick mason by occupation, as well as a good carpenter and a blacksmith, and also farmed on the side. Along with music, Nolan gained an appreciation for these trades from his father, and learned basic woodworking and smithing skills from him.

When asked, out of his ten siblings, why he was the only one to continue with music, Nolan replied,

> I don't know. I just liked my dad's sound of the violin, you know, and I asked him to play the fiddle of a night.... So he took enough interest in me — he made me a little wood violin — just kind of whittled it out, you know, and then he showed me the scales, I guess that's what you call it, isn't it? Do-re-mes? Showed how to get it on the violin. That's all he showed me and I practiced that for — well, I don't know how many months — before I accidentally stumbled on a tune. "Mississippi Sawyer." And when I did that anything I could think of I'd play. I was about twelve or thirteen years old. Naturally they didn't have radios back then [and since there weren't a large number of other musicians around] anything that I knew was something I heard him play, you know.

By playing guitar with his father, Nolan learned these tunes, as well as "Hopping in the Buggy," "Old Christmas," and "Silly Bill."

Musicians in Nolan's community never traveled far outside of their own local area. In the 1930s, the radio helped broaden his repertoire. Music by the Tobacco Tags, Monroe Brothers, Hoosier Hot Shots, Sons of the Pioneers and J.E. Mainer, on WBT-Charlotte or WPTF-Raleigh, all emanated from the family radio at dinner time. And some of those tunes found a place in Nolan's guitar or fiddle tune bag.

Nolan Johnson left school after the ninth grade, and worked briefly as his father's assistant. If not for Levi Johnson losing his sight and being forced to retire, Nolan would have followed him into the building trade. Instead, Nolan Johnson tended his father's farm until being drafted into the army in 1941. After getting out of the military at the end of World War II, Nolan went to barbering, and retired in 1980. He married Dorothy Treva ("Dot") Harris (born 1916) of Thomasville in 1947.

Nolan had quit music upon entering the service; this may have contributed to the preservation of his father's pieces in Nolan's playing. With Dot on the ukulele, he picked the fiddle up again around 1960: "I learned there was a place down below Trinity at a store on Saturday night was making music. One of my sisters lived down where that was and she told me about it so I got to going down there and listening and picking up a few tunes and I got interested and so that's how it happened. I never had lost all my interest but I did not do it for so many years."

Through an association with the late Henry Rohde, Nolan also learned to build and repair violins, an avocation which he followed up until a few years ago. His love of a good instrument, and the craft which produces a violin, has helped to deepen Nolan's affection for the instrument, and added to the distinctive sense of tone in his playing.

Although Nolan had been influenced by the fiddlers popular when he was growing up, he never lost a love for the old pieces that his father played. Tunes from Grand Ole Opry Star Arthur Smith and Nashville fiddler Tommy Jackson like "Florida Blues" and "Run, Johnny, Run" resided alongside selections popular twenty to thirty years before Johnson's birth. One reason Nolan Johnson has retained the music of older generations in his repertoire may be because he had not had to satisfy the needs of dancers nor the tastes of contest judges. For unlike most musicians, Nolan has never played for many dances ("It's too much like work"), nor entered fiddlers' conventions. He has never been very public with his music, preferring to play within the confines of his family and close neighbors. This made Nolan Johnson an anomaly in his locale, and probably the only fiddler playing the pieces of his father's generation.

Jam Sessions

It is just a short distance between the informal private music sessions occurring in people's homes to the public jam sessions and performances that take place in outbuildings and community structures. All of these share an easygoing spirit and an unpredictability of just who might attend (although there are regular musicians, dancers and audience) and of the quality and quantity of the music. What sets these jam sessions apart from those like Nolan Johnson's is that they are open to the public.

These sessions come and go. As people pass through the cycle of life's events, music becomes less important, jobs and family take up a greater part of their time, and those sponsoring the sessions become weary of the responsibility.

The late Wade Walker (March 5, 1915–December 29, 1988) lived among musicians. Although he never played an instrument himself, he did everything he could to promote those amongst the community with a talent for music. As he said, "Ever since I could walk [I have been interested in country music]. I think I inherited it from my daddy. He could sit up all night and listen to string music. I don't play anything. I'm a great listener." Walker's friendship with banjoist and raconteur George Pegram provided the impetus toward an organized event. Wade's wife Oberia Walker recalled that the couple first heard George playing for the Farmer square dance in the mid to late 1950s: "Well, after we met George Pegram, that was when Wade really wanted a place big enough to invite friends in, you know, and have him to come and play, and then Clegg Garner would play with him, you know."

In the 1960s, the Walkers began holding gatherings every two or three weeks

Left to right, "Tommy" Parker (banjo), Tommy Walker (guitar) and Mark Walker (fiddle). These three musicians provided the core of the band that entertained at jam sessions held by Wade Walker, father to Mark and brother to Tommy Walker. Tommy Parker holds his father's banjo. Randolph County, 1990.

during the cool months until Wade's death in 1988. On Friday nights, from 7:30 or 8 P.M. until 10:00 or 10:30 P.M., approximately 70 to 75 people would gather at a building on Wade's property to make music and dance. Sometime along the way, Wade and Oberia Walker's son Mark (born January 2, 1953) took up the fiddle and joined in with the music making. Mark was inspired to play the fiddle by watching Lost John Ray, who played with George Pegram. In 1980, Mark Walker started learning from Fred "Speedy" Marley from Staley, who worked with Mark at Klaussner Furniture. Saford Hall, another musician who fiddled for the dance at Farmer, also provided some instruction. "I had always been fascinated by the fiddle and I knew there would be somebody to play [that style of music] with," Mark told me. "Rock 'n' roll, or other modern music, you need to do it in a big way. Old time and bluegrass, you can sit and pick on your porch." Eventually, the Walker jam session band grew to include Mark on fiddle, Oberia's relation Ray Betts on guitar, Wade's brother Tommy Walker (May 10, 1925–February 2, 1992) on guitar, Tommy Parker on banjo, Wade's nephew Steve Bingham on bass, Reid Thornburg on harmonica, George McDowell on harmonica, Johnny Walker (Wade and Tommy's great-nephew) on guitar and spoons and Jerry Talbert on mandolin.

Mark Walker describes the band's repertoire: "We try to, you know, play some pretty good songs for 'em to dance to, and then when the Tommys get a little tired there, we'll play a slow one or two. But most of the time, you know, we'll try to play something where they can dance to."

Wade had one rule: "There won't be any drinking because I won't put up with that. Some come with their children. They're not embarrassed by somebody saying bad words or drinking 'cause I just wouldn't allow that at all" (*Nuggets*, 46–48, 51–53).

Opry's

A more organized version of the public jam session moves the music onto a stage and imposes a structure onto the occasion. Folklorist Amy Davis, who has written extensively about these organized jams, defines public music sharing sessions as "oprys." To differentiate these performances from jam sessions, Davis mentions "a master of ceremonies, a sequence of performers, an audience, and a sound system" (3). "Opry," supposedly a signifier for a country version of grand opera, is derived in this case from the name of the most famous country music radio program of them all, WSM-Nashville's Grand Ole Opry (Davis, 4). Only one of the many live radio variety programs to proliferate in the years before World War II, the Opry and the other shows of the same mold provided the blueprint for local country music shows, including those in the Piedmont of North Carolina. The imitation of the famous Opry treads a fine line between conscious and unconscious parody. In some ways, the emcee, performers, and audience are pretending that they are a part of a bigger,

Left to right, musicians "Buck" Holt (guitar), Maynard Perry (guitar), "Zeke" Reitzel (banjo), David Watson (electric bass) and unknown electric guitarist. This jam session was held at Linen's Service Station near the Randolph and Alamance County line around 1983. Courtesy Zeke Reitzel.

more famous show, knowing all too well of the humbleness of their surroundings. On the other hand, these audiences enjoy the attempts of community members at serious music making as much as if they were attending a professional show. Some of the local Piedmont "oprys" includes Charlie's Barn between Siler City and Pittsboro in Chatham County (Friday nights), Brown's Ole Opry, Jimmy Johnson's (Davis, 115), the Kimesville Fire Station in Alamance County (Davis, 113), Eleazor, and the Rand Ol' Opry.

The opry at Eleazor takes place in a building in southern Randolph County built by Leonard Simmons on his property. Opened in 1986, on Friday evenings, Leonard hosts an open stage that is free of charge, and Saturday evenings, he hires professional bands to perform, with admission charged. Simmons' building is an archetypal homemade structure for jam sessions and "Opry" alike, an amalgam of particleboard, cinder blocks, and tin. Church pews and other cast-off furniture fill the structure. At one end is a stage with a sound system, and at the other, a refreshment stand.

Brown's Ole Opry is located on a farm owned by the Brown family near McLeansville. There is no charge for admission as the musicians are not paid, although donations are collected in order to cover other expenses. Advertisement is through word-of-mouth. Brown's began in the 1940s as a public jam session led by fiddler Will Brown. These feed barn sessions stopped when they grew too crowded. In 1979, Brown's son Charlie began inviting musicians to come play in a tobacco barn on his property. Friday evenings, from 7 until 11, a very consistent group of musicians and listeners gather for performing and clogging. In fact, bands will often call in advance to make sure that they'll have a performance slot. Charlie has added onto that original building over the years. Improvements have included replacing the dirt floor with one of concrete, along with the addition of a stage, a sound system and kitchen. Charlie passed away seven years ago, but his family members have carried on with the Opry (Davis).

Begun in 1993, Liberty's "Rand Ol' Opry" stands in contrast to Brown's Opry, and is another level up from even Eleazor in organization. Saturday evenings, from 7:30 to 11, is performance time. As Amy Davis has written: "[This] Opry employ[s a] professional house band, lead singers and feature a variety of guest entertainers.... The founder, ... Grady Hockett, ... [has] quite a bit of experience in the country-music world.... Grady Hockett performed for many years with the house band at the Renfro Valley Barn Dance" (Davis, 32, 116).

FOUR

"I Can't Remember When I Didn't Go to a Square Dance"

"I like to square dance. [My wife] and I used to go, but we never said nothin' about it. Some people think it's wrong to square dance, but it ain't. It's just good clean fun. Drinkin' is what's given it a bad name. They ain't a thing wrong with square dancin' and it'll keep you young."

— John Tussey III

Any community event would be incomplete without an organized dance of some kind. In the Piedmont, dances followed agrarian events such as corn shuckings and tobacco curing. Dancing is documented back into the later part of the eighteenth century, although North Carolinians have probably danced since the time of settlement before the American Revolution.

Over the last two hundred years of Piedmont life, inhabitants have practiced a "single dance" (known these days as "clogging," "buck dancing," "tapping," and "stepping") tradition that is found in both Anglo and African American culture. Calvin Henderson Wiley, writing about Alamance County, seems to be describing this style of "showing off" when he writes

> I followed the sound of a fiddle, and found myself at the door which opened into the public saloon. As no one met me to welcome me in, and as it was rather moist to wait long out of doors, I followed the example of others, and was soon wedged so tight in the middle of the passage, that I could move in no direction, and could scarcely turn my head.... Through a door on one side, I saw into a room, around the sides of which men and women were packed together as if put up for exportation, and in the centre of which some young folk were dancing, each one having about eight inches square on which to cut his capers [Wiley, 12].

73

These members of the Waynick family are pictured during Reconstruction, just after the Civil War. They wear parts of Confederate uniforms left over from the conflict in this demonstration of "step" dancing and banjo playing. In order to hold the dancer still enough for a sharp photograph, a stand (whose base can be seen clearly) is used at his back. Rockingham County. Courtesy North Carolina Office of Archives and History.

Sometimes, as Marvin Gaster has described, the dancer would provide his own music. At other times, as shown in the photograph of "Uncle Jim" Scotten, musicians would play and dancing occurred as accompaniment. If a musician was not available, rhythm was "patted" by the dancer or by a friend. Commonly found in African American tradition of the Piedmont, patting has been less frequently described by whites. Leonard Eubanks, an Anglo-American musician from Chatham

County, characterizes this practice in the 1930s, interestingly associating the dance style with blacks:

> I had a first cousin, … his name was Bernice Whitaker. Boy, I'm a telling you right now, man he could kick the sand, buck dancing, nothing in the world but what I call "ole nigger buck." Law, he could just cut that stuff now. I patted for him, you know, just kept a rhythm going [with slapping hands] if he didn't have no music, you know, just pat him apiece. I've seen him buck dance with a pair of rubber boots on.

Organized Dancing in Years Gone by

Organized dancing, done in lines, squares, or circles, has existed in the Piedmont since the earliest times of colonization. These figures, based on old world forms, were executed by couples, directed or "called" by one of the dancers, and accompanied with whatever music was available. Guion Griffis Johnson, in his book *Ante-Bellum North Carolina*, writes of the occasions where dancing occurred during the antebellum period:

> In some communities "dance frolicks" were held as often as twice a week, on Wednesday and Saturday nights. The young men would "gallant the girls" to the frolic, and dancing would last until midnight. The musician would be a local fiddler who would also call out steps. Amid the sound of merry laughter and the cry of "Salute your partner," "cut the pigeon wing," the dance would proceed. Mint-sling, blackberry acid, and cider were served between dances and not infrequently the men also had their whiskey and brandy [93].

"Uncle" Jim Scotten fiddles for his granddaughter Blanche's dancing on the porch of his Holly Springs home outside the town of Coleridge. Randolph County, 1930s. Courtesy Wil Scotten.

R. R. Michaux tells about dancing in the middle Piedmont during the same period, with an obviously jaundiced eye:

> Now about noon at such gatherings a young fellow would take his "best girl" up to a cart where cakes and cider were to be had, and treat her.... Then would come a dance. Having selected a suitable place in the grove, and about a fifth rate fiddler taking his stand, some would enter the contest for the championship, two dancers at a time, competing one with the other, while near by a squad of white and colored mixed, would engage in playing marbles. Later on, fisticuffs would be in order [20–21].

Dancing continued unabated through the 1800s. J. M. McCorkle, born around 1875, wrote a column for the *Salisbury Post* in the years after World War II. Often, McCorkle would discuss music and dancing in times gone by.

> The students of Davidson College, when I was one of them, visited Charlotte at every opportunity ... I bought a guitar at E. M. Andrews' Music store, and learned to play the "Spanish Fandango," and a few chords....
> In later years both Charlie Snide and Tom Martin learned to play that guitar, and so far excelled my best efforts, that I gave it to Tom. It then became the leading instrument in "Martins one-man band...."
> For informal dances [in the 1890s] we often had a one-man band in the person of ... old Tom Martin. Tom was for many years the janitor at the Davis and Wiley Bank.... Tom fashioned a "contraption" to hold a harp in his mouth, a sort of frame work of wire and string, so that both hands could be free to manipulate a guitar, and with a bell on the floor to tap with his foot, he furnished the music for many dances.
> A little later still, Tom Martin, Pink Johnson and two or three other of their associates, organized a larger band with two violins, a flute and a big bass fiddle.

House Dances

Most Piedmont dwellers I interviewed remembered the house dances from between the first part of the twentieth century and World War II. As Kermit Brady recalled, "Every time they got together, somebody'd want to dance a little and it was alright if they did. It was more or less entertainment for the neighborhood."

Musicians would sit in a doorway between two rooms so that the couples could dance on either side of them, increasing the size of the dance. Stamina and ability were important qualities for players, as each dance would often run fifteen to thirty minutes. Here's how various community members recall these house dances:

> On Saturday night when we'd have the playing of music, the neighbors would all gather in, far and near, to hear the music and sometimes, where there'd be homes that they could have square dancing. In my Daddy's day they'd have the dance in a barn. They'd clean the feed out and have a barn dance, they called it.... And when it was cold weather ... the musicians had to put on extra clothing to keep warm.

And usually along with this the musicians got first choice at the jug. That kept him warm.... And they figured I reckon that it'd pep you up and make you play faster.

[Then] they got to building bigger houses. They'd take the furniture out of the living room and we'd have the whole house in there for dancing. Usually it'd just be in one room of a house, but they could pack a whole lot of people in there, twelve or fourteen in a room. They'd put cornmeal on the floor to make the dancing better. And in summertime, they'd be outside. They'd have square dances, and the Baptists kind of condemned them a little bit, but they'd have them anyway. They played a lot of those old songs, like "Chicken Reel" and "Mississippi Sawyer," and "Old Ninety-Seven" was coming in. If it was a pretty big group, then we went on out across the porch and around the house and come back in — when you were grand marching. But all the time, you were hearing the music as you went by [Jones and Babel interview; Saunders and Whatley].

Worth Winslow grew up in Caraway, a Randolph County community. His parents met in Oakboro, where Winslow's father was providing the music for a Saturday evening square dance using just his fiddle and harmonica. Worth's older brother Sandy Claude Winslow (May 29, 1905–August 1970), played banjo in a finger picking style with his father, as did neighbors Roscoe Parker and Howard Snyder. Worth had fond memories of the house dances held during the 1920s and 1930s.

We lived about a mile from my granddaddy. We had to cross the creek on a foot log. When we crossed the creek, we had to carry our instruments. My daddy would carry his violin, my brother would have his banjo, and we'd go up to our granddaddy's house. They had a big one room upstairs in his house. And we'd put a poplar pole six inches in diameter right in the center of the room downstairs to keep it from falling in, you know. And when the dance was over, they'd take the pole out. Well, it would be about — I'd say a thirty by forty room, a big room. And we'd have thirty or forty people up there sometimes. That would be mostly on an occasion, like the Fourth of July, Christmas. Doc Hartsell was the one that called for the special events, and he would come from Oakboro. My daddy'd drop him a postcard the last of the week and tell him that they were going to have a dance, to come on up Saturday. And he'd spend the night with us and go back on Sunday.

One time, we had that room full of peas— I'spect it was three or four foot deep, you know, just in the hull. And he told us, he said, "If you'll beat them peas out and clean that room up, we'll have a square dance." And so, you know, the boys— they'd get together and get out there and beat 'em up and throw the hulls out the window. And we'd have it.

And we'd have square dances at home —family square dances. My daddy'd tell my sisters to bring some of their friends with them home from school and spend the night. They'd bring five or six girls and then we'd invite the boys in and we'd have a square dance. And one of the neighbor boys, Clarence Snyder he'd call the figures, you know [Nuggets, 39–40].

Leonard Eubanks, from outside Pittsboro, had similar experiences playing and dancing in homes around Chatham County.

Well at a square dance, they'd be four, you and your wife, me and my wife, my girlfriend and me and your girlfriend and you would be a couple. Well us four would go right there. We'd all be in a circle and then when [the caller said] "Four couples out!" well you'd come out and I'd come out and they'd be four of them that join hands and he say, "Lady round the lady and the gent go slow" and "Lady round the lady and the gent don't go," and that's the way it went.... He had to stand out there to do the calling of the figures. Well I don't know some of them might could have danced and called figures. A first cousin of mine [Herbert Herndon] used to call and he'd dance and call figures....

Now way back, even before my time, my Granddaddy King [Faddy K. King, April 20, 1861–December 27, 1936], the one that played the fiddle, used to call. Then there was a Wright man that called down there and was standing back a calling and of course they'd drink a little whiskey and he got pretty high along towards the last of the dance, way over toward midnight, my granddaddy said he'd done forgot the figures and he'd say, "North door, south door, east door," that's all he could say. He'd done got lit up pretty good....

Six or eight couples would be about all that [a house] could really [hold].... The biggest one I was ever at was the sheriff of Chatham County's house, Sheriff Miliken. And the living room was about 20 x 20 [feet]. Had about 16 or 18 couples on the floor. We got a figure caller out of Sanford, Joe Ledbetters. There wasn't no just dragging your feet, you know, back there we used to dance, you know. I'm gonna tell you right now when that music was really rolling, boy, it wasn't making all the racket "tickity-tackity-tickity-tackity" around there, but the way it's run, you know, it was pretty.

Leonard met his first wife at a dance following a corn shucking, when dancing might occur any night of the week excepting Saturday or Sunday, which went against everyone's beliefs.

They'd cut you off at 12 o'clock. The only time they ever danced on Sunday, it was at Julie Perkins', it was way on down toward Farrington. And I was playing and dancing too and there was an old fellow there playing a fiddle with me and Will Council, Ed's brother, Lester. The lady of the house, she said, "Now ya'll gonna dance til 12 o'clock and I mean you ain't dancing nary minute over." Well, man, we was dancing. It went on up to about 10 o'clock, he went there and turned the John Brown clock back to nine. What made it so bad, somebody else didn't know he had turned it back and on about 11 o'clock they went there and turned it back. So we was dancing next Sunday morning at 2 o'clock, we was dancing right on. She never knowed the difference.... It was near 'bout day when I got home. That was in 1931, I believe, about a year before I got married.

In some communities, religious beliefs prohibited dancing, so the gatherings were called "drycorn parties" after the children's game that resembled adult dancing. In other places, children were not allowed to attend dances because they got in the way.

Janet Miller Gillean loved to dance when she was growing up. If Janet wasn't dancing, she was playing music for those gathered around her brothers. Most Saturday evenings through the wintertime, Gillean could be found at a house dance. "I'd rather square dance as to eat when I was young!" she recalled. However, there came a time when Janet's father decided that she should stop attending dances. At first, he objected to Janet's brother taking her to a home of a family with a bad reputation. Finally, his religion got the best of him, and he stopped Janet's dancing altogether. Mrs. Gillean tells the story:

> We went to church one Sunday.... And we had had a dance on Saturday night
> before we went to church on Sunday. And the preacher preached on "the road to
> heaven was too straight and narrow to have a dance hall on it." So, goin' home that
> day, Papa said, "Well, girls, you've had your last dance." So, he wouldn't let us have
> any dances anymore 'cause that preacher preached like that.

Most musicians wouldn't try and support themselves on the money made playing for house dances. Usually a hat was passed and the resulting contributions were
divided up between the caller and the players. In the farming communities of the Piedmont, this was just about enough to pay for gas or a new set of strings for an instrument. Robert Eugene "Bob" Roberson (June 28, 1906–1999) played for house dances as
a teenager around the Snow Camp community in Alamance County. On one particular evening, the caller passed the hat as usual. But, when the time came for the musicians to collect their pay, the caller had absconded with their money, never to be seen
again.

Occasionally, however, additional monies were offered by the assembled community. Kermit Brady tells of a house dance that happened before World War I. Henry
Brady was a popular area fiddler, especially because his wife Martha Ann (nee Sea-
well; March 11, 1855–March 14, 1937) was a figure caller. One night "they had played
for this dance and got tired and quit. He was puttin' his fiddle up. And this fella come
over and told 'em, 'play us one more set, I'll give you fifty cents.' And he played it,
one other tune for the crowd."

Things were different around the mill towns of North Carolina. Bill Allen, who
did cotton mill work in Alamance County, and Fred Foster, from the mill town of
Cooleemee in southern Davie County, remember that the money from music making could be a significant addition, or even substitution, for a weekly wage. While
the mill paid $7.40 to $11 a week in the 1930s, a musician could come away with
$3–$12 for a night of dance music.

Public Dances

Dances also took place in public buildings, although less people remembered
attending these events until after 1940. These occasions shared some similarities
with country house dances, but seemed more open to modern day "improvements"
and outside influence. Homer Keever writes of dancing in the last quarter of the
nineteenth century in Iredell County, which reflects the imprint of upper class society:

> During the Trading period the old line churches were still opposed to dancing,
> but the newer elements in Statesville were not. The 1874 Landmark noted that the
> young men of the town had sponsored a "hop" in Stockton Hall. In 1883 an Italian
> string band was brought from Charlotte to play for a dance in Mott's warehouse.
> The next year there was a dancing school in the Iredell Blues' armory. Then in 1886
> a Terpsichorean Club hired the Italian string band and rented Stockton Hall for tri-

Left to right, Hubert Lohr (banjo), "Shorty" Cruise (string bass), Olin Berrier (banjo) Ernest Harrington (fiddle), Raymond Waisner (guitar), Tom Cooper (guitar) and Russell Smith (caller). This dance occurred at the Lion's Club of Lexington, and, judging from the decorations, probably was around Christmas. Davidson County, December 1947. Courtesy Jeanne Beck.

weekly dances. In the late 1890's a more formal German Club sponsored the dances and provided for dancing lessons [310–311].

In the twentieth century, Piedmont newspapers reported several organized dances before World War II. These public dances showed their modern touches. In Siler City, this meant the incorporation of up-to-date dance steps. "In early August of 1914 a cement floor was put down in the garage building at 124 East 2nd Street. To initiate this improvement a dance was held there at which around one hundred people were present. This was primarily a square dance but some innovative couples demonstrated the one-step and the hesitation" (*Sylvanian*, 40).

There are other accounts of youngsters at house dances and fiddlers' conventions dancing the Charleston.

Olin Berrier

When dances moved out of homes and into public halls, no band was busier in the western Piedmont than that of Olin Gilmer Berrier (February 25, 1899–May 27, 1990). The Berrier family was originally from Germany and moved to Switzerland and then to Pennsylvania in the 1700s. Olin is descended from the three Berrier brothers who left Pennsylvania for Davidson County in North Carolina. Olin's grandfather, Hiram Randleman (born 1839), played the fiddle, and his father, Jacob G. Berrier (October 5, 1867–February 28, 1946), started the banjo in the "hammer" style when he was twelve years old. Jacob's first cousin, William Henry Berrier, also fiddled, as did William's son Elmer.

Olin Berrier grew up in the Ebenezer community of Davidson County, the oldest of four siblings. The family lived a rural lifestyle common for the time. His father farmed, growing cotton as a cash crop, along with wheat, corn, and molasses cane for food, cultivating at least forty acres. As dry goods stores didn't come in until the 1910s, his mother, Victoria C. C. Tussey (1872–1931), spun the fabric for their clothes.

Olin's first musical instrument was the French harp (harmonica), at about the age of nine or ten. As he remembered:

> Well, the way I learnt to play a French harp, my daddy put me in draggin' wheat land [with a horse] one mornin'—we always drug it so we could make a good job of sowing it. Well, I'd bought the harp the night before from a fellar and didn't know how to play it. And I thought, "Well, I'm going to take my harp along to see if I can play it." And when I come in to dinner I could play three tunes.

He began playing the banjo soon afterwards. His first instrument was a simple affair; Olin paid Walt Everhart, a boy two years his elder, fifty cents for it. His teacher was an older neighbor, L. Artis Koontz (December 7, 1892–May 2, 1968). Olin eventually learned to play with his thumb and finger "steady handed," up picking the banjo. Some of the tunes Olin played were "Home Sweet Home," "Tater Pie," "Sweet Bye and Bye," "When the Roll's Called up Yonder," "Jesse James," "Little Log Cabin," and "Golden Slippers." After Olin began to play the banjo, his father "got after" him about why he didn't learn the organ instead, like his sister Ester. Olin answered that you couldn't take the organ with you like you could the banjo. He also picked up the autoharp, the Hawaiian guitar, the ukulele, the mandolin, the guitar, the tenor banjo, and the bass fiddle. "And we run out of instruments then," Olin said, somewhat tongue-in-cheek, "and I believe with all the different ones, it was eleven different instruments. Started off with the French harp and ended with the old big bass."

In 1917, Olin Berrier began working as a mechanic, eventually going into business for himself. He also farmed at night after getting off work in the garage. Berrier married Bessie Leonard (March 17, 1902–January 26, 1987) on May 12, 1920, moving with his new bride into the home he built on Leonard Road in June of 1921. Olin and Bessie Berrier had three children, Leonard Gilmer, born February 18, 1921, Margret (called "Micki"), born August 28, 1923, and Elva Jeanne, born September 5, 1926. With Bessie and the children, Olin formed a family band in the late 1920s or early 1930s.

Olin was proud of their music making: "If things had just kind of been right and if there hadn't been a depression, I think our family could have been like the Carter Family. We got together every Saturday till the Army got Leonard. Then I had to go out and form my own band" (Berrier and Brown and Michael; Berrier and Michael; *Greensboro Daily News*, June 29, 1958: B12; Census; Glenn Tussey; Cemetery Book).

During this period, the Berrier family would hold house dances. Olin's daughter Jeanne Beck remembers those occurring at the end of the 1930s. These were not organized square dances with a caller, but more like a jam session where some of the audience would round dance and Charleston. "Some of Daddy's farmer friends that played the violin, the banjo and whatever," tells Jeanne.

> Some of them were actually kin people, they would come on Saturday night [after supper until 11 P.M. or 12 midnight] and we would roll up the rugs and people

Left to right, Olin Berrier, with the violin, his wife, Bessie (guitar) and their children Leonard (five string banjo), Micki (mandolin) and Jeanne (ukulele). Both Micki and Jeanne excelled on the piano and Leonard became a caller with his father's square dance bands. This photo was taken in front of the home built by Berrier on Leonard Road in Welcome, Davidson County, summer 1931. Courtesy Jeanne Beck.

> would come from miles around. Mostly, they could hear it, because you didn't have that many houses then, you didn't have that many trees, and the music carried and they'd say, "Oh, they're making music over at Olin's house."

Olin Berrier "formed his own band" when a local fundraiser was needed for Franklin Roosevelt's 1933 presidential campaign. Thus began his career providing the music for public dances.

> They wanted to make some money at Lexington and some of them suggested trying a square dance. Then they come to see me and see if I would play it, and call it for them. And the first one was right across the street yonder where my cousins used to have that big old garage in there, a Pontiac and Buick place. And they filled that thing until no more people could get around. And it went over so good, they decided to have one over at the club the next week and the same thing happened over there. [So, eventually] we took over the recreation center in Winston-Salem every Tuesday night. Thursday night we would go to Rural Hall and play up there. Friday night we would come to the American Legion down here [in Lexington] and Saturday nights, it was the Lion's Den [Lion's Club].

These early dances might attract fifty to seventy-five people a night, who each paid twenty-five or fifty cents to attend from 8 P.M. until midnight.

The public dances started in earnest with the prosperity following World War II. Mildred Southern, a Texan who attended Appalachian State University in Boone, North Carolina, with Olin's daughter Micki, was hired by the Winston-Salem Recreation Department to teach the newer style of western square dance calling. Six people took the courses in 1946 and 1947, including Micki's brother Leonard and Micki's husband Russell Smith (March 11, 1919–1980). Both Leonard and Russell went on to call dances with the Olin Berrier band (Berrier and Brown interview). The City Recreation Department also sponsored dances at the Hanes Building on Indiana Street.

Olin seems to have used different bands depending either on the locale or upon the availability of musicians. For the five years following World War II, one of Berrier's groups used Ernest Harrington (March 20, 1903–November 21, 1997) on fiddle, Thomas Raymond Waisner (August 11, 1905–September 13, 1965) and Tom Cooper on guitars, Hubert Lohr on banjo, and Shorty Cruise on string bass. Ernest Harrington was originally from Iredell County and worked at the Winona Cotton Mill. Tom Cooper had recorded with his cousins Dewey and Clay Everhart as the North Carolina Cooper Boys (see Chapter Seven) and had been a long-time musical acquaintance of the Berriers. Olin had heard Hubert Lohr on a High Point radio station, and recruited him for his groups (see Chapter Nine). And Cruise was a well-known local musician in Lexington, having led a band during World War II that included future Berrier associate Floyd Morrison.

Another of Olin's groups, called Dick Smith and His Night Owls, consisted of Dave Beck on guitar, Dick Smith from Winston-Salem on fiddle and Miles Calloway (from Winston)/stand/up bass, along with Olin on banjo. Russell Smith called with both of these aggregations (Leonard Berrier started calling with Olin when Russell Smith quit around 1950 or 1951). Dave Beck, another of Olin's son-in-laws, remembered how they'd "load that old sound system up [in] Olin's old 1937 Oldsmobile ... and we put that old bass in the center ... inside the car and there would be four of us sitting in there with it and we'd load the amps and stuff in there...."

Berrier also included his daughter Jeanne in his early square dance groups, as the volume of her piano playing could be easily heard over the sound of the dancers. Jeanne Beck remembers

> As I grew older, probably 14 to 15 years old, I accompanied the band with the piano (Leonard remembers this to be four or five years later, in 1945). We started the dances at the American Legion and by then, I could play the piano very well by ear. This was an every Friday night affair and believe it or not, I made my spending money that way, which probably didn't amount to $5 a night but that was great bucks then. We would play for dances in Winston-Salem. We played at the [roof garden of the old] Robert E. Lee hotel which was big stuff then and we played a couple of nights for Salem College for the girls to have a square dance and I was right in there with him, playing the piano.

In fact, Olin Berrier became so successful, that he couldn't handle all the requests for his services. So, Olin would refer the work to others in his musical circle (Berrier and Michael interview; Berrier and Sowers interview).

Phillip Eldridge Hege (February 9, 1923–March 3, 2002) had been one of Olin's competitors, but decided at that time it would be better to join forces with Berrier. Phillip's father, Fred Henry Hege (1892–1976), was born around Yadkin College and worked at the Erlanger Mill. Fred played banjo in the down-picking style, and performed mostly around home for his own amusement. Born in Lexington, Phil started playing music at the age of eight, learning guitar at the same time as his brother

Lloyd (born 1926). When Phil Hege got married in 1941, he was playing with bass player and caller Gene Carnet's band. Around 1953, Phil followed his brother, who had originally performed with Olin in the late 1930s, into Berrier's band. At that time, Olin Berrier could expect to draw two to three hundred dancers at the American Legion on Friday nights. Phil and Olin also played on Saturday nights in a skating rink for a Mr. Kearns, who owned an awning business in High Point. The pay at that time had risen to $15 a night for the caller and $10 a night for each musician. The four to five hour nights were hard work, but Hege preferred it to other jobs: "You know, when you're doing something you enjoy, it's work, but it don't hurt you like it does when you've got a boss-man looking over you or telling you to do something."

None of these dance musicians made their living from music. Jeanne Berrier used her pay for spending money, while the other band members employed their music earnings to supplement an income from working in a mill or garage. Phillip Hege took his dance pay to feed his family. He recollects,

> I had a pretty rough time convincing my wife to go to the Lion's Den with me on Saturday night. She says, "I'm not going down there because some of those people might take a drink,"' you know. I said, "Well, hon," I said, "If you'll go with me a few nights and just get you a seat and sit down," you know. And I said, "We can go to the A&P store and buy our groceries next week and not have to bother my paycheck [from the Mill]." And she went for about three or four months and then later, she started square dancing and she danced for the rest of her life. And she really loved it.

For the next fifteen years or so, Olin Berrier spent his weekends playing for dances. The membership of his band remained fairly stable into the 1960s. Floyd "Diddle" Morrison (born February 25, 1923 in the Surry County town of Elkin) met Olin Berrier back in 1947. Although he sometimes played with Olin, Floyd didn't bring his guitar on a permanent basis to the group until the late 1950s. Morrison had come to Lexington at the age of five, and had become interested in music after seeing the Monroe Brothers play local schoolhouses. His brother-in-law got him started by showing him guitar chords. "About everybody wanted to play the guitar" back then, remembers Morrison. Floyd Morrison worked at the Erlanger Cotton Mill from the age of 18. "One time I quit the mill and started playing with Jack Sparks. That was back during World War II. I quit and we toured that summer, theaters." When Sparks left for California, Morrison went back to the mill.

Leonard's son Len, who had grown up surrounded by his grandfather's music, was added on mandolin to follow Raymond Waisner's replacement, Curly Blake, in the late 1960s. A music student of Morrison's, Andy Lawrence Prevette (born November 10, 1941), helped out the band as a substitute on a variety of instruments and finally joined in 1968.

Even when life interfered, the dances never stopped. Leonard Berrier tells of calling a dance the evening after the birth of his son, and passing out cigars. Friday nights at the American Legion in Lexington were displaced by dances at the Kernersville VFW. Saturday dances moved from the American Legion in Winston-Salem to the Welcome Civitan Club and then to the High Point Recreation Center.

Left to right, Raymond Waisner (guitar), Olin Berrier (banjo), Leonard Berrier (mandolin), Phil Hege (guitar), "Shorty" Cruise (electric bass), with Leonard's son Len in front (mandolin). Olin Berrier's band was still playing area square dances in the second half of the 1960s. This photograph was made at the Berrier home in Welcome, Davidson County, around 1966. Courtesy Leonard Berrier.

By the 1970s, it was getting harder and harder to support a live square dance band. Although the money was good when it could be gotten, the number of venues that saw the need for live music had diminished. Floyd Morrison mentioned how hard it was to work at the cotton mill on Friday, go and play a dance Friday night, get home at 2 A.M., get up and work Saturday at the mill, and then play another dance Saturday evening until 2 A.M. Sunday morning. By his own account Olin Berrier hadn't been home on a Saturday night for the last forty years. It was time to retire (Leonard Berrier and Brown interview; Olin Berrier and Michael interview; Olin Berrier and Betty Sowers interview).

Farmer and Denton

Since the 1950s, rock and roll, television, and other activities have drawn participants away from square dancing. One of the few remaining public square dances in the Piedmont is held in the southern Davidson County town of Denton. Descended from the Farmer Dance begun after World War II, this monthly event still uses acoustic old style string band music to accompany dancing. From 1947 until 1965, the Clegg Garner String Band played for dances the first and the third Saturday nights in Farmer at the Grange Hall and the second and fourth Saturdays in the Denton School gym (see Chapter Eight). Other bands covered the remaining two Saturdays in Farmer. The Grange building was an Army barracks bought at the end of World War II, and moved from Goldsboro to behind the Farmer School. The admission fee for the dance, at first around a quarter to fifty cents, was used to pay for the cost of the building.

Worth Winslow was a big supporter of public dancing in Randolph and southern Davidson County since World War II. His memory goes back to the first Grange dance: "I can remember the time over there at Farmer, we had more than forty cou-

Above and top: Tommy Beanblossom calls as the dancers promenade to the music of the Oak Tree Boys at the Denton Civic Center, Davidson County, 2000.

ples on the floor at one time. And N. M. Lowe was calling at that time with no mike — we didn't have no kind of sound system. Didn't know what it was. They'd run 125 to 150 people sometimes every Saturday."

Neureus M. Lowe began calling the dances at Farmer in 1957. "[I learned to call] just by observation," revealed Lowe, "going to the square dances and listening to Doc Hartsell and Shorty Cooper, [who was] from up between Greensboro and Reidsville. I called over twenty-five years at the [Farmer] Grange" (*Nuggets*, 21, 24, 27–33).

When the Denton dance ended in 1965, the Garner Band quit the Farmer dance as well. Since that time, various musicians and callers have worked the event. In 1975, the Farmer dance went to twice a month, ending at the beginning of 1991. Worth Winslow told me it stopped because "there was not enough people coming. They went on to the other kind of dancing. Rock and roll and that western dancing."

The Farmer dance was resurrected several years later, but was discontinued when the Grange Hall was deemed unsafe. Out of the ashes of the Farmer dance came the idea for the dance eventually held at the Denton Civic Center. The house band for the Denton Dance is the Oak Tree Boys, led by fiddler Dean Lewis Maines (born March 22, 1929). Born in Sparta, Alleghany County, and raised on a farm in Gap Civil, close to the New River, Dean got the bug to play at age thirteen from Earl Crouse, who worked on the family farm in the summertime. Because of the lack of local fiddlers, most of his repertoire came off the radio. "See, they'd play it one time," said Dean, "and it might be two or three weeks before you'd hear it again. You didn't have tape recorders or anything like that. Just had to learn it by ear that's the only way." Maines played for square dances in Sparta on Saturday nights at the local school gym, with musicians like Del Reeves (guitar), Ernest Jones (mandolin), and Larry Richardson (banjo). Dean moved to the Silver Valley area in 1956, working first as a carpenter and eventually for the Sapona Country Club, retiring after 15 years. He married Ruby Pearl Miller of Randolph County in 1957 and the couple had a son, Tim (born February 17, 1961). Dean had stopped fiddling when he left Sparta, but he started up again in the 1970s when Tim became interested in the guitar.

Neal and Debbie Leonard of Thomasville began the Denton Dance in September of 1996. Currently, the dance occurs on the third Saturday of each month. The hall holds about 100, but normally about 50–70 people attend. For each dance, the house band alternates with a guest group. The Oak Tree Boys, along with the Maineess, features Scott Arnold on banjo or mandolin and Mike Plummer on bass. Recently, Matthew Nance, a descendant of two members from the original Farmer band, has joined the Oak Tree Boys (Worth, 12–14).

Uncle Henry's Favorites

It is just by fate that Marvin Gaster favors the lead style of banjo playing preserved by his Uncle Henry over the newer, "flat chord" back-up style that had grown up in the late 1920s and 1930s, and the bluegrass sounds of Gaster's late teenage years and early adulthood. Marvin is one of the last purveyors of this two-finger lead style, which uses multiple tuning and confines the melody notes to the index finger.

The Gaster family has a long history of involvement with music and dancing, dating back to at least Marvin's great-grandfather, "Fiddlin' John" Morris Francis Gaster (1853–1942). John's determination to learn music was demonstrated by his practice sessions. Due to his father Big John's hatred of music, they were conducted on the roof of one of the outbuildings on the family farm. "Fiddlin' John" moved to Sanford around the turn-of-the-century to work in the Father George Cotton Mill. While living in town, he won a prize in at least one fiddlers' contest (by dancing and playing at the same time). "Fiddlin' John" Gaster's son, also named John (August 23, 1885–February 15, 1969), was nicknamed "Dancing John" for his abilities and predilection toward hoofing.

Dancing while playing may or may not have been a common practice. Leonard Eubanks remembers the practice as rare: "My granddaddy [Faddy King] was the only man that I ever seen of all them fiddle players he could dance. Now you talk about a dancing man and playing that fiddle all the same time and never miss a note, he danced not like a clog dancer but he danced on his tiptoes [makes a sound like dancing] and playing that fiddle."

Marvin Gaster remembers that both John Gasters

> loved to dance. And all of them could dance. The last sister, she was 94 when I went to see her, his ["Fiddlin' John"] last daughter by his first marriage, she was born in 1881. When we walked in, she got straight out of a chair without pushing and danced a step or two. [John Morris Francis' mother] was Francis Kelly, and I've never seen a Kelly that didn't dance or play music in this section.... They were all dancers.

There are two stories that bear repeating about Dancing John. One is that John had instrumental talent, but couldn't bear to play music and miss out on dancing. The other relates to his seventy-fifth birthday party, where John danced on a 2x4 board while balancing a glass of water on his head. When asked by a younger family member if he could always do this, he replied that in his youth he could do the same with the board turned up on its end!

Marvin comments that Dancing John's style of flat footing has disappeared:

> It was just a single dance, you know, done mostly on the toes, double timed. Some people call it flat footin' now, but you don't see anybody that can do that the way they danced. It was just light footed. My granddaddy said once that anybody who ever let his heel touch his floor wasn't much of a dancer. And they were all skinny, wiry people too. There was no wasted timber in any of those Gasters or the Kellys that they descended from.
>
> I remember Uncle Henry said that one night they thought John was gonna kill himself dancing. Uncle Henry said that he finally told John that if he was gonna dance anymore he had to get him another banjo picker because he was give out. He said "I couldn't play anymore" and that "my fingers were numb."

Marvin Gaster poses for the camera. Sanford, Lee County. Photograph by Hal Tysinger; courtesy Marvin Gaster.

Marvin Edward Gaster was born in Sanford, North Carolina, December 21, 1934. His parents, Carlton Gaster (September 15, 1915–December 1, 1944), a plumber, and Virginia Belle Odom (born February 15, 1917), had their roots in the farming communities of rural Lee County. The Gasters, of Dutch descent, had come into North Carolina through Wilmington in the 1740s. Marvin's father played the guitar and sang songs like "There's An Empty Cot in the Bunkhouse Tonight," "Take Me Back

to Colorado," and "My Buddy." A brother, Harry Olan, followed Marvin on February 26, 1937. In 1942, the family pursued wartime employment opportunities in
Georgia, and Marvin was placed in the care of his father's Aunt Alice and Uncle
Henry, who were childless, on their farm southwest of town. Initially, this was
considered a temporary arrangement. However, over time, Marvin became attached
to his aunt and uncle, and the youngster became invaluable to the couple. So,
rather than rejoining his parents and brother, Marvin Gaster was raised by the Per-
rys.

Born in the part of Moore County that later became Lee County, his great-uncle
by marriage, Henry Perry (March 14, 1893–1968), had moved to Sanford in 1909.
Marvin recalls

> His father Oren Zeddy Perry came from Chatham County and he came down
> to work in the turpentine business. That was the heyday and the last hurrah for the
> tar pitch and turpentine. When [Henry] was sixteen, he left home and took a job
> [working for] Sanford Sash and Blind at ten cents an hour, ten hours a day, six days
> a week.

Henry married Marvin's great-aunt Alice Gincy Warner (January 2, 1890–1973)
in 1913. The couple moved out of Sanford in 1919 onto the farm where Marvin lives
today.

While residing with his aunt and uncle, Marvin was inducted into a culture of
"workings" and music. With its roots extending back into the early nineteenth century, this world of communal cooperation integrated dances, called "frolics" (including live fiddle and banjo music), within functions such as corn shuckings and land
clearings. Fiddle contests, held in the earlier part of the twentieth century at the Sanford Opera House and above Efird's Department Store, and after 1920 in school auditoriums as fundraisers for the new school buildings, were also pervasive. "If they
were neighbors close by, they would swap labor in that community," tells Marvin
Gaster.

> A hog killing went into the second day and they would get through about din-
> ner and then they would clean up in the afternoon. Some of them would walk back
> home, change clothes and come back and then that night they would have what they
> would call a frolic. It would usually last all night long. You know, talking about that
> basic toughness, I remember a lot of people talking of that generation who'd dance
> all night and walk home in the daylight and hook up the mules and work. Just like
> sleep was something you could do without.
> There was Chris Spivey's aunt [Pearlia "Pearl" McNabb Spivey Smith (Sep-
> tember 22, 1881–August 13, 1972) played fiddle and banjo] who was the last one of
> that generation to die and her father was a Civil War soldier, and she talked about
> them going to a frolic in old Morristown. She said, "Yeah, I remember one night
> Papa came in when I was a little tiny girl and said that Will Oates shot the lamp out,
> came in and just boom, with a pistol and shot the lights out."
> Now, John Williams [1867–1947] was the oldest fiddler I ever heard. And
> he was also the only one I ever saw that had his fiddle in a white flour sack;
> he didn't have a case, and it was hung up on the wall, just throwed it up there sort
> of.

In Sanford one day, the teenaged Marvin Gaster passed by the local music store and saw a banjo in the window. Even though he was unaware of his musical heritage, the boy felt an overwhelming desire to purchase the instrument. Using money he had saved up from a tobacco crop and funds from the small government payments the family received as a result of his father's death in 1944, Gaster procured the banjo: "So, I went and bought it and Mr. Chears put it in a brown paper dry cleaner's bag."

When the young Gaster got the instrument home, his uncle asked to see it. Up until that time, Marvin was unaware that his Uncle Henry had once played music. "He'll play 'Mr. Catfish,'" Marvin was told by his Aunt Alice. Before even unpacking the groceries from the car, Henry had struck up the aforementioned tune. "You know, the next morning I woke up with him picking the banjo," recalls Marvin. Marvin later found out that Henry had quit music sometime in the 1920s. Uncle Henry gave two reasons. According to Marvin

> He stopped playing because he got afraid that he would end up an old drunk. His words were, he got to the place he liked whiskey too good. The other reason was that he got sick and tired of somebody coming up and saying play so and so, and when he would start playing, they would just walk off. He said that that was kind of insulting he thought, so he just got away from it.

From that point on, Marvin practiced when taking dinnertime (midday) breaks from his farm work.

> We'd come in and take the mules out and feed 'em, and go to the house. Just as quick as I could, I'd just wash my hands, I wouldn't wash my arms if they were dirty, and run out on the front porch and get a few minutes with the banjo when I was learning. And there was nothing I wanted to copy or listen to on the radio and there were no tapes or such as that, so I just … I imagine that was a slow process, too. It seemed like it took a long time for me to learn "John Hardy," which was the first one.

Under the tutelage of his uncle and other local musicians, Gaster learned to play.

> Like for a year or two, [Uncle Henry] played considerably and that's when I began to pick up things. He would not show you anything. About the music, he said, "If you can learn to play, you will. If you can't learn to play, you won't never learn"— which was exactly right.
>
> He took a lot of pleasure in the fact that I had got that banjo and played, and he would get the thing out till I got to where I could play pretty good and then he sort of put it away except at Christmas. He'd tell me to get my fiddle — I was messing with the fiddle just a little — and we'd go through the motions. I could play something sort of like "Old Molly Hare."

Aunt Alice was also musical. Marvin relates

> My very first recollection of any type of music was that of my great aunt, Alice Perry, singing little ditties such as "Bye Bye Baby Bunting," or some other similar

songs. I remember, as the childhood years passed, what a cozy time it was to get out of a warm bed to smell good things cooking for breakfast, but most of all to hear her sing and hum the many songs she knew.

As Marvin grew into adulthood, local life gradually changed away from the old-time ways and the old-time music. Rural electrification came in 1947; frolics had already moved from farmhouses to public halls. The younger generation got away from the melody style as rendered by Uncle Henry. Instead of using their bare fingers, remembers Marvin, they wore picks and

> played the banjo strictly in chords with no licks [Marvin calls this "flat-chording"]. I've heard Uncle Henry say more than once that nobody played the guitar back in his day, the fiddle and banjo was it. The [younger musicians] seemed to hold the old music in utter contempt. Donald Foster almost condemned his daddy Brown Foster just over the music. [And], you know, his daddy was a great banjo player.
>
> The last [house dance] I ever saw was [in the 1940s] at a man named Walter Wicker's. He had a big house, four rooms down and four rooms up, you know, one of those with a hall in the middle, and Earl Wicker [fiddle player and Walter's first cousin, September 7, 1913–December 11, 1980], a man by the name of Roland Lemons [guitarist, 1920–1989], Chris [Christine or Christian] Spivey [1920–1982, guitar], and Howard Conder [born February 9, 1920, banjo], played in that hall and there were dancers in the two rooms on each side. And there were about four couples in each one. That fascinated me to no end. Because they were together with each step and it was just like a huge "clunk-clunk-clunk," the square dancing, as they went through that and the music, and that was the first time I ever saw anything like that. But they had a corn shucking up there. And then, it seemed like they sort of went away from the playing and the dancing, the times changed.

W. Earl Wicker became Marvin's second musical mentor. Marvin warmly recalls Wicker's first visit.

> One night, when I was about fifteen or sixteen, a car horn tooted out in the yard. I went to see and it was Earl Wicker and his lumber truck, an old green Ford, and he says, "Boy, how about playing a little dance with me tonight?" And so I went and it was one of those frolics at Sandall Wall's house. It was a big house, big rooms and they danced kind of the same way, we played out in the hall.
>
> Earl had a lot of effect on me and I want to give him the credit for that. He was very, very patient.... Earl would say, "Boy, let's find that chord." And that's imprinted on my mind that it's important to do it right. And he helped me find a lot of things that sometimes I use now when I'm playing with a fiddler and just need to get those little touches. Earl Wicker is responsible for that. He liked "Dill Pickle Rag" and all kind of blues and waltzes. He could make a lot of hymns sound real pretty too. "What A Friend We Have in Jesus," he played that in C. Earl played in B and Bb and C, which these other people did not do. He was a very, very talented man. I guess you'd call him a swing fiddler because, like "Five Foot Two," I have never heard anybody play that type of song any better than Earl Wicker could play it. And he didn't like the old music. He was of that generation around here, at least in this section, who just threw it away.
>
> I recollect that we went to Hoffman one night [to a fiddlers' contest], and that

place was packed full and we won everything. Earl Wicker won the fiddle, I won the banjo, Harvey Johnson won the prize for singing and we won first band prize. I played a guitar song that I won it with, "Steel Guitar Rag." But anyway, I got first prize and there were seven or eight banjo players.

Earl Wicker weighed about 260 pounds and was about 6 feet 4. Wade [Yates] was talking and said he bet his fingers were about an inch or so around. But, he was a huge guy. The last [fiddlers' contest] I went to locally, when we walked out on the stage, I started slipping my fingerpick on and it fell off, bounced about twice and Earl's big size 14 just crushed that thing. I caught up with him, picked it up and said, "Earl, talk a little bit or something because I've got to get this thing straightened out." And if Earl said a sentence, he talked real slow, so he did a little describing and I kept on. I never did get it straightened out back right, but I was ready. Now, that was the last one that I went to, and that must have been about 1954. But it was thirty-five cents for adults and children, you know, free.

But they were fundraisers. There were three schools in this county and that's what they did. What were we going to do? Go home and sit and look at each other and watch the fireplace and that was it. There was no TV. The radio, we always had programs we listened to faithfully, but there wasn't much to do. You could just pack a place full. The auditorium I remember just being ringed around every time with people standing up against the walls because the seats were full. So it was a pretty big thing. Always on a weekend, Friday or Saturday.

Marvin eventually graduated to better quality instruments. In about the tenth grade, he acquired a Kay banjo. In his senior year of high school, he went back to Chears and bought a Gibson RB-100. "Uncle Henry thought he had never heard anything sound that good," says Marvin. In the late 1940s, Sanford secured two radio stations, WEYE and WWGP, which featured bands including the young Marvin Gaster: "I played for about three years on those, both of them. I was in a period of flopping around. I's starting to practice to try to play bluegrass, getting a third pick. I never could get that pick to work; of course, I've been glad of it ever since."

Marvin also played with groups for dances at the VFW on Friday nights and at the Woodman of America on Saturday nights.

When I was in high school I played at Goldston and Pittsboro for about two years, played with Alton Williams (1910–1993), and that was Pittsboro on Friday night and Goldston on Saturday night. And we picked up some good money, probably averaged $12 or $13 a night. It was always 50-50, the musicians got half. I played more with [Alton Williams] in those teenage years than anybody. I played every week at a dance. Minimum wage back then was fifty-five cents and I usually made thirty dollars or thirty-five dollars a week on Friday and Saturday night. I made $18.75 one night, and there were men working for less than that the whole week supporting a family. I was rolling in the dough when I was in high school until it ended.

Marvin Gaster married Catherine Ann Patterson April 9, 1954. By the late 1950s, further changes, like the automobile and drive-in movies, drove out public square dancing and private music making. By that time, Marvin was raising his children and his music took a back seat to familial responsibilities. Farming and teaching

Marvin Gaster with the banjo and Sarah Smith at the piano were voted "Most Talented" by their graduating class at Greenwood High School in 1952. Courtesy Marvin Gaster.

school filled the rest of his time. As Marvin Gaster tells it: "I think the Woodmen's Hall stopped about the year I married, and the VFW and the American Legion had some sometimes, but it just played out."

By the late 1960s, Marvin Gaster began playing again in earnest. He recalls

> When I started back, I played with [Harnett County fiddler] Lauchlin Shaw, and that was about '68. Lauchlin came and played a couple of square dance sets up at a man's named Alton Green's about two miles away and I'd never seen him. But he was a heck of a fiddler. The man who was picking the banjo with them was Eb Collins, and he said, "I know you play the banjo. How about playing with this man? I don't know him and I'd rather not." So, I played some and we talked. That is kind of when I got started back. Probably eighteen years I would say. We played dances at Dickerson's towards Chapel Hill for eight years, nonstop every Saturday night. We never missed. They had a dance up there on Christmas Day one time, we went. My wife had a fit, and there weren't but just a handful of people there either. And we played a lot at Bahama at that time, you know.

In the 1980s, with his children "flying out of the nest," Marvin struck out on his own, devoting himself to the fiddle and attending fiddlers' gatherings, music festivals and jam sessions. Marvin credits "Mr. Shaw who introduced me to festivals such as Fiddler's Grove, and I heard music that I had never heard the likes of before." Music making just intensified when Gaster retired from teaching school in 1993. During this same period, the music bug finally bit Marvin's brother Harry, who took up the bass and began to accompany Marvin on his musical travels.

Today, Marvin Gaster, with his banjo and fiddle in tow, is a familiar sight at southern fiddlers' conventions. He is often in the company of fiddler J.P. Fraley or banjoist Will Keys, another master of the up-picking two-finger style. He is particularly attracted to younger musicians, like Robert Mitchener, fiddler Palmer Loux, and "all the Philly crowd." Richard Hartness is another of Gaster's musical companions. Hartness has musical and kinship ties to Lee County, which makes their relationship that much more special. Rich, along with his then-wife Beth on guitar, accompanied Marvin to win first prize at the Eno Fiddlers' Convention. Marvin finished in the money at the prestigious Clifftop competition in the summer of 1995 and has also taken home awards from Fiddler's Grove.

FIVE

"Music Made the Day Seem Grander"

*"There is no more pleasure-giving feature in a town than
a good band."*

—*Wayne County Herald* March 23, 1899 and Kreitner 4.

In a time when Piedmont society was based around the cycles of farming, school sessions would run in the cold months, when there was a lull in farm chores. Rural schools opened sometime in November and ran until anytime from the end of February into the beginning of June. The more rural the school, then the shorter the session would run. The larger "college" and "academies" would hold longer or multiple terms, and would stay open for most of the year.

One event that was sure to involve the whole community was the school closing, or "exhibition," as it was then known. Music was an integral part of the commencement celebration, which often stretched over several days. Addresses by clergy or politicians, speeches by the students, and a covered-dish supper were all features of the actual graduation day. Both brass bands and string bands had their place during the occasion. However, there seems to have been little crossover between the schools employing brass and those using string ensembles. It appears that the larger, urban, and more well-to-do institutions employed the services of the community's brass band, while the smaller, rural, and more modest schoolhouses utilized the string aggregations.

On the day of the graduation ceremony, the band would arrive in its wagon, and lead the children around the schoolyard to the schoolhouse porch. In between the speeches, recitations, declamations, and dialogues, the band would play selections from its place on the end of the porch. The band members might have been paid a small honorarium. At the very least, the musicians would get a meal for their troubles.

Newspaper coverage and oral histories provide a picture of exhibitions from the late nineteenth century through to the time of school consolidation in the 1920s and

Fiddler Matt Rayle and banjoist Charlie Pegram "make music" for an unidentified school exhibition near Colfax in Guilford County circa 1890. Courtesy Dorothy Pegram.

the 1930s. Kathleen Craver, an educator, writer and local historian in Davidson County, describes the decorated stage outside of the schoolhouse, the speech making, and the musicians on their bandwagon:

> Most of the old schools had no hall that could accommodate the crowds of commencement day. Boys and girls and their teachers and parents labored to make the porch stage a thing of beauty. Posts and poles were interlaced with wire to which were tied boughs of cedar and garlands of running pine and even bunting and crepe paper. Spectators sat beneath a rough arbor or protective roof of greenery.
>
> Music did far more than break the monotony of speech making, for it made the day seem grander. In fact no commencement or exhibition could amount to much without a band, brass or string. Most people felt that money for hiring band was well spent. Men and boys who made up the bands were more amateur than professional. What a thrill it was to ride in the high old band wagon along a country road to a country school…. A fiddler or two, a drummer, a couple of horns, and maybe a banjo made up the band.
>
> An aged man told me about the part a band played…: "When we heard the music coming, we lined up two by two. When the prancing horses with red tassels hanging from their bridles came into view, and we could see the musicians as well as hear them, we started marching. We marched and marched and marched, around the school, and through an arch we had previously hung with green boughs" [125–6].

Calvin Henderson Wiley, in his book about Alamance County circa 1775, gives an early impression of exhibition day, filled with some accurate details and many literary exaggerations. Note how, even then, the fiddlers led the celebration.

The end of the session was near at hand, and as it approached, the exhibition became the absorbing topic of conversation with old and young. It was similar to our modern commencements, being a grand gala day, when there were public exercises by the students, and which were witnessed by the parents of the scholars, and all others who took an interest in the cause of education.

It was in the month of April…. At an early hour the seats were filled by the ladies; and the boys, awkwardly wearing their fine new clothes, were shivering in the house, looking wistfully at the gathering crowd, and feeling like culprits who were that day to be led out to execution. All the patrons of the school, and all their relations—all Alamance, with a sprinkling of gallants from distant parts, were there…. At ten o'clock in the morning the curtain rose, and Corny Demijohn, marshal for the day, and arrayed in a suit of faded uniform, stepped out upon the stage…. Next after Marshal Corny came two negro [sic] fiddlers, then the students, ranged two abreast, and, lastly, the clowns or fools in masks and comic dresses, and acting as lieutenants. Uncle Corny, conscious that every eye was bent on him … and the point of his sword resting on his shoulder, strode off with the step of an ancient Titan; the fiddlers, feeling as Uncle Corny did, scraped away as if they were performing the grand finale of all mortal fiddling; the clowns, believing they were the objects of general attraction, acted accordingly, and each student, thinking that he himself fixed every gaze, felt his heart throb within him, and envied the courage and coolness of fiddlers and commanders. In this way the column marched off to the spring, and performing a circuit, wheeled, and started to the house….

After the eloquent efforts of two or three of the smaller scholars, and after the playing of two or three animated tunes by the fiddlers, the rising of the curtain disclosed Ben Rust, who, with a series of low bows to those in front and at his sides, advanced to the edge of the stage. Here he halted, made another profound and oriental salaam, and smiling on the crowd generally, and winking specially at two or three of his friends, the loud tones of his stentorian voice suddenly burst on the astonished audience like a clap of thunder, and Ben was soon some distance in the oration of Cicero against Verres….

Henry Warden, by his assistance, had composed an original address on the wrongs of the American Colonies, and this, according to the first design, was to conclude the exercises of the day … a fervent prayer from the Rev. Dr. Caldwell ended the ceremonies of the day [57–60].

We'll pause in our look at string bands in the Piedmont to examine a parallel musical movement that involved some of the same musicians and musical families. Piedmont brass bands performed for school exhibitions, as well as many of the other community celebrations utilizing fiddlers and banjoists, so it is important to tell their story here.

Brass Bands

The roots of America's brass band movement lie in the northwestern part of North Carolina's Piedmont. In an unpublished article, Steve Terrill quotes Moravian historians Knouse and Crews in describing this predecessor to the "band craze" of the late nineteenth century:

> Brass music played a special role in the Moravian settlements. A continuation
> of the German Stadtpfeifer tradition, the Moravian brass ensembles announced spe-
> cial services, welcomed visitors, announced deaths, accompanied hymn singing at
> outdoor services and funerals, and marked events of note throughout the commu-
> nity. The ensemble would often mark someone's birthday by "blowing them up" early
> in the morning. This Aufblasen also happened on festival days to wake up the peo-
> ple and to remind them of the special nature of the day [Knouse, 18].

The Moravian brass bands of the period from the middle to late eighteenth century were succeeded by a national band movement. As brass band historians Kenneth Kreitner and Victor Greene have written:

> Brass bands spread rapidly through America in the decades before the Civil
> War, and even more so afterward, as a large industry developed to mass-produce
> their instruments and music.... By the nineties, town bands were "discoursing sweet
> music," ... in thousands of cities, towns, and even tiny villages all over the country
> ... local brass ensembles emerged ... and became essentially civic institutions, sym-
> bols of community identity as well as performing units. Supported both by public
> and private sources, including societies of many sorts, such as local industries, busi-
> nesses, and lodges, by the late 1800's they were evident in nearly every town in the
> country [Kreitner, 2; Greene, 16].

One must not underestimate the specifically Moravian, and more generally German, influence on Piedmont brass groups. German areas throughout America seem
to have produced the most musicians or best bands (Greene, 18). The City Directory
credits the Moravian cornet band organizing in 1830, and local Salem newspapers
mention brass bands as early as 1851. The Moravian settlement at Salem produced
the 26th North Carolina Regimental Band, organized in 1862, a group that served
the Confederate Army during the Civil War.

The true golden age for the brass band movement in the United States occured
between 1870 and 1930. Victor Greene estimates there were 2,300 American bands
in 1872, over 10,000 in 1890 and almost 20,000 by 1908. According the Greene, at the
turn of the century, most communities in the United States had a brass band (18–19).
This coincided with the prime period for school exhibitions, where community bands
competed with the less formal string groups for work at commencements. Brass bands
dwarfed their string counterparts in size. Most brass groups had between sixteen to
eighteen members (Kreitner, 131).

Brass instruments were highly suited to outdoor celebrations. Their music was
loud, and carried across a long distance. The groups were portable, either traveling
on a bandwagon or on foot. And brass bands were plentiful. Bands were sponsored
by towns and textile mills, although it is hard from newspaper coverage to differentiate between the two because of the overlap between mill organizations and local
governments. The membership for these assembledges were far from stable. Brass
groups were always breaking up and reforming, losing one instructor and gaining
another.

Brass bands were found at other community events as well. Grange, Masonic,
and fraternal picnics, weddings, temperance celebrations, fairs and holiday festivities

such as those held on the Fourth of July all employed the services of brass groups. Community concerts were also an expected part of the band's performance season, as the local citizenry provided money for uniforms and instruments.

The Lexington Silver Cornet Band existed from as early as the summer of 1887 through at least 1903 (*High Point Enterprise*, June 24, 1887: 3; *Dispatch*, January 21, 1903: 5; March 1903; April 8, 1903: 5). A letter to the editor in the Lexington *Dispatch* titled "Our Band Boys" reflects on how that band represented their community when discussing the condition of uniforms for the Cornet Band:

> Now we all know that the young men who compose this band have worked hard to make a success of it. This they have done, but it has required great effort on their part and considerable outlay of money…. As the June commencements for 1892 will soon be here and before our boys go out to play for any of them they should have new uniforms, as their old ones are beginning to look like a Confederate officer's uniform at Lee's surrender. I think we owe it to them and believe with the proper effort is made the debt will be paid and I suggest the band appoint a committee at an early day to wait on our citizens and see if they cannot raise money enough to buy them New Uniforms [*Dispatch* April 21, 1892].

The newspaper's appeal must have carried some weight, as the Lexington Silver Cornet Band had their new uniforms for the 1893 commencement season. (*Dispatch*, March 30, 1893: 3)

Band wagons were used by both string and brass organizations. The Salisbury Cornet Band owned an ornate red and gold painted bandwagon with four horses (McCorkle), and the Lexington Concert Band used an immense red bandwagon. Stringbands had to rely on their neighbors for a more modest but no-less decorated set-ups. Michael String Band member Frank Everhart built their wagon at his home on the Monkey Bottom (now called Pine Ridge) Road in the Arnold community of Davidson County. The wagon's body was painted a light green and its wheels and tongue a bright red. The animals were dressed in black leather harnesses trimmed in brass, their bridles decorated with red tassels. The band would be seated on the board benches that lined each side of the wagon, facing each other as they played (Greene, *Homespun*, 37–8; Orrell and Greene interview).

Like stringbands, the amateur brass bands drew their members from all walks of life. The star cornetist of the Statesville Cornet Band for 1884 was the local butcher, John Finley Harbin (Keever, 311–312). Charles Young, a member of the 1900 Union Cornet Band, was later mayor of Lexington in Davidson County (*Dispatch*, April 28, 1909: 3). And, obviously, mill town bands were heavily populated with textile mill workers.

Brass and string bands may have served similar community functions, as well as shared membership and customs. It was highly unusual, nonetheless, for the two to share an event's spotlight, let alone for one to benefit the other. However, at least one event did combine the two, the "Fiddlers Convention and [Brass] Band Concert" promoted by the Ramseur Concert Band. The group had existed for at least eight years when, on Friday, April 5, 1912, the band took over the Ramseur auditorium for a convention and concert. The event was structured much like other fiddlers' conventions (see Chapter Six) (*Asheboro Courier* March 28, 1912: 8).

Land sales were another event that utilized both brass and string bands. On April 9 and May 14, 1924, R. T. Blackburn's Fiddling Farmers performed at land auctions by the Bolich Company of Winston-Salem. There was no shortage of hyperbole from a writer at the *Twin City Sentinel* in describing the arrival of Blackburn's group:

> "The Fiddling Farmers," as Lon Bolich has termed them, played for about fifteen minutes this morning to a big crowd of folks in front of Owen's drug store, on Third street, before going to the land sale conducted by the Bolich Company, on the Hollow road, north of the city. Had the men kept on playing it is very likely that an old-fashioned Virginia reel would have been going in the street, as Allison James, Lon Bolich and others began to slide their feet across the sidewalk in graceful fashion, but the cessation of the music cut the dance off short. The players demonstrated to the crowd gathered that they were real old-time fiddlers. One bystander listened attentively to one number, remarking at the close that he had not heard it for twenty-five years. The fiddlers were R. T. Blackburn, Tom Samuels, Lum Sapp, Bill Gray and Bill Blackburn, all Forsyth county men [*Twin City Sentinel*, 8].

String Bands

String bands played for commencements during the same period as brass bands, from the 1880s until 1930. Unincorporated settlements with names like Eagle Hill, Ellis Crossroads, Trading Ford, Needham Grove and Maple Springs sponsored educational institutions that utilized string rather than brass groups.

Unfortunately, stringed instruments like fiddles and banjos were much quieter than their brass counterparts, and were less suited to concerts for large audiences or in noisy situations. This gave the string bands two choices. One option was for the bands to play at schools with enrollments on the smaller end of the scale, and therefore, including a more moderate audience at graduation. A second option was to combine several string bands into one, making a super group that was many times larger than the normal ensembles employed for agrarian events, house dances, fiddlers' conventions, and the like. Often, these larger bands used the bass drum borrowed from brass orchestras to increase the group's volume.

There were those situations where bands were made up of whatever instruments and instrumentalists could be gathered from the immediate vicinity. The *Asheville Courier* reported on the 1906 commencement for the Bombay Institute, located four miles southwest of Farmer in Randolph County. The orchestra consisted of Sherrill T. Lassiter, director and pianist (later a teacher at the Farmer public High School), violinists Bernard Varner and Walter Lyndon, cornetists Eck Loflin and Reggie Varner, trombonist Carl Lyndon, tenor violinist Walter Hill, bass violinist Rufus Lassiter, mandolists Floyd Lassiter and J. L. Cranford, and banjoists Tony Johnson and

Carl Nance, who was then a student at the school (Denny, 76). One can only imagine the sound of this group or what selections they chose to render. Nance and Johnson were part of a popular area string band that included fiddlers Jake and Lee Miller, two of Lee's daughters on the autoharp, and Carl's two sisters (probably Mattie and Essie) on autoharp and piano. This band also played at school exhibitions, including those held at the New Hope school.

Small, community string bands, used to a routine of birthday parties and square dances at people's homes, made only slight changes to their repertiore and performing style to play the modest school graduations throughout the Piedmont. Every settlement seemed to have had a number of musicians. These ranged from Charlie Harrison Williard (circa 1860–1945) in Guilford County, Alamance County's "Fiddling Clapps" led by Michael Elihue Clapp (March 2, 1865–July 12, 1938), the Jubilee Band of fiddler Charlie Barnes, Sam Barnes on banjo, Frank Lanning on tambourine, Frank Forrest on guitar, and Cleve Orrell on bass drum in Davidson County (Orrell/Greene), the fiddling brothers Ben and Joe Brown with banjoists Carl Stanley, Sr. (November 22, 1895–January 16, 1981) and Clyde L. Chriscoe (October 28, 1906–June 16, 1983) on the Rowan and Moore County border, as well as Claude Murray, Henry Hampton "Hamp" Bray (September 14, 1881–February 14, 1958) and Newton H. "Newt" Hicks (July 8, 1890–November 9, 1973) on fiddle and banjo in Randolph County.

As with other community events, school commencements were ripe with mishaps that provided the material for humorous stories. One such tale is about the Murray family who farmed ten miles south of Burlington. James Alson Murray (no relation to Claude; August 7, 1847–October 30, 1915) was lead fiddler with the band that included his sons Solon Lorenzo (the first born, September 1868–December 19, 1922), William Leach "Buck" (January 6, 1871–May 14, 1928), Andrew Clay (known as "Ank," March 6, 1876–July 28, 1937), James Martin (November 9, 1878–January 1941), and Eusebious Alexander (nicknamed "Sebe," December 17, 1881–January 16, 1963). The Murrays performed within their community at the usual mix of parties, picnics and exhibitions. On one such occasion, at the Friendship School, a boy brought the band a fruit jar full of homemade white liquor, and all the members took a big swig. When the time came to play, the Murrays launched into their first tune and never stopped. When someone tried to cue them to conclude by asking Alson why they were playing the same piece over and over, Al replied that it was "all they knew!" (Newton, *Alamance County Legacy*, 317–318).

It appears that the less plentiful and smaller rural African American schools also followed the tradition of having string music at graduation time. Pleasant Hill School, a school for black children, held exhibitions that were open to whites. Charles Cheek can not remember if their stringband was made up of Anglo or African American musicians. One school that did have a black stringband was Glover's School, an African American institution affiliated with a black church located four miles from Bennett toward Siler City.

Michael's Reeds-Shiloh String Bands

One of the largest string groups playing school exhibitions was based in the Davidson County settlement of Reeds. Ross Michael co-directed the band with Cicero Leonard, and practices were held at Michael's home near the Shiloh Church. Organized in the 1890s, some of the schools where the band appeared included Happy Hill (March 1903), Burkhart (April 1903), Oak Hill (March 7, 1903), Swearing Creek (February 25, 1908), Brooks Hill and Reedy Creek for school exhibitions and commencements at Fork Church, Advance, Yadkin College and Green's School. The band also performed at picnics for the Mocksville Masons, Darr Hill, and Royal Shoaf. During an exhibition, the band might break into "Pretty Red Wing," "Will There Be Any Stars in My Crown," or "My Country 'Tis of Thee." One of the last times the band played in public was for the Mill Knob Exhibition of 1924. The Michael String Band featured David Franklin Everhart (December 29, 1855–September 12, 1943), his son Earlie Fletcher Everhart (May 27, 1886–December 12, 1983), Jacob "Jake" Pickett and Albert Leonard on fiddles; Arthur David Tussey (June 15, 1890–November 25, 1939), John Everhart, John Leonard and Sherman Leonard on banjos; Ed Fritts on the tambourine; and Ad Craver on bass drum.

The Tussey family were of Swedish descent, having immigrated to America in the mid–1600s. The family landed in Delaware, migrated to Pennsylvania, and came

The Reeds Shiloh (or Michael) String Band, riding their bandwagon to a school exhibition. The drivers are band directors Cicero Leonard and Ross Michael. The musicians include Arthur Tussey and Sherman Leonard (banjos), Jake Pickett, Frank Everhart, Earlie Everhart and Albert Leonard (fiddles), Ed Fritts (tambourine) and Ad Craver (bass drum). Circa 1910. Courtesy Betty Sowers and Hugh Greene.

to the Jersey settlement in what is now Reedy Creek in Davidson County around 1790. Arthur Tussey's grandfather, John Tussey II (1826–1887), was possibly a dulcimer player and Arthur's brother John and sister Clattie credit their father, David Lee Tussey (1863–1908) with teaching the boys to play music. David's oldest son, Harvey Lee (1884–1971) learned to pick the banjo, and his brother John Tussey III (September 25, 1894–May 24, 1987) took up the fiddle.

David Lee made Arthur his first banjo when his son was eight years old. In 1913, Arthur married Lona Temple (August 16, 1890–April 2, 1957) from Reedy Creek and settled on the Arnold Road. Lona also played banjo, which she probably learned from Arthur so that the couple could play music together (both played banjo in the finger picking style). The only of Arthur's children out of nine who showed an interest in music was Ruby (born 1920), who played the mandolin (Greene, *Homespun*, 37and 38; Tussey and Tussey; *Lexington North State*, February 12, 1908: 1).

The Whitehart School Band

Just north of Thomasville, in the eastern part of Davidson County, is the community of Whitehart. By 1917, the small school was holding exhibitions featuring its own area string band. Solomon William E. "Dad" Walker (May 21, 1874–December 17, 1965) and his son (Emory or Emery) Ray (December 7, 1903–October 22, 1976) fiddled for the band; Walker's brother Laurie (August 11, 1888–December 20, 1955) or Jacob M. Hilton (July 4, 1897–November 25, 1957) played the banjo; Dad's daughters Wanda (born 1915) and Margaret (born 1908), his nephew Dolan and niece

The Whitehart School Band at school exhibition time. As mentioned, this large a band was necessary to be heard by all those assembled at school closing time. Left to right, the musicians are Emory Walker (fiddle), Laurie Walker (banjo), Jacob Hilton (banjo), James Walker, Chiney Emanuel (bass drum), unknown (fiddle), Wanda Walker (guitar), Early Jones (banjo), Margaret Walker (guitar), Andy Meredith (banjo), Dolan Walker (guitar) and "Dad" Walker (fiddle). Whitehart, Davidson County, circa 1930. Courtesy Gladys Jones Craven.

Lucille strummed guitars; Dolan's brother James (December 25, 1915–February 1, 1984) played mandolin; Early Boston or (Bonson) Jones (December 3, 1884–June 1, 1946) played either fiddle or banjo; and "Chiney" Emanuel was their drum beater. In addition to playing for the exhibitions and the dances that followed the ceremony, the Walkers also provided the music for parties and ice cream suppers, mostly in the summertime.

Of German descent, the Walkers came from Forsyth County, where the community of Walkertown is named for them. In 1910, Dad moved his family to join his brother in Thomasville, and joined the city's police force. Dad Walker may have also worked as a brick mason during this period. Nine years later, Dad moved out of town to a farm in Whitehart. After Emory contracted mumps in 1934, the band stopped playing for public events, subsequently only making music around their various homes.

School consolidation coincided with Emory Walker's illness. The closing of small, rural one- and two-room school buildings, to be replaced by large, centralized educational centers, brought the practice of engaging community string and brass bands for graduation exercises to an end. Some missed the old time exhibitions and tried to revive the custom. But, the era was over. The old exhibition, with its string bands and brush arbors, was left behind at the abandoned schoolhouses.

SIX

"The Fiddlers Fairly Lifted the Roof with 'Mississippi Sawyer'"

"People used to appreciate music. Back then, there was nothing to go to. This was a treat. To be able to hear somebody putting on a fiddlers' convention was very exciting, and they just followed it."

— Dorothy Pegram

Music as a competition, fiddling as a battle. A strange contest, perhaps, but one that has existed even as the fights are good-natured ones. In music, there is no democracy. True, rural string band music by design can be played by almost anyone with the desire and need. However, there are always musicians who rise above their community, who outpace their peers and their competitors. They provide the inspiration for everyone else, the standard for others to try and match and even surpass.

It is hard to know how far back communities were holding fiddling competitions. Bob and Alf Taylor, two brothers from East Tennessee, ran their opposing campaigns during the 1886 Tennessee governor's race as if they were in a fiddlers' contest. The siblings carried musicians with them on campaign stops (if the two weren't playing themselves!) to gain the public's attention. There are other scattered accounts detailing musical contests, as well as folkloric tales of playoffs with the justice system or the devil, throughout America's post–Civil War period. By the early days of the twentieth century, we can definitely say that organized public fiddlers' conventions had begun in earnest.

As historian Gail Gillespie and folklorist Wayne Martin have written:

> Detailed accounts of fiddle contests suddenly began to crop up in Southern newspapers of the 1890s. Suffused with nostalgia, these article celebrated "olde tyme" fiddlers who played the tunes "our grandmothers danced to." Since the turn of the century was a time of disturbingly rapid change, pining for the good old days was probably quite natural. The year 1900 was a watershed in which for the first time

Gathering of musicians from Snow Camp in Alamance County, held in the state capital of Raleigh. July 1923. Courtesy Bob Roberson.

> American urban dwellers began to outnumber those in the country. In the growing cities of the South, new musical terms like ragtime, Dixieland and jazz were replacing older kinds of music. Aware of the rapid change, newspaper writers described "old time fiddle contests" in loving detail ... all the while emphasizing the quaint handlebar mustaches, mud-covered boots and old-fashioned rusticity of the fiddlers [*Raleigh Fiddlers' Convention*, 7].

North Carolina was no different from the rest of the south (see for example, Cauthen, Joyce H., *With Fiddle and Well-Rosined Bow: Old-Time Fiddling in Alabama*, Tuscaloosa: University of Alabama Press, 1989, 163–200). Like other southern states, conventions held in public places begun to garner newspaper coverage during the initial decade of the twentieth century.

The first large convention to receive ink in Piedmont newspapers was held in Raleigh, the state capital, as an annual event. From 1905 until 1914, Labor Day Monday meant there would be a fiddling contest on the grounds of the Agricultural and Mechanical School (now North Carolina State University). The gatherings were the brainchild of William Johnston Andrews (March 1, 1871–December 1942), the son of a Southern Railway vice president and brother to a mayor of Raleigh. Raised in the capitol city, "Buck," as Andrews was known, had held many public positions. After serving as secretary to Senator Matt Ransom, who was the U.S. envoy to Mexico during Grover Cleveland's administration, and head of an iron foundry, Andrews ran the Raleigh Electric Company, nowadays known as Carolina Power and Light. Buck was head of the Electric Company when he initiated the fiddlers' convention, but there seems to have been no tie in between his employer and the event.

Unlike many of the other contests held during this time, the first "North Carolina Fiddlers' Convention," as Buck Andrews named it, was planned as an outdoor affair. However, rain moved the event from Pullen Park on the school's campus into its large auditorium. Whether it was weather or other reasons, the 1907 contest was the only one held outside, the rest more typically occupying the A and M auditorium.

Another characteristic that set this event apart from its competitors was the unique way the contestants traveled to the event. As reported by local news coverage:

> Preceding the contest in fiddling a large number of the fiddlers went through the city in a big wagon, provided by Mr. Busbee, who lives in the country, the conductor of the team being Mr. John U. Smith. On the sides of the big wagon, which was drawn by a $600 pair of mules, was a notice of the contest, and over this could be seen the heads and faces of the fiddlers [*News and Observer*, September 5, 1905: 4 and Gillespie and Martin].

The Raleigh contest, as far as indicated in the *News and Observer*, was not a fundraiser for some deserving local institution, nor designed to earn money for a private citizen like Buck Andrews. The newspaper reportage does not even mention an admission charge.

For the years that attendance figures are known, the audience averaged around 500. Strangely, considering the number of contestants drawn by other contemporary contests, an average of five fiddlers per year are all that are listed in the newspaper coverage. Unless these are just the finalists from eliminations held earlier in the day, this is an extraordinarily low number of competitors. These are just some of the ways in which this event early in the 1900s differed from the majority of contests held between 1905 and 1924.

The individual deserving top honors in the promotion of early twentieth century conventions in North Carolina, and therefore codifying their structure and policies, was C. Z. Whitaker of Oak Ridge in northern Guilford County. For a brief period at the end of 1907 and the beginning of 1908, Whitaker's contests were the talk of the Piedmont.

Charles Zack Whitaker (February 9, 1876–November 3, 1950) was born in Durham, one of twelve children by David Wesley Whitaker (August 24, 1840–January 18, 1918) of Wake County and Carrie A. Freeman (May 28, 1847–March 16, 1918), a Randolph County native. David Whitaker founded a number of county newspapers, and was running a periodical that did job printing for tobacco concerns when Zack was born. Between the ages of ten and fourteen, Zack Whitaker worked as a printer for Bull Durham smoking tobacco. Zack also loved music, and took violin lessons from a German he remembered only as Professor Folson. His real musical mentor was Joe King, who organized and taught children's bands in the city. Whitaker apprenticed to King, doubling on the violin and cornet. After a yearlong stint on the *Durham Morning Herald*, a fifteen-year-old Zack Whitaker followed his brother Early to school in the Guilford County community of Oak Ridge (Whitaker, *My Memories*).

When Zack was nineteen, Will G. Kirkman founded Oak Ridge Institute's music department. The musically inclined Whitaker must have been a welcome member of the first Oak Ridge Band and Orchestra, and he appeared on alto horn in the former and as a trombonist and violinist with the latter. The music department also floated

A group gathers for a public square dance, possibly sponsored by the postal workers, in the old gymnasium at Oak Ridge in Guilford County. Left to right, they include post mistress Pearl Linville, dance caller Gene Parrish, Opal Peeples on piano, Clyde Pegram on fiddle, Obie Peeples on banjo, Roy Osborne on guitar, Zack Whitaker on cello and an unknown postal official. Circa 1940. Courtesy Francis Allred.

a ten-member mandolin club, and enrolled two banjo and nine guitar students to boot. The 24-member band and 28-member orchestra gave their first public concerts on May 27, 1895; Kirkman was a featured soloist on cornet. The groups also played many of the leader's own compositions (Kirkman, *The O.R.I. Band and Orchestra Journal*). Local communities enlisted their services and other public performances followed in the years to come. Zack Whitaker remained a vital member of the music department, and, around 1897 or 1898, took over its directorship from Kirkman.

In the days when conventions were locally organized affairs, C. Z. Whitaker decided to promote events across the State. Between November of 1907 and March of 1908, Whitaker staged fifteen known contests throughout the Piedmont. Zack was affiliated with another eight events, either as a promoter or attendee; several might have been imitations of Whitaker's conventions. Another twenty-eight contests are mentioned in North Carolina's newspapers during this time, although the promoters for the majority of these are unknown. The amount of fiddling activity is amazing; the Asheboro Bulletin commented that "Fiddlers' Conventions have had a great run in the State this season" (February 6, 1908: 3). That Zack Whitaker was involved with a full half of these conventions was a remarkable achievement.

His goal was lofty: to organize a statewide fiddlers' association in order to pre-
serve the old style of fiddling and the old time tunes. This association would include
committees to manage conventions at the local level, and would present local winners at a yearly statewide event. Zack Whitaker would call his events "Ye old tyme
fiddlers' convention" (*Union Republican*, December 5, 1907: 6; *Greensboro Record*,
December 14, 1907: 1; *Alamance Gleaner*, January 30, 1908: 3; *Tarborough Southerner*,
February 20, 1908: 1 quoting *Argus*, February 12, 1908; *Twin City Sentinel*, March 12,
1908: 1).

As Whitaker told various newspapers of the period:

> I have studied the musical situation in North Carolina, especially in the rural
> districts and find the interest in music very much retarded. The old veteran has laid
> his fiddle on the shelf in the dusty cutty; the young chap has never caught the spirit....
> These conventions are to resurrect the fiddle, to make him get down his fiddle,
> teach his boy the old tunes so there will be more music and better music in old North
> Carolina than has ever been before. (*Charlotte News*, January 4, 1908: 1)

To this end, Zack Whitaker set about gathering the fiddlers and staging the conventions. He wrote to local officials throughout the state, stating his purpose to form
a fiddlers' organization and asking them to list any musicians from their area. Zack
prepared a poster and handbill with his own drawing of an "olde tyme fiddler" for
distribution in local communities. Whitaker talked with newspaper reporters, providing them with quotes and copy about his fiddling contests, and also placing advertisements to reinforce his purple prose.

C. Z. Whitaker couldn't perform this task alone and recruited various individuals to aid him in his quest. J. R. Blackwell of Winston-Salem, who became secretary and treasurer for the Winston fiddlers' association, helped promote the
Winston-Salem and Salisbury events. Whitaker's brother Early and Hebert H. Low-
ery of Kernersville worked on the Mt. Airy contest, and James C. Rotan of Winston-
Salem went along with Whitaker for eight of the conventions. Rotan even emceed
one event (*Charlotte News*, January 8, 1908: 5; *Tarborough Southerner*, February 13,
1908: 1 and 2; *Union Republican*, November 28, 1907: 6; *Salisbury Post*, December 3,
1907: 7; *Western Sentinel*, March 13, 1908: 5; *Winston-Salem Journal*, November 21,
1907: 1; *Concord Times*, January 6, 1908: 3; *Twin City Sentinel*, January 13, 1908: 8;
Statesville *Landmark*, January 7, 1908: 5; *Webster's Weekly*, January 16, 1908: 5).

It all began just before Thanksgiving of 1907. Despite the bad weather, when the
appointed day arrived, the assembly of bow shakers and the size of the audience on
Wednesday, November 20 was so great that the Winston-Salem Elks Auditorium was
reserved for the following night. After the decision to establish a permanent committee to run future events (*Union Republican*, November 28, 1907: 6; *Journal*,
November 22, 1907: 1), Zack looked toward other venues.

Throughout this season, large turnouts greeted the promoter. As had occurred
in Winston-Salem, at many stops, second days were added. Whitaker's success was
clearly delineated in Raleigh, the hometown of the North Carolina Fiddlers' Convention. Zack's event drew far more musicians to the Academy of Music than Buck
Andrews had been able to get to A and M's auditorium. The Raleigh gathering was

singular in including a "barn dance" as part of the proceedings (*Western Sentinel*, February 7, 1908: 5; *Twin City Sentinel*, February 5, 1908: 8). Only in the old state capitol of New Bern did Whitaker falter. At that contest, the audience and promoters were present at the appointed time, but, strangely, no musicians showed up and the event had to be canceled (*Twin City Sentinel*, February 28, 1908: 1).

While working toward the establishment of the structure for his fiddling empire, another tact Whitaker would take was the founding of a musical newspaper. Zack drew upon the knowledge of his father, as well as his own publishing experience, to install a printing plant at his home in Oak Ridge. The weekly paper initially appeared during the first week of April, and featured local news items as well as serving Whitaker's fiddlers' association.

Whitaker's efforts inspired Colfax, Red Springs, and New London to hold events. While Zack rested up, musicians filled the Colfax grade school under the direction of Messrs. W. E. Tucker and S. J. Fugua, on Saturday, March 1 (*Twin City Sentinel*, March 3, 1908: 8) and the auditorium at Red Springs on March 2. W. M. Ivey and Reed Reeves gathered fiddlers on Wednesday, March 4, to benefit the new building of the New London High School (*Stanly Enterprise*, February 27, 1908: 1 and 3).

By the second week of March, Whitaker was back promoting his fiddlers' conventions. Zack's influence was apparent at the Glenola contest of Saturday, March 14 (*Asheboro Courier*, March 19, 1908: 5). On March 11, 12, and possibly 13, bow pullers invaded the Granite City Theatre in Mt. Airy, filling the theater even though the March weather was uncooperative (*Mt Airy News*, March 5, 1908: 3; *Western Sentinel*, March 13, 1908: 5). Sanford held its own event at the Opera House on March 21, appearing to be one of Whitaker's promotions even though his name was not mentioned in any surviving publicity materials (*Sanford Express*, March 20, 1909: 3).

However, the convention season was drawing to a close. By the end of March, farmers in the Piedmont would be preparing for planting, schools would be closing, and a musician's attentions were turning toward the work of the coming spring and summer. Luckily, Whitaker had accomplished what he had set out to do. He had organized committees to help run local conventions and gather musicians, assembled statewide lists of fiddlers, and raised the public's awareness for fiddling in North Carolina.

From the earliest days of this effort, one of Zack's goals had been to stage a statewide event where the winners of local contests could face off against each other. He promised at the Charlotte event that "When all the local conventions are concluded, the prize winners will hold a State convention to settle the championship players of North Carolina" (*Observer*, December 22, 1907: 6). When in Raleigh, he suggested that the championship might be held in that city (*News and Observer*, February 16, 1908: 13). At the conclusion of his contests for the 1907–1908 season, as he told the *Winston-Salem Sentinel*, "a state fiddlers' convention will probably be held in the near future.... The place has not been selected yet. Winston-Salem could get it" (*Twin City Sentinel*, March 11, 1908: 8).

But either North Carolina's newspapers lost interest in Whitaker's fiddlers or this was the end of Zack's noble effort. On Friday, March 21, he performed at a local convention in East Bend with W. C. Hill, and attended another East Bend contest a month later on Easter Monday (*Twin City Sentinel*, March 21, 1908: 8 and April 21, 1908: 1). D. W. Whitaker, Zack's father, became seriously ill around Easter, although it would be purely speculation to attribute the end of "Ye Olde Tyme Fiddlers' Association" to his father's illness. In May of 1908, C. Z. Whitaker participated in a Winston-Salem concert sponsored by the local chapter of the Daughters of the Confederacy. He revisited the location for his triumphant fiddlers' convention along with a number of the participants— Laurie and Billy Hill, "Mockingbird" Lineback, George Prim and Bob Blackburn — to benefit local Confederate Veterans. (Laurie Hill served in the War and might have instigated this event [*Western Sentinel*, April 24, 1908: 5; *Union Republican*, May 14, 1908: 6]). Whitaker also moved his newspaper from Oak Ridge to Winston-Salem at the month's end (*Union Republican*, May 28, 1908: 6). But no statewide contest was forthcoming.

To anyone's best knowledge, C. Z. Whitaker never staged a grand conclusion to his contests, and gave up on his idea for an ongoing, statewide fiddlers' organization. And when the Winston-Salem committee held their 1908 competition, many familiar names graced the stage of the Elks' Auditorium, but Whitaker was nowhere to be found (*Twin City Sentinel*, December 12, 1908: 3, 7–8; December 14, 1908: 1; *Journal*, December 13, 1908: 2 and December 15, 1908: 1, 6).

What defined these fiddling events and how were they organized? To begin with, Whitaker, although classically trained, tried to differentiate the fiddling heard at his events from the violin playing of classical music. Newspaper coverage carefully mentioned that "none need hesitate to enter in the belief that contest is meant for those who read violin music," "no violin solos or anything of a classic nature was allowed," and that "only old time fiddlers will be admitted to the contest" (*Western Sentinel*, November 1, 1907: 5; *Charlotte News*, December 23, 1907: 4; *Dispatch*, December 18, 1907: 7). Some writers and audiences concurred with these sentiments. One area publication weighed in with its concern about authenticity when it noted, "The Winston affair was a rather modern event under an old-time name, but we're disposed to lay money that the Salisbury affair is to be the genuine old-time stuff" (*Landmark*, December 20, 1907: 1). The promoters played on local pride, when proudly they insisted that "This is no traveling troupe, but citizens of this and surrounding counties ... playing the music of long ago and living over their boyhood days" (*Mt Airy News*, March 5, 1908: 3). At the Lexington contest, "The announcement that no violinists were admitted to the convention was greeted with applause" (*Dispatch*, January 29, 1908: 5). And a writer for the Tarboro newspaper equated fiddling with patriotism when he expressed the racist sentiments that "There won't be any violin obligatos [*sic*], virtuosos, valydalydyspepsiendo business, but plain old fashion fiddlin'.... Perugginni, Paginini, Paderoughski, none of those old Dagos or Deitschers will be in it against this aggregation of talent..." (*Tarborough Southerner*, February 20, 1908: 3). The *Western Sentinel* and the *Twin City Sentinel* also ran the headline "Ye Olden Time' Handlers of the Fiddle and the Bow Make the Greatest Hit of the Season."

Only several newspaper articles mention any of the rules for these competitions, although those surviving may very well be typical of all the events. Included were the stipulation that any instrument could be used as accompaniment, that the total number of contestants would decide the length of each performance, and that a musician may perform even if he didn't wish to compete for the prizes. One newspaper advised, in an unintentionally comical manner, that "No entrance or admission fee will be charged any fiddler who enters the contest, or takes part in the program, as some have consented to take part, and do special stunts, such as mimicking [sic] birds, geese, screaking [sic] pump, cane mill, fox chase, crow like a rooster, etc., who will not contest for a medal" (*Union Republican*, November 14, 1907: 6).

Fiddlers were asked to deliver a list of the three tunes they would perform in advance for inclusion in that evening's printed program. The program book also included James Whitcomb Riley's poem "The Old Fiddler" and listed an "Old Fiddlers' Directory" to the contestants (*Greensboro Patriot*, November 27, 1907: 7; event program in private collection of Frances Allred; *Twin City Sentinel*, November 18, 1907: 8; *Winston-Salem Journal*, November 17, 1907: 8).

Judges were chosen from prominent members of the community. Only one convention boasted that those holding judgment were also fiddlers, although one musician judged at both Winston-Salem and High Point (*Western Sentinel*, November 11, 1907: 5 and November 22, 1907: 8; *Twin City Sentinel*, November 21, 1907: 1; *High Point Enterprise*, December 4, 1907: 1 and 3; *Charlotte Observer*, December 19, 1907: 8). Mostly, judges came from each locale and were not part of Whitaker's package deal.

There were a great variety of prizes offered as well. Sometimes, money pure and simple was taken from the receipts and handed to the winning musicians. Other instrumentalists, such as banjoists and guitarists, were rewarded as well. Generally, prizes were given for best lead fiddlers (which I take to mean melody), second fiddlers (which I take to mean harmony), and others including banjo, guitar, dancer, worst fiddler, and specialty (which was a catch-all category). Prizes mainly started at $10 for first-place fiddlers and worked their way down from there; first prizes given for other instruments and skills were half that amount. Three of Whitaker's conventions rewarded the top fiddlers with "medals ... [of] solid gold ... not to cost less than $2.50 or more than $10" (*Western Sentinel*, November 8, 1907: 5; *Greensboro Patriot*, November 27, 1907: 7). Finally, a contestant might walk away with a knife, umbrella, picture, or hat as a reward for being the "ugliest man," "most comical fiddler," or "fiddler making the most fuss." Local merchants were always looking for advertising opportunities, and donating merchandise to the convention was always cheaper than giving money (*Record*, December 11, 1907: 1; *Charlotte News*, December 19, 1907: 10). On one occasion, "a fine fiddle bow was given by the Dixie Music Company [of Winston-Salem] for the participant receiving the greatest applause" (*Journal*, November 22, 1907: 1).

Admission ran from 25 to 50 cents (*Western Sentinel*, November 11, 1907: 5; *Charlotte News*, January 4, 1908: 5; *Dispatch*, January 15, 1908: 4; *Argus*, February 6, 8, 10, 1908; *News and Observer*, February 16, 1908: 6; *Tarborough Southerner*, February 13, 1908: 1 and 2; *Mt Airy News*, March 5, 1908: 3). The local newspaper published the budget for the High Point convention. It included receipts of $385.75, $20 of which went for prizes, $19 for printing and advertising, $10 to rent the auditorium, $2.75 for circulars, $16.92 to board musicians at various hotels, and $47.95 for "railroad fares" (I presume for the competitors). Dr. Hill and his daughter were paid $20 to entertain, and Zack Whitaker took $47.95 for his time. This left a "profit" of $189.38 (*High Point Enterprise*, December 25, 1907: 1).

One way to guarantee a good turnout was to donate a portion of the proceeds to a worthy local institution. Some of the beneficiaries included Winston-Salem's Twin-City Hospital, fire departments in High Point and Salisbury, the Confederate Monument Fund in Reidsville, the Greensboro Civic League and Raleigh Associated Charities.

When the big day arrived, many of the fiddlers were already on the premises. In order to guarantee their attendance, out-of-town participants would leave plenty of time to complete the trip to the convention site. Whitaker wanted them there anyway, in order to clarify the rules, order of play, and other particulars of the evening, as well as running through the overture and acquainting accompanists with the contestants. Toward that end, visiting musicians were "entertained" with room and board and even train fare provided by the promoters.

These events were major happenings for the communities visited by Whitaker. They benefited legitimate area organizations. Often, the mayor himself would address the gathering, as happened at four of these events. One, a fiddler himself, even aided in the judging!

When the doors opened between 8 and 8:15 P.M. on the appointed nights, with the exception of Charlotte's first night, which was hampered by a severe storm earlier in the day, auditoriums and opera houses were filled (*Charlotte News*, January 7, 1908: 5; *North Carolinian*, February 20, 1908: 2; *Charlotte Observer*, January 8, 1908: 10). An audience of one thousand people was not unusual for these gatherings, with some nights approaching fifteen hundred attendees. The two-day Charlotte contest drew 1100, Winston-Salem's dual event drew 1,700 and Greensboro drew around the same as Winston (*Greensboro Patriot*, December 18, 1907: 1 and January 8, 1908: 7; *Winston-Salem Journal*, November 21, 1907: 1 and December 18, 1907: 5; *Salisbury Post*, December 12, 1907: 1; *Greensboro Record*, December 14, 1907: 1; *Charlotte Observer*, December 18, 1907: 12 and January 8, 1908: 4; *High Point Enterprise*, December 25, 1907: 1; *Western Sentinel*, January 10, 1908: 4; *Charlotte News*, January 8, 1908: 5).

When the curtains parted, all the fiddlers competing would be assembled on stage, drawing their bows in unison. The group, averaging around fifty, but, at some events, swelling to over eighty bow wielders, filled the hall with their anthem, the fiddle tune "Mississippi Sawyer." The applause greeting the musicians was deafening. (*Winston-Salem Journal*, November 21, 1907: 1; *North Carolinian*, February 20, 1908: 2; *Western Sentinel*, November 22, 1907: 8; *Twin City Sentinel*, November 21, 1907: 1; *High Point Enterprise*, December 25, 1907: 1; *Charlotte Observer*, December 19, 1907: 8; *Landmark*, January 17, 1908: 3). After the audience regained their composure, local dignitaries and the evening's master of ceremonies sounded words of welcome. Then, the competition began in earnest. Each fiddler took his (or, in the case of Charlotte, her, where Mrs. S. G. Sharpe earned fourth place and was the only female fiddle contestant in all of Whitaker's events) place on the stage. The player might attempt his selections solo or would bring along a group of other musicians, with banjo, guitar, piano, or another fiddler the particularly popular accompaniments in those days (*Charlotte News*, January 9, 1908: 2; *High Point Enterprise*, December 25, 1907: 1; *Charlotte Observer*, December 19, 1907: 8; *Landmark*, January 17, 1908: 3). There were some humorous moments, as many of the performers, unused to so large a platform, would either be intimidated by their surroundings, or, more likely, completely ignore the size of the audience and act with the charm and impunity of sitting on a back porch or in the midst of a room filled with dancers.

Although a few of the fiddlers were Whitaker's good friends and took the time to attend multiple events, by and large the fiddlers and their accompanists were particular to the locality where the contest occurred. With the exception of the cities of the western Piedmont — Statesville, Winston-Salem, High Point and Greensboro, which were relatively close together — musicians did not travel from one event to another. Their work schedules, familial responsibilities, and the vagaries of travel kept this from happening.

If the contestants could all be herded on and off of the stage by 11 P.M., then the competition would be completed and the judges would retire to decide on the winners. If there were still fiddlers left to perform, the event would continue into a second evening, structured much like the first (*Charlotte News*, January 8, 1908: 5; *Greensboro Patriot*, December 18, 1907: 1). When the last bow had been drawn and tune played, a few of the non-competitors or perhaps even some of those hot from the contest would entertain the audience. Sometimes, the spectators were so wound up in their seats that they attempted to join in with the proceedings. At the Charlotte convention:

> When the party of musicians was sending forth upon the midnight air the strains of "The Arkansas Traveler," Mr. [Ben] Powell [one of the fiddlers competing] finally could stand it no longer. For a minute or two he twitched and fidgeted in his chair. Then he leaped to his feet on the stage and began executing a pigeon wing to the rioutous [*sic*] delight of the audience, which howled for more [*Observer*, January 8, 1908: 4].

Then, the judges would render their verdicts, the list of winners would be read, and the prizes awarded. There might be a closing number, such as "Home, Sweet Home." Possibly, the fiddlers would continue their meet well into the night, unable or unwilling to leave such a large gathering of their compatriots at the conclusion of the evening's organized event (*Journal*, November 22, 1907: 1).

If there were any doubts about the success of Zack Whitaker's conventions, the *Charlotte Observer* put them to rest. Following their city's convention, an unidentified journalist commented that "If anyone ever imagined that Charlotte people are too citified, too modern, too cultured, or too anything else to enjoy the music of the fathers, five minutes spent last night in the new Auditorium was enough to disabuse his mind" (*Observer*, January 8, 1908: 4).

A great majority of the fiddlers and other musicians who appeared at C. Z. Whitaker's conventions remain names in newspaper articles, with no significant biographies attached. Others are known through their activities outside of these contests. Some, through their own audacity and outrageous claims, commanded the attention of audience and writers alike.

One of the fiddlers competing at the Winston-Salem contest, a salesman at the Piedmont Furniture Store, issued the challenge for any "second fiddler" (harmony or back-up fiddler) to try and beat him. Local newspapers reported the dare, mentioning that its source, one George William Prim (born March 1867), had been playing "by ear" since the age of five, "and he claims that he has never heard a piece of music played on a fiddle that he could not listen to and play the second to perfection" (*Western Sentinel*, November 8, 1907: 5). At the convention, Prim accompanied a number of the other fiddlers in the competition, as well as entertained while the judges tallied the votes with "an imitation of the 'old cain [*sic*] mill.'" He came in first in the second fiddle contest at Winston-Salem and Greensboro (*Winston-Salem Journal*, November 21, 1907: 1; *Western Sentinel*, November 22, 1907: 8; *Twin City Sentinel*, November 21, 1907: 1; *Greensboro Record*, December 24, 1907: 1) and captured second place at High Point and Salisbury (*Western Sentinel*, December 24, 1907: 3; *Carolina Watchman*, December 25, 1907: 3). Prim also appeared at the Statesville convention (*Landmark*, January 14, 1908: 3).

Another star of the Winston-Salem event that later accompanied Zack Whitaker on his travels was W. C. "Uncle Billy" Hill from the mountain settlement of Rutherford College. Other members of his extended family were musical, and he was often in their company. At Winston-Salem, he and his uncle, Dr. Lauriston Hardin "Laurie" Hill (January 30, 1837–May 13, 1921) of Germanton, took turns entertaining during the judges' break (*Journal*, November 22, 1907: 1). Dr. Hill had been a surgeon assigned to the 53rd North Carolina during the Civil War (*Landmark*, January 28, 1908: 1). At the 1916 reunion of the troops held in Birmingham, Laurie Hill led an "old-time fiddlers' convention" ("Old Fiddlers' Contest During Reunion," *Confederate Veteran*, 93).

W. C. Hill gained much of the audience's support with his playing in the competition. The *Journal* reported, "W .C. Hill's 'Twinkle Twinkle Little Star' aroused the audience to the highest pitch. Dr. Hill is up in years, but his age would not be betrayed by the manner in which he handles the fiddle." The audience also supported the decision to declare Billy Hill the winner of a prize violin bow. Laurie and W. C. Hill swept the competition away on that first night, capturing first and second respectively in lead fiddle (*Winston-Salem Journal*, November 21, 1907: 1; *Union Republican*, November 28, 1907: 6; *Western Sentinel*, November 22, 1907: 8; *Twin City Sentinel*, November 21, 1907: 1). Billy Hill, sometimes with his uncle in tow, followed Whitaker to several other conventions, appearing at Greensboro, High Point, Salisbury, Charlotte and Statesville. "The Hills and others," wrote an unnamed reporter, "accompany Whitaker to all the gatherings as specialists. As we understand it they do not contest for the prizes but of course get a part of the proceeds." The newspaper also commented that, "Dr. L. H. Hill of Germantown, and Mr. W .C. Hill, of Rutherford College, were the finest players. The only criticism that could be made is that they come dangerously near being violinists" (*Landmark*, January 17, 1908: 3). Billy was not a contestant at Lexington, even though he did perform (*Dispatch*, January 22, 1908: 4), but did compete at Mt Airy in March (*Western Sentinel*, March 13, 1908: 5).

R. T. Blackburn (see Chapter Five) competed in his home area at the Winston-Salem, Greensboro, and High Point conventions. Robert Blackburn, in fact, earned himself an encore at Winston with "Old Sallie Goddin" [*sic*], and a razor (!) at Greensboro for his efforts. Blackburn, a left-handed fiddler from Kernersville, specialized in the "Mockingbird"; his son Bill (born around 1880) was also a fiddler (*Journal*, November 22, 1907: 1; *Charlotte News*, December 19, 1907: 10).

The public took special notice of juvenile fiddlers. Common knowledge tells performers never to follow animals or children onto the stage, and fiddlers' conventions are no exception to this rule. Three young bow pullers who received the public's favor at Whitaker's events were Charles Grady Graham from Barber in Rowan County; John Thomas Jones, the son of Greensboro's sheriff; and Master Lindsay Kester (or Kestler), a twelve-year-old from Winston-Salem (*Western Sentinel*, December 20, 1907: 7). Grady Graham was seven years old when he entered four of Whitaker's conventions and an equal number of other local events during the same season. Because he was too inexperienced to beat the adult fiddlers, the audience, on several occasions, "passed the hat" (took up a collection) for him (*Salisbury Post*, December 5, 1907: 1 and December 12, 1907: 1; *Western Sentinel*, March 20, 1908: 1 and January 3, 1908: 3; *Charlotte News*, December 30, 1907: 2; *Landmark*, January 21, 1908: 3; *Twin City Sentinel*, March 27, 1908: 8).

"Trick" fiddling has had a history of mixed success at fiddlers' conventions. Sometimes, the playing of the instrument in unconventional ways (i.e.: behind the head, between the legs like a cello, holding the bow between the knees and rubbing the fiddle on the bow, and soon) has been barred from "serious" contests. Trick tunes, as well, have had ambivalent responses from judges and organizers. These pieces, which purport to represent the sounds of birds, animals, or machinery, are variously barred or rewarded, depending on the particular event.

One player who gained his reputation and nickname from a rendition of ("Listen to) The Mockingbird" was machinist Edward E. Lineback (or Leinbach) (born October 1870). From Winston-Salem, Lineback appeared (but didn't compete) at that city's event (*Western Sentinel*, November 22, 1907: 8; *Twin City Sentinel*, November 21, 1907: 1) and at the Statesville contest (*Landmark*, January 14, 1908: 3). At Greensboro, "Ed Lineback ... play[ed] with the bow beneath first one leg and then the other and even went so far as to place the bow between his knees and draw the fiddle across the bow, never losing the least fraction of time in the operation" (*Western Sentinel*, December 20, 1907: 7).

Lineback challenged High Point's audience that, "if [I] can't go so much like a mocking bird on the fiddle that one thinks he is in the presence of a real bird, [I] guarantee to have your money refunded" (*High Point Enterprise*, December 11, 1907: 1). Lineback also assembled what he called "the Linebach Musical Comedy Company," which included his wife Bertha (born December 1879) on piano, his ten-year-old daughter Edith on mandolin, and eight-year-old son Charles Edward on "violin-cello" to perform locally (*Journal*, December 13, 1908: 2 and December 15, 1908: 1, 6; *Western Sentinel*, May 19, 1908: 5; Census).

Dancing was a feature of all the conventions. Often, a member of the audience, used to moving his feet in time to the music, just had to get up and cut a few capers. Sometimes, dance was included in the competition. Nowhere did dancing captivate the audience more than at the Statesville event. As readers of the *Landmark* learned:

The specialties were the feature of Friday evening's contest. [The] Blankenship brothers ... are star performers. Two of them appeared on the stage in working clothes and without coats. One, a heavy-weight, picked the strings of a zither, worked a triangle with his foot and a harp with his mouth all at one and the same time, singing a little if the occasion required, while the others sang. In addition, they are all fiddlers or banjo pickers, or both. One of the brothers, also a heavy-weight, did a dancing stunt which he called "The Buzzard Lope," imitating the movements of a vulture when it is about to attack a carcas [sic].

The Woodruff brothers ... danced some more, and another dancer was Mr. W. W. Carter, of Chambersburg township, this county. Mr. Carter also played the fiddle.... At the afternoon performance Mr. Ed. Freeze, of Iredell, 70 years old, gave a good exhibition of the dancing of his boyhood days [January 21, 1908: 3].

As one- and two-room rural public schoolhouses were closed to make way for new, consolidated schools, string-band music was dropped from school graduation exercises (see Chapter Five). On the positive side, in order to maintain these new school buildings, revenue was needed to supplement that supplied (or not supplied) by government. And banjos and fiddles were used to earn these monies.

Before these new public schools were built, the only halls available for community gatherings were courthouses in smaller county seats and opera houses, fraternal halls and academy or college auditoriums in larger locales. Once the move toward consolidated schools began in the 1920s, school assembly halls became an alternative site for events. Local parent associations saw fiddlers' conventions as a good way to raise the necessary funds needed for school upkeep and the purchase of equipment.

School halls were used for fiddlers' conventions as early as 1907, when C. Z. Whitaker utilized the High Point graded school auditorium for his December 19 event (*High Point Enterprise*, December 4, 1907: 1, 3). Zack Whitaker was at least the inspiration, if not the promoter, for the Kernersville, Mooresville, and Glenola graded schools' 1908 events. All three locations were the benefactors of the events, with Mooresville using their share of the funds to "purchase blackboards and curtains" (*Twin City Sentinel*, February 8, 1908: 8 and February 26, 1908: 5; *Asheboro Courier*, March 19, 1908: 5). Eleven additional fiddlers' conventions were held during the winter and spring of 1908 in school auditoriums, as reported by Piedmont newspapers. Seven were fundraisers for the sponsoring schools. Several used the receipts to paint their school buildings and at one event, "to be applied to the new building of the New London High School" (*Asheboro Courier-Tribune*, January 9 and 16, 1908, and February 13, 1908: 1; January 16, 23 and 30, 1908: 10; February 13 and 20, 1908: 5; February 20, 1908: 12; March 5 and 12, 1908: 5; *Randolph Tribune*, December 3, 1931: 1; *Observer*, February 21 and March 19, 1908: 8; *Ansonian*, February 25, 1908: 3; *Twin City Sentinel*, March 3, 1908: 8). Interestingly, a 1913 Advance Academy fiddlers' convention raised money to build an outdoor exhibition stage, and the Car[r]away school held a contest in conjunction with their 1908 school commencement (*Davie Record* April 2, 1913 and *Asheboro Courier*, April 2, 1908: 8).

According to anecdotal evidence, the heyday for schoolhouse fiddlers' conventions was the 1920s and 1930s. Unfortunately, the newspapers of the period were not as enamored of fiddling as they were during the first decade of the 1900s. Whereas the articles about Whitaker's conventions covered many columns and were spread over many days, these latter-day schoolhouse events received scant coverage if any. Often, the only mention would be in advertisements placed by the school betterment association in advance of the contest. At the conclusion of the competition, an organization was lucky if the newspaper listed the winners' names.

By and large, these contests were run by the schools themselves, or, through proxy, by the Parent Teacher Association or under the banner of the School Improvement Fund. It is somewhat conjecture to imagine that these were more local affairs, held in less central locations than the Whitaker conventions of earlier times. It also seems to have been common for a school to hold more than one event during each school year. Of course, in the days before air conditioning, these were cool weather events, which probably left November through May as the prime months for the contests. From the little coverage available, admission prices and prize money seems to have changed little from prior days.

A typical school-sponsored fiddlers' convention of this period was held at the Skyland School on April 17, 1924. At 8 P.M. on the appointed date, fourteen musicians gathered to compete. Echoing the way Whitaker began his 1907 and 1908 events, all the musicians played "Mississippi Sawyer" to begin the evening. This practice had been discarded by the 1920s, as the *Twin City Sentinel* noted by calling the opening "novel." Over the next two plus hours, R. L. Grubbs introduced the players. When the smoke had cleared, Ralph McGee had walked away with the first prize for fiddle, followed by F.M. Stultz. Jessie Grubbs and D. W. Patterson won the "violin" prizes, as both fiddle and violin music was allowed at this event. Sid Allgood, who recorded the next year for Okeh Records, beat J. H. Itol, Jr., in the banjo competition. The school planed to hold another convention after Easter (*Twin-City Sentinel*, April 19, 1924: 24).

Leonard Eubanks attended several Chatham County events in the late 1920s. During this time, his grandfather, Faddy King, a fiddler and local convention promoter, began taking Leonard with him to contests. Leonard remembers:

> Back in the '20s or '30s, there wasn't no whole lot of stuff going on like you got going on now and when you had a fiddlers' convention, you had a crowd. When I looked out over yonder at Durham, it looked like looking out over a 10-acre field and all I could see was people's heads. I said, "Good gracious alive" to myself. If I had looked at them, I don't believe I could have picked a lick. There was a great big building and that thing was full and I couldn't tell you how many there was there.

Although the amounts offered for prizes at the fiddling conventions of 1900–1940 seem small, and participants commented that they weren't competing primarily for the money, their actions point toward the importance for musicians of their winnings.

Several banjoists paid for their first "real" instruments with their prize money. In 1908, after playing for about fourteen years on a homemade banjo, Carl Nance

Carl Nance displays the banjo bought from Sears with his contest winnings, circa 1908. Courtesy Glee Arnold.

(February 29, 1884–October 10, 1980) of Randolph County ordered one from Sears for $15.75. As Ralph Bulla later related:

> Three nights after receiving his banjo from Sears and Roebuck, he and [Jake] Miller competed in a fiddler's convention in Ether and both of them won first prizes in their different categories. [Carl] made enough prize money at three fiddler's conventions to pay for the prized banjo [Bulla, 9a].

When I interviewed Snow Camp's Bob Roberson, he gave Nance's story with a different twist:

> Back in them days they had a lot of fiddlers' conventions ... they'd have 'em around the schoolhouses.... When I was in my late teens [in the mid–1920s], I bought

me an old banjo and paid five dollars for it. And back then, you'd get a pretty good banjo for five dollars. And we went over here to Anderson High School one Saturday night and played a fiddler convention. And our band won the first prize. And I was the only banjo player there. And the man that was the master of ceremony, he wanted to discard the banjo prize 'cause I didn't have no competition. And our manager said, "You can't do that, I got a banjo player here." So, I got up and played a couple of tunes, made my five dollars and paid for my banjo.

Hubert Lohr was always in dire financial straits when he attended conventions. His son, Jack, says, "He'd go to a fiddlers' convention with just enough gas to get there and he would have to win to buy gas to get home. And he's done that more than one time. And he'd always win as banjo soloist or whatever."

Even though C. Z. Whitaker had been unsuccessful in his attempts to form a statewide organization, Whitaker was not out of public music making quite yet. Along with playing area dances (see Chapter Four), he reappeared with his band as the promoter of local conventions. Zack may have had a hand in both the Germanton school contest of May 1924 and the one at the North Grade School of Winston-Salem held in early 1925 (*Twin City Sentinel*, January 26, 1925: 4; February 12, 1925: 2; May 13, 1925: 7, 13). Whitaker promoted a contest at Oak Ridge on December 15, 1933, and also drew the illustration that adorned the convention's flyer. Billy Prim, one of Whitaker's star performers from the turn of the century, was there as well.

Prim had been raised in Yadkin County's East Bend township. His father, Enoch B. Prim, worked as a carpenter and farmed; his mother, Mary (possibly Jane), stayed at home and raised the children. Bill Prim married in 1896; by 1900, he was farming in Meadows township of Stokes County. Bill left farming to sell furniture, moving over to the manufacturing end as early as 1913, when he relocated his family from Winston to High Point. In the early 1920s, Billy Prim left his wife and four children, but seems to have continued to live around High Point (Census; High Point City Directories). By 1930, he was living with his sister in Surry County. Billy had kept up his friendship with Whitaker and also grew close to Charlie Pegram's family. Dorothy Ray Pegram (born January 21, 1918), Charlie's daughter, was part of her family's performing troop, playing second violin to Prim and dancing at conventions. She remembers Billy Prim accompanying fiddler Sidney Flynn, who would appear on stage in drag! Prim lived with the Pegrams for several years before his death in the 1940s, returning to his Mt. Airy home before passing away.

Zack Whitaker had known the Pegrams by the time he was promoting his first fiddlers' conventions. Charles Lee (March 22, 1874–March 22, 1963), a few years older than Whitaker, was known in the area for his banjo playing. Charlie attended six of Zack's 1907 and 1908 contests, winning second place at Statesville and capturing first at Salisbury, where he may have been the only banjo contestant (*Carolina Watchman*, December 25, 1907: 3; *Charlotte Observer*, December 19, 1907: 8 and January 19, 1908: 2; *Winston-Salem Journal*, November 21, 1907: 1; *Charlotte News*, December 19, 1907: 10 and December 30, 1907: 2). Charlie's brother, Carl Luther (February 27, 1887–February 20, 1960), fiddled in his youth and competed at Whitaker's Greensboro convention of 1907 (*Greensboro Record*, December 18, 1907: 1).

Billy Prim, as he looked in the 1930s. Courtesy Dorothy Pegram.

But it was Clarence Clyde Pegram (July 18, 1890–November 20, 1958), the youngest brother, whom Zack Whitaker knew the best. Clyde studied under Whitaker at the Oak Ridge Institute and played in the school's orchestra. Soon after attending Oak Ridge, Clyde departed for Cincinnati to enroll in that city's Conservatory of Music. Besides the violin, young Clyde also learned clarinet. Clyde Pegram served in the military as a musician, assigned during World War I to the 81st division, 321st Infantry Band in Europe. In France, Clyde found the violin of his dreams. It was labeled as a Vuillaume, and Pegram thought so much of the instrument that he named

The Oak Ridge Academy Band, assembled on the school grounds. Student Clyde Pegram is the seated violinist, with friend and bandleader Zack Whitaker holding a baton to his left. Oak Ridge, Guilford County, circa 1910. Courtesy Frances Allred.

his son William (born October 12, 1946) for the maker. Clyde Pegram returned to America and performed with dance orchestras at Moore's and Vede Mechum Springs, Southern Pines, Pinehurst, and other North Carolina locales. He went back into the military between 1921 and 1925. After his second enlistment, Clyde stayed close to home. He helped out on the family farm and took care of his elderly parents.

In the 1930s, the Pegrams played a large part in Whitaker's public life. Clyde played square dances and conventions with the older man; Carl would emcee the fiddlers' events and Charlie's family would take on a large part of the responsibility for promoting Zack's and their own contests around Guilford, Forsyth, and Randolph counties. The family would take flyers to the sponsoring schools, sending them home with the students. The Pegrams would also notify those they considered "good musicians" to invite them to their events. Charlie Pegram was the driver and his wife, Bertha Ethel Coltrane (February 8, 1894–July 8, 1962), was in charge of the door and handling the money. Dorothy and her siblings would be on stage, either dancing or playing as the Redbirds. Dorothy learned to fiddle from her uncle Clyde, sister Sue (born April 16, 1916) played piano, brother Wallace (known as Bill; born September 23, 1923), picked the tenor banjo, and their friends, brothers Virgil and Glenn Rahne played the tenor banjo and guitar, respectively.

Three schoolhouse conventions that began in the 1920s were held in the southern Davie County mill town of Cooleemee, at Star High School in eastern Montgomery

County, and at Union Grove High School in northern Iredell County. All survived World War II, one ending sometime after the war, another mutating into a different current-day event, and a third continuing to this day unabated.

Jim and Lynn Rumley of the Cooleemee Historical Society trace the town's first fiddlers' convention to the initial decade of the twentieth century. The *Cooleemee Journal* reports a 1923 event in the "auditorium of the new school," although it is unclear if this indeed was the start to the twenty-plus year run of contests (*Cooleemee Journal*, March 21, 1923). *Journal* editor James Crawford Sell (1865–1940), reports the paper, was the convention's organizer by September of 1924, which was held on (more or less) the third Saturday of September during its initial stretch. Interestingly enough, the convention was billed as a statewide event (*Twin City Sentinel*, September 12, 1924: 6 and September 19, 1930: 18; *Western Sentinel*, August 28, 1925: 2, September 17, 1930; *Davie Record*).

According to the Rumleys, the Sell family was from Stanly County. J. C. Sell moved to Lexington, where he had some hand in the Lexington Fiddlers' Convention (although he is not mentioned in any newspaper coverage that I have seen) and newspaper. In 1906, Sell opened the Cooleemee newspaper under the auspices of Erwin Mills, who controlled much of the town (Chaffin, "An Astute Observer of Life." *Salisbury Post*, June 12, 2001). When J. C. Sell died in 1940 from injuries received in an automobile accident, his son J. C. Sell, Jr. (born around 1919), known as "Bud," took over the fiddlers' convention.

Cooleemee's first postwar convention reflected the great changes that had been taking place in country music. Performers included Harvey Potts, on the "electric Hawaiian guitar," and prizes were given in the "Best Electric Guitar" category. The local Lion's Club was now sponsoring the event, as similar organizations were promoting contests throughout the Piedmont. Admission had risen to 85 cents for adults and 35 cents for children. An unknown writer proclaimed that "This will be a convention which the whole family can enjoy" (*Erwin Chatter*, October 1946: 1).

The Star Fiddlers' Convention began sometime between 1925 and 1927, and was held during those early years on the first Saturday in March. It is hard to know much about this event's history. This area of Montgomery County suffered from a lack of local newspapers and from scant coverage in other Piedmont publications. In addition, the current sponsors of the contest have not retained any memorabilia from early contests.

Oral history names C. V. Richardson, now deceased, as the master of ceremonies for those initial meetings. Banjoists Ira Britt, a local, and Fred Franklin, from High Point, competed against each other at the first couple of conventions held at Star. Teddy Roosevelt Trogdon (June 12, 1907–August 25, 1997) of Franklinville in neighboring Randolph County was a fixture at Star for many years. Trogdon competed as early as 1930, and won so many guitar prizes over the next twenty or so years that he was barred from competing and hired to judge (*Asheboro Courier*, March 6, 1930: 5).

The school's PTA, aided by J. W. Murray, promoted the contest in the high school auditorium, which held one thousand people. When Murray's wife contacted the newsreel company Fox Movietone News about the event, a film crew was dispatched to the 1932 convention. The *Asheboro Courier* reported that two of the contestants, "Mr. Renigar of Asheboro and Mr. O. Daniel, of Liberty ... are consequently in the picture" (*Asheboro Courier*, February 27, 1930: 1 and March 3, 1932: 7). After viewing the film clip, guitarist Fred Olson further identifies banjoist Glenn Davis in the assembled group of players. Star continued until at least 1996, when I last attended the event.

North Carolina's most famous fiddling event of recent times is held in the tiny town of Union Grove in the foothills of the Western Piedmont. As northern musicians invaded the upland south, searching for traditional music at festivals and fiddlers' conventions during the "folk boom" of the 1960s, Union Grove was identified as one of their primary destinations. In the 1970s, the original event literally crashed and burned under the weigh of several hundred thousand visitors. Drugs were openly sold, and gangs of bikers ran amok, setting portable toilets on fire. But another, more low-key event emerged, phoenix-like, from Union Grove's ashes, which still exists today (Keever, 453–454).

The seeds for the Union Grove contest were planted in the Statesville courthouse conventions of the early 1900s. Sheriff J. M. Deaton promoted these local events from 1912 into the 1920s, the first of two which included the Van Hoy band. In December of 1912, the brothers Henry Price (January 22, 1887–July 19, 1976) and John Web[b] Van Hoy (August 26, 1880–June 25, 1943) captured third in the band competition with the fiddle and "harp" duet of "Whistling Rufus," a popular song written by W. Murdock Lind and Kerry Mills and published in 1899. J.W. also took the first fiddle prize. At the February 1913 convention, no prizes were awarded (the profits were divided among the contestants), but the newspaper mentioned "The Van Hoy band, J. W. Van Hoy and Chas. Echerd, accompanied by Miss Weber on the piano." The unknown writer also commented "Mr. Van Hoy comes dangerously near being a violinist.... He can play fiddle music all right but he doesn't pat his foot," meaning that J. W. used the long bow and vibrato associated with classical music (music and fiddlers' convention articles in Iredell County Library scrapbooks; Keever, 453–454).

Henry Van Hoy married Ada Casey (November 30, 1896–October 13, 1989), conveniently also a fiddler, on November 30 of 1896 and began teaching at the Union Grove School. The first Union Grove Fiddlers' Convention was held in 1924 as a fund-raiser to support the high school the Saturday night before Easter. At first, the contest was not a large affair, and the initial event only netted the school $50 (Seeger; music and fiddlers' convention articles in Iredell County Library scrapbooks). Historian Homer Keever wrote that

> By the 1930s, though, the Union Grove Fiddlers Convention with Henry P. Van Hoy as master of ceremonies had become a North Iredell institution. It grew and grew, first into a second hall in the library, then in 1949 into the old wooden gymnasium, and finally [by 1962] to a large tent on the school grounds, with each band playing at three places [453–454].

The convention showed a steady growth throughout the decade of the 1950s. The 1953 event grossed $1,200. The 1954 Union Grove convention was spread over three days and three halls. Twenty-five hundred people witnessed a total of 137 musicians making up the 34 bands competing for the three first places. The winners that year were Earl Cheek and the Sons of Kannapolis, George Pegram (the well-known banjoist, singer, and raconteur; see Chapter Eight) and his Brushy Mountain Boys, and the Blue Ridge Buddies (music and fiddlers' convention articles in Iredell County Library scrapbooks). An attendee to the 1956 Union Grove paid seventy-five cents to enter the halls (music and fiddlers' convention articles in Iredell County Library scrapbooks), which grew to four by 1957. The 1958 competition included 47 groups (music and fiddlers' convention articles in Iredell County Library scrapbooks). Some other participants in the '50s included L.W. Lambert's Blue River Boys (see Chapter Eleven), fiddler Esker Hutchins and the Surry County Ramblers, and fiddler Burt Edwards with son, banjoist Billy Edwards, originally from the mountains of southwest Virginia (Scancarelli, Union Grove LP).

By 1960, Henry had retired and turned his duties over to son James Pierce Van Hoy (July 20, 1917–May 16, 1997). Over two hundred musicians graced the various stages that year at Union Grove, comprising 55 bands from six states and the District of Columbia. Fifteen hundred dollars was raised for the school that year, which marked the beginning of the invasion by outside musicians (Seeger; Keever, 453–454; music and fiddlers' convention articles in Iredell County Library scrapbooks). The '60s marked a large decade of change for the United States, and these changes were reflected in the audience and participants at the Union Grove Convention. This was no more apparent than at the 1964 and 1965 gatherings. In 1965, 75 bands competed before a total audience of 8,500. In an effort to appease the changing tastes of the "local" audience and the mixed nature of the spectators between the indigenous and outside attendees, a "modern" (I assume this means electric instruments) band category had been created, which was won in 1965 by the Stokes County Ramblers from King, North Carolina. This was by no means unique to Union Grove. Drummer Ed Blair remembers playing with a rock band at the 1961 Siler City Fiddler's Convention; it was his first public performance. Back at Union Grove, a bunch of Yankees, the New York Ramblers (from, not surprisingly, the New York City area, with the exception of their guitarist, Eric Thompson, who was from California), won the top band prize in 1964. This group included David Grisman, the pioneering bluegrass mandolinist who went on to spearhead a musical movement titled variously "newgrass," "jamgrass," or "new acoustic music."

Regional bands, however, continued to hold their own with the judges and the audience. As was the case with other southern fiddlers' contests of the 1960s, the newer bluegrass music groups, with Earl Scruggs-influenced banjo, hot instrumental solos, and fast tempos, were judged in the same category as dance fiddle-led old time ensembles rooted in prewar musical styles. The newer style bands dominated at Union Grove, and included the Mountain Ramblers of Galax, Virginia, led by James Lindsey and featuring the fiddling of Otis Burris; various groups including mandolinist Dewey Farmer from Kannapolis, including the Blue Grass Mountain Boys; the Friendly City Playboys of Winston-Salem, including Billy Edwards picking the "Scruggs-style" banjo; and banjoist L. W. Lambert's assorted groups (music and fiddlers' convention articles in Iredell County Library scrapbooks; Seeger).

During the 1960s, Easter weekend at Union Grove became a meeting place for like-minded string band musicians from throughout the upper south and the northeast. It was at Union Grove that Doc Watson first met the folklorist Ralph Rinzler, who introduced the pioneer flat-picking guitarist to northern, urban audiences and wider fame. Rounder Records, now the largest independent record label for bluegrass and string band music, began to issue a number of recordings made during the convention. These included albums by George Pegram and West Virginia fiddler Clark Kessinger.

The problems brought about by the changes that had racked America in the 1960s affected this tiny Piedmont community as well. As historian Homer Keever wrote:

> By 1970 the Fiddler's Convention had grown too large for the school, criticism was rising over the rougher elements that were appearing, and the county board of education withdrew permission to hold it in the school. J. Pierce Van Hoy ... moved the event to his farm near Winthrop Church at the intersection of Interstate 77 and Highway 901. Folk musicians from all over the United States discovered it and came in droves to the three-day event, camping on the Van Hoy farm and nearby. It became more than a fiddlers convention. It became a "happening...." Some estimates of the crowd there in 1976 ran over 100,000 [453–454].

Fiddler Bill Hicks, later a member of North Carolina's Red Clay Ramblers, attended the 1970 event. At the time, he reported that

> In 1970 the freaks were in the majority. There were plenty of excellent mountain musicians— Tommy Jarrell was there, and white-bearded John Hilst from West Virginia, and Kilby Snow, and of course George Pegram. But the audience was almost entirely composed of long-hairs [sic], and the band which tore the tent apart was the Raleigh-based New Deal String Band. The 46th Annual Union Grove was the first at its new location. In the old-time band competition, the Spark Gap Wonder Boys from Brookline, Mass., won first prize. The Constitutional Wiretappers, with John Burke on the fiddle and Durham's Jim Watson on guitar, placed second in the same category. The Fuzzy Mountain String Band [of which Hicks was a member], also of Durham, took fourth prize in the old-time category. There isn't a farmer or a grey hair in the whole bunch. Other winners included: banjo, Roger Sprung of New York; guitar, Tom Edwards of Siler City; fiddle, Joe Drye of Galax. The best bluegrass band was Jim Holder's Border Mountain Boys of Statesville.

At the same time that Pierce Van Hoy continued taking his convention further and further toward a "happening," his brother, fiddler Harper Austin Van Hoy (born August 6, 1922), established the nearby "Fiddler's Grove" Convention and campground. Harper had wanted to host a more family friendly affair, while keeping the best aspects of the old fiddlers' convention started by his father. For the first few years, he went head-to-head with Pierce, and both events kept to the same schedule Easter weekend. Eventually, Harper moved his event to Memorial Day weekend, when it still runs today (Keever, 453–454).

Pierce Van Hoy, however, was not so lucky. Bill Hicks aptly describes the end:

About 4 years later Pierce's Union Grove died of gluttony, exploded by a attendance of 200,000 or so people, most of whom had no interest at all in the music but
were just looking to party. The festival under these circumstances required the attendance of the entire NC Highway Patrol — and they had other things to do that Easter
Weekend.

A newspaper article about a fiddlers' convention in High Point in 1985 was written in reaction to problems with such conventions at Union Grove: "But unlike other
similar conventions held across the state, this one is geared for the whole family. That
means no bonfires, drugs, weapons or disturbances please. And no pets, either" (*High
Point Enterprise*, "City Fiddlers' Convention Geared for Whole Family," June 12, 1985:
D1).

Postwar changes precipitated a period of decline for the local schoolhouse
fiddlers' conventions. The evolving role for music in Piedmont society brought about
the death of many indoor events. The 1960s saw the rise in outdoor summertime contests. Rather than the one-day events promoted in schoolhouses during the school
session, the outdoor conventions were multi-day affairs, more the type of festival that
Union Grove had became.

But many events soldiered on, giving countless musicians their first experience
on stage, or their initial opportunity to see a legendary musical instrument like a
Martin guitar or Gibson banjo. Charlie "The Devil Went Down to Georgia" Daniels
got his first exposure to the public at Piedmont conventions, as did many others.

Although fiddlers' conventions were still held in school buildings, the schools
themselves had stopped relying for these events for financial support. As PTA sponsorship fell away, local civic organizations such as the Civitans and Lions started new
contests. For a time, the pre-war string band music coexisted and competed alongside the newer bluegrass sounds. Eventually, bluegrass entirely replaced the fiddle and
banjo music of days gone by at the schoolhouses. By this time, however, the heyday
for winter conventions had passed, replaced by a few select large regional camping
events held during the summer months.

SEVEN

"Mountain Folk Music Is Being Recorded Here"

The large phonograph companies have come to the realization that what the people who own machines really want is not so much classical music by Madame XYZ, but real honest to goodness music furnished by real everyday people, who know how. Representatives of the various large companies are scouring the country trying to unearth new talent, or old talent that has been overlooked.

—*Twin City Sentinel*, April 28, 1924

Rural Southern music makers got the first inklings that their performances might bring them fame (if not always fortune) when the nascent record business issued the first commercial recordings of string band music. There are many apocryphal stories of instrumentalists and singers, upon hearing the attempts of their brethren, contacting companies such as Columbia, Victor, Edison, and Okeh because "they could do better" than what was being presented on those first country discs of the 1920s. Eventually, the recording concerns would bring their mountain to Mohammed, setting up field sessions within the very region that provided the best musicians for their string band series.

The Piedmont's first true country musician to make records, Ernest Thompson, was also a pioneer within the whole field of country recording. Signed by Columbia Records in reaction to the rival upstart Okeh's success with Southern fiddler and singer John Carson, Thompson's records never brought him the lasting fame Carson earned from his efforts. Instead, Ernest Thompson became a forgotten footnote, typical of the majority of the first generation of country music recording artists.

Ernest Thompson, the blind singer and multi instrumentalist, as he appeared around the time of his recording sessions for Columbia. Circa mid–1920s. Courtesy Roy Snider.

Ernest Thompson: Forgotten Pioneer

Ernest Errott Thompson was born February 20, 1892, in Clemmons, North Carolina. Winston-Salem (then two separate municipalities) was just to the north of the Moravian settlement. Ernest's rural upbringing was typical for the area and the time. Ernest's youngest sister, Agnes Ersley (born July 28, 1900), described their farmstead in marvelous detail:

My daddy had a green thumb. We had every fruit tree you can imagine. He planted cherries, black walnuts, and chinquapins. We dried fruits. We had a barn made out of logs, stables, a threshing floor, and it was filled with food for the cows, hogs, and chickens. The only things we bought were kerosene oil, and salt and sugar and pepper. And in the spring, father would buy one hundred pound of white sugar, and mother would do her canning and her preserving and things like that. We were poor, but we never were hungry or cold.

Although Agnes Thompson paints an idyllic picture of the family's lifestyle from the vantage point of eighty years later, several tragedies of Ernest's youth shaped his adult life. Agnes recounts a story from before she was born:

One time he got burned real bad when he was a little fella. He was just at the walking stage when we were hog-killing one day. He wore dresses like all children did then and caught afire. Mother was in the basement when she heard him scream. She ran upstairs and grabbed a bucket of water. She knocked Ernest down from throwing water on him, putting out the fire. He had scars on his face, and he breathed enough fumes and heat that it scorched his throat and voice box. The fire changed his voice to a certain extent.

A more severe event occurred when, at the age of fifteen, Ernest began losing his sight. Several different family stories explain the cause of his blindness. Thompson worked in a sawmill as a teenager, and one family story traces his loss of vision to splinters that flew into his eyes from the cutting operation; a variation on this tale has the heat from the mill affecting his vision. Other family members attribute his loss of sight to disease. His school records list scrofula, a form of tuberculosis, as the cause of his blindness. Regardless of its origin, the loss of vision occurred over about ten years. By 1920, Ernest's blindness was complete and his disease widespread enough to warrant the removal of his eyes. He was fitted with glass prostheses, which he is sometimes pictured wearing. Even with the loss of his eyes, Thompson remained fairly independent. "He never, never forgot a voice," claims his sister. "If you went to see him one time, he could tell who you were." Family members also comment on his sense of humor and his love of practical jokes.

With chances for a normal career diminished by his impairment, Ernest applied in December 1911 to the Governor Morehead School in Raleigh. Founded in 1845, the school catered to the special needs of its blind and deaf pupils. It had been created out of the fear that an indigent blind population would be dependent on government financial support, and these worries had increased by the first decade of the twentieth century. The result was the Compulsory Education Act for the Blind. As an outcome of the 1908 provision, the state actively recruited pupils, swelling student enrollment to what was then the highest level in the history of the school. This may be one reason for Thompson's attendance. Another must have been his and his family's desire for him to become more independent. Thompson attended the Morehead School for two years. Like some other blind musicians who later recorded, he was trained to make mattresses and brooms and to read and write Braille. He also learned piano tuning, and upon returning to Clemmons, he attempted to lead a normal life by utilizing those skills. But the attraction of music making had become too great.

The one bright spot in Ernest's teenage years had been his introduction to music, which probably occurred before he entered the school. Although neither of his parents was musically inclined, they owned an early Edison cylinder phonograph, and Ernest learned many songs from the Edison Company's records. In addition, his father acquainted him with the guitar. "Daddy brought home a guitar one time when we were just little folks," recalled Agnes Thompson. "He said, 'The one who learns to play it can have it.' So, Ernest said, 'Well, I'll learn to play it.' And he's the one that got it." Thompson's picking style, common for the period, used his thumb to hit the bass notes—photos often show him wearing a thumb pick—and his fingers to brush or up-pick for the strum. When Ernest acquired a better guitar, he passed his original one on to Agnes and gave her lessons in the rudiments of the instrument. Eventually, Burney Edgar (born November 12, 1895), the youngest boy, joined on the cello with Ernest and Agnes in their music making. The three of them, along with Russell Stylers on banjo and Agnes's good friend Mattie Boner on guitar, formed a loose confederation, the Dixie Band. Such amateur instrumental ensembles were common throughout rural America at the time. As Agnes recalls, "We'd sing and play on Saturday nights. We made our own entertainment. People would come out and sit on their porches while we played, and they'd serve refreshments for us."

During this period, Ernest started to expand his musical skills. He is pictured with a mandolin and was probably fiddling as well for local house dances in this stage of his development. Thompson also began his street performing at this time. Agnes describes these scenes vividly:

The Dixie Band assembles before the camera. Left to right, Mattie Boner (guitar), Russell Stylers (banjo), Agnes Thompson (guitar) and her brother Ernest (mandolin). Clemmons, Forsyth County, circa 1920. Courtesy Faye Fritts.

A lot of times when he'd be out there playing, people would gather around him. During the First World War, a lot of soldiers would come home on leave. Quite a few of them would sing with Ernest on the sidewalk. He'd sing "It's a Long Way to Tipperary" and all these songs, like "Smile Awhile." All those people who listened would pay him for singing. That's the way he made a living.

Street buskers were extremely common during this time period. With the exception of tuning pianos or making brooms, few options were available to a sightless person of Thompson's background. Whether it was Ed Haley in Kentucky, Gary Davis and Blind Boy Fuller in the Carolinas, or Willie McTell and Riley Puckett in the Atlanta area, blind virtuosos dominated street corners throughout Southern cities and towns. Moreover, many individual players traveled widely. David Evans reports on McTell: "In July and August he would usually follow the tobacco season in towns like Statesboro in the eastern part of [Georgia] and in the Carolinas, playing in the tobacco warehouses." For both Willie McTell and Ernest Thompson, the fall of the year, after farmers had sold their tobacco crop, was a lucrative time.

Street performing influenced Thompson's music in several ways. He developed the skill of singing and playing loud enough to be heard over traffic. This served him well later on, when recording acoustical discs for Columbia Records, and may have helped him secure his record contract in the first place. Ernest's tenor vocals on his recordings have a shouting quality that possibly came from projecting on the street. His guitar and banjo styles leant toward simplicity, which also may be a result of his busking. Street appearances also influenced his repertoire toward the popular tunes of the day.

In another move toward stability and independence, Ernest Thompson married during this period. His bride was the former Bettie Viola Houser (January 14, 1889–January 12, 1964), who was several years his senior. The couple set up housekeeping at 200 Gregory in Winston-Salem. Ernest continued to attempt a legitimate career tuning pianos; he may have also taught music.

Unfortunately, his marriage did not provide the support he sought. Bettie had problems that came to a head after only four years with Ernest. She suffered a breakdown, and on November 11, 1921, was admitted to Broughton Hospital in Morganton, where she was to spend the remainder of her days.

With Bettie and Ernest's mother, who had died in 1920, both gone, Thompson began a nomadic existence that continued until the last years of his life. He also continued to develop his skills on guitar, harmonica, banjo, fiddle, Hawaiian guitar, and piano. "He was a one-man band almost," said sister Agnes. "He sometimes even used his feet to beat a drum. Cymbals, too. He played them all at one time." Through his appearances, Ernest achieved local and regional fame. Performances on the streets around the tobacco warehouses of Winston-Salem sustained him when he stayed locally. Schoolhouse shows supported him as he traveled between the homes of various members of his family. Musician Roy Arnold, born in 1921, recalled:

> I can remember, I think it was before I ever started to school, that over here at Cedar Springs [School, in southeastern Davidson County], they was a blind man that would come about once a year and he played — oh, ever so many different string

One-man band Ernest Thompson poses with his musical arsenal. Thompson holds a guitar with a harmonica in a rack around his neck. A fiddle and banjo-ukulele (banjo body with a uke neck) rest in front of his bass drum, with a zither on top. Continuing to the right are a mandolin, cello, autoharp (front), tenor banjo (back), five string banjo and lute banjo. Forsyth County, circa 1930.

> instruments. And, people in the community would go in and listen to him play. I was too small to know whether you paid to go in or whether you just give him a donation or what, but I can remember him being over there at the schoolhouse and hearing that.... It was a treat to hear the string music that he could play, you know, and I don't even know what the man's name was or where he came from or anything, but he would come around about once a year and play music.... I can remember it for about a year or so and that was back when I was just real small. It would have been in the early twenties, along '23, '24, '25, along in there....

This is how Ernest Thompson must have spent the three years after his marriage ended, when a representative of the Columbia Record Company came calling.

The record company executives sitting in New York City did not have a clue as to what rural audiences would buy. They had to rely on the recommendations of those on the front lines: Southern storeowners and regional sales representatives like Polk Brockman and William Parks. Nothing beat standing across a sales counter from a farm or factory worker to learn about local musical tastes. Being Columbia's Atlanta representative, Bill Parks was commissioned to bring examples of Southern singers and instrumentalists to New York. In April, Parks brought Thompson, along with the duo of Eva Davis and Samantha Bumgarner, to Columbia's studios on the top floor of the Gotham National Bank Building. The *Twin City Sentinel* of Winston-Salem recounted the story of Ernest's discovery in an article obviously written upon Thompson's return from New York City:

> Last Tuesday Ernest Thompson was a farmer living on a small track of land near Tobaccoville. This morning [April 28, 1924] he is an employee of the Columbia Phonograph Company, having made 44 records [only twenty-one are listed in company logs], at the salary of $100 a week and expenses.
>
> It all happened this way.

William S. Parks, regional representative of the Columbia Phonograph Company ... came to Winston-Salem last Tuesday in his quest. He stopped by the Rominger Furniture Company [the local Columbia dealer] and Mr. Rominger told him of one Ernest E. Thompson, who was a born musician. Mr. Parks hopped into an automobile and drove out to Thompson's farm. There he discovered a blind man, sitting in the doorway of a humble home. The blind man was Thompson.

Sitting there in the warm April sunshine, Thompson played and sang a number of old southern melodies and folk songs. The more he played and more he sung, the more convinced was Mr. Parks that he had found the man he was looking for.

It did not take much argument to persuade Thompson that he ought to go to New York immediately. He played before the officers of the Columbia Company there and they pronounced him great....

The records made are from selections on the harmonica, the guitar, the banjo and vocal.... Thompson plays well on twenty-six different musical instruments, and on his next trip there will be records made from some of the others [this never occurred].

On his next trip to New York, which will be within the next few weeks, Thompson will play before the microphone of the Broadcasting station WEAF. The Columbia Phonograph Company uses the station every Tuesday and Thursday evening.

Thompson's recorded repertoire from those first sessions runs counter to the common image of the country rube performer. Rather than emphasizing old English ballads or Celtic fiddle pieces, Thompson, as did many of his contemporaries, favored Tin Pan Alley compositions of a recent vintage. With the sheet music of popular songs invading rural areas, his generation was the first to digest this particular batch of pop Americana. These compositions, altered by country performance standards, mixed with the earlier canon to form a new core repertoire for rural presentation. However, it is probable that these tunes did not come to Thompson via sheet music; anecdotal information, his performance style, and his blindness point toward cylinder recordings as Ernest's source for popular tunes. Early popular recording stars Cal Stewart, Collins & Harlan, and Harry C. Browne may have had more to do with Thompson's style and repertoire than any published notation.

The majority of the 21 tunes Ernest Thompson waxed in April had popular origins. Nine were copyrighted during his lifetime; one, "Don't Put a Tax on the Beautiful Girls," was only five years old. Several others had recorded antecedents. "The Wreck of the Southern Old 97," on which Thompson accompanied himself with twelve-string guitar, had been a Henry Whitter release on Okeh earlier that year. Harry C. Browne had recorded "Climbing up the Golden Stairs" for Columbia in 1917. And both Riley Puckett and Henry Whitter had beaten Thompson to the punch by recording "Chicken Roost Behind the Moon." On the other hand, Ernest's "Red Wing" and "Snow Deer" were the first recorded country versions of both of those pieces and may have helped to establish them as standards.

Thompson's interpretations of Tin Pan Alley songs differed from those of popular singers. His vocals were a cross between the trained light-parlor style popular on early recordings and the natural "head voice" of an "unschooled" country musician. He sang in the direct, unadorned manner common to other rural performers of the period. If anything, Ernest under interpreted songs, with a lack of vocal ornamentations and embellishments. His guitar accompaniments were also simple, using a bass-strum pattern. Both vocal and instrumental styling lent a naiveté to Thompson's performances. Although the record companies eventually steered away from previously copyrighted pieces to favor those newly composed or in the public domain that they themselves could claim and profit from, it is conceivable that Columbia's employees directed Thompson toward songs with obvious written origins. Columbia may have feared music that was unknown, and the Tin Pan Alley compositions were a known quantity. But it's just as possible that, for Thompson, the choice was instinctual.

In the publicity blitz that followed Ernest's first recording sessions, Columbia ran his photograph in the June issue of the *Talking Machine World*. After announcing his signing, they continued with the following claims: "Mr. Thompson has entered forty-three … contests and had to be satisfied with forty-two first prizes and one second prize. In the latter contest the first prize went to a lady (a relative of one of the judges)…. Mr. Thompson has played for ex–Presidents Roosevelt, Taft, Wilson and a list of other national celebrities that sounds like reading a copy of Who's Who."

By the end of the month, Ernest's first release, "The Wreck of the Southern Old 97" with "Are You from Dixie" on the flip side, was available for sale in Winston-Salem. Rominger's Furniture ran a large advertisement in the Twin City Sentinel to announce the recording.

Thompson's records must have sold well enough to warrant more sessions. He returned to New York City and to the Columbia studios in the fall of 1924. This time, he was accompanied by his niece Connie Faw Sides (October 14, 1906–April 21, 1987), the daughter of Ernest's sister Rosa Lee (born January 3, 1886). It seems probable that her proposed role in her uncle's second recording trip was as his guide. However, once in the studio, the decision was made for her vocals to grace two records. It was her only attempt at making music professionally.

The team of Riley Puckett and Gid Tanner, Columbia's first country recording artists, was also present at that session, and they alternated matrix numbers with Thompson and Sides. Ernest recorded six pieces on September 9, eight with Connie on September 10 and 11, five solo sides on September 11, and one final cut on September 12. Thompson and the Puckett-Tanner duo each waxed "Whistling Rufus"; in fact, three log numbers only separated the two recordings. Of the 20 cuts, Thompson again favored songs of recent origin. Seven were written after the turn of the century. Several of the pieces he featured later became popular in country music. "Silly Bill," published around the time of the Civil War as "Common Bill (I Hardly Think I Will)," was later recorded by the Hillbillies. Uncle Dave Macon made a version of "When You're All In, Down, Out" for Bluebird in 1937. And Connie Sides' version of "In the Shadow of the Pine" was the first recording of what was to become a standard.

It is possible that a friendship between Riley Puckett and Ernest Thompson developed at the sessions. Thompson's niece, Mary Thompson Snider, recalled that the Skillet Lickers, the band including both Puckett and Tanner, accompanied her uncle to the family's Lee County home. They were so mean, she contended, that her father, Ernest's brother Rufus, made them sleep out in the barn. Puckett and Thompson came from similar backgrounds. From the small Southern town of Alpharetta, Riley Puckett grew up outside of a metropolitan center (Atlanta). He was born sighted but was blinded by misapplied medication as a baby, and attended blind school (Georgia Academy in Macon), where he studied piano. However, through his appearances on Atlanta radio station WSB, Puckett had a better regional reputation than Ernest when he stepped up to Columbia's microphones, and Puckett's records made him a bigger star.

The period following his recording dates constituted Thompson's most successful years as a musician. During the mid to late 1920s, he was able to replace the low-quality guitars he had been playing with a model L-4, just one step down from the top of the Gibson Company's guitar line. He also commissioned the only two studio portraits of him that survive. The Columbia publicity department frequently reproduced one; the other was possibly made for but never used by Columbia. Ernest usually owned an automobile and would get his friends to drive him to engagements.

Thompson's releases continued through 1924 and into the first half of 1925. In the fall of 1924, Columbia Records featured him in a booklet called *Familiar Tunes on Fiddle, Guitar, Banjo, Harmonica and Accordion*. Columbia catalogues prominently displayed Thompson's records, with 15 releases highlighted in the *Old Familiar Melodies* booklet from September 1925, and seven of his newest records from the 1924 catalogue below his photograph in a June 1926 publication. His version of "Alexander's Ragtime Band" backed with "The Mississippi Dippy Dip" was the inaugural release of Columbia's famous 15,000 "Hillbilly" series, one of the first and most famous devoted exclusively to rural Southern music.

In the fall of 1925, Ernest traveled to Virginia for a four-day booking at the Danville Fair. The *Danville News* advertised his in-store appearances at Benefield, Motley and Company: "For this week we will have with our music department Ernest Thompson, who will sing for you all the old favorites, which we have on the Columbia Record. You can also hear him at the fair ground in his show 'Floyd Collins in the Sand Cave.'"

L. B. Clarke, who a year later made records for Columbia, managed Benefield's music department. Although Clarke was a country music devotee and predisposed toward having Thompson perform, in-store demonstrations to promote his Columbia recordings were probably a common occurrence for Thompson.

Ultimately, despite all the publicity common to other rural singers, Ernest's later records did not sell well. Whereas accountings are not available for his early releases or for budget label equivalents of the same titles, sales figures for Columbia's 15,000 series of "Old Familiar Tunes" show Thompson's records sold one-quarter to two-thirds the number for the average selling disc. Four of his releases sold fewer than 4,000 copies, the worst sellers being the two discs featuring vocals by Connie Sides. According to Dave Freeman of Rebel Records, from his research at Columbia, Thompson's biggest "hits" were "Whistling Rufus" b/w "When You're All In Down and Out" (7,101 copies), "Weeping Willow Tree" b/w "Sylvester Johnson Lee" (8,967 copies), and "The Old Time Religion" b/w "I'm Going Down to Jordan" (9,567 copies). Of course, these recordings came out before phonographs became widespread in rural areas. Nevertheless, even taking other factors into account, Ernest's sales still pale when compared to Gid Tanner and Riley Puckett's "Be Kind to a Man When He's Down" b/w "Don't Grieve Your Mother" (10,925), "The Arkansas Traveler" b/w "Fox Chase" (22,000), or "John Henry" b/w "Georgia Railroad" (45,000). Eventually, Columbia's country releases averaged sales of 20,000–30,000 copies, with their biggest sellers moving upwards of 300,000 pieces.

Needless to say, when Tanner and Puckett, with their newly formed Skillet Lickers, recorded again in 1926, Columbia did not include Thompson in the session. Electrical recording had made the loud voice of a street singer unnecessary, and string bands, like the Skillet Lickers, replaced solo singers as the vogue. Additionally, as Ed Kahn comments

> From the outset, the record companies were looking for new sounds, [and] new songs.... They knew that the supply of traditional material was not inexhaustible, so when the supply ran out, they sought artists who could provide new and fresh material that would appeal to the same audience that had been buying rural recordings up to that time. It was more common for artists to make a few recordings and fade back into their former obscurity.

By 1930, Ernest Thompson had returned to obscurity. Musical tastes began to become more sophisticated. Rather than being "Forsyth County's favorite musician," Ernest became a well-known local personality appearing on Winston-Salem city streets. That winter, he set out to visit Burney's family, who lived briefly in Indiana. While there, he made one further stab at a recording career, on Gennett, and the fame he hoped it would bring him.

For his trip, Ernest took along a companion, fellow musician Boyden Carpenter (February 26, 1909–1995). Born in Sparta and raised around Cherry Lane, North Carolina, Carpenter had his greatest musical success in the mid–1930s, when he spent two years working on WPTF-Raleigh for Crazy Water Crystals. Known as the "Hillbilly Kid," Boyden toured with Mainer's Mountaineers and the Monroe Brothers. He was best known for the song "Saving Up Coupons" (see Chapter Nine). Although Carpenter had only played with Thompson a few times, Ernest chose Boyden to accompany him on the trip. When Charles Wolfe interviewed Boyden Carpenter at his Winston-Salem home, he recalled the details of their journey:

> Thompson ... used to play [in Winston-Salem] on the street at Brown's Warehouse, and around down there. I learned the idea of putting my harmonica in a rack when I'd seen him do it.... He wanted me to go with him, he had some people that lived out there in Fort Wayne. And we just played along, we stopped in towns along and played and we'd take up a collection. We stopped at a hotel in Bluefield, West Virginia, and we hitched on out and went into Huntington, Charleston and [from] Charleston up that road there to Fort Wayne. And [then me] and him hitchhiked then and we come back to Richmond and went over there to the [Gennett place].

The pair spent two days in Richmond, in January, for their first Gennett session. Thompson mostly recreated pieces originally waxed for Columbia in 1924. Boyden spelled Ernest and recorded two sides, "Bring Back My Blue Eyed Boy" and "Billy Boy"; both were rejected. After the session, Boyden continued on to Chicago, and

Ernest wintered in Fort Wayne. Thompson was to return one other time to the Gennett studios, in March of that year. Unfortunately, possibly due to the technical problems that were all too common at Gennett, the pieces cut that time were all discarded.

Thompson's timing could not have been worse. In 1930, the record industry was in abysmal shape. Sales dropped from 104 million records in 1927 to just 6 million for the year 1932. The Starr Piano Company discontinued their Gennett imprint at the end of the year Thompson recorded. His one supposed release for the company, instrumental versions of "Sparrow Bird Waltz/Good Old Summer Time" b/w "Are You From Dixie/Swanee River," must have sold poorly, if it was released at all. A copy of the 78rpm record has never, so far as is known, turned up.

Sometime after his visit to Indiana, Ernest met the woman with whom he would spend the remainder of his life. Cora, possibly middle name Lee and last name Pistollious, like Ernest, was an itinerant street performer, although, unlike Ernest, Cora was partially sighted. The pair arrived in Baltimore, Maryland (possibly Cora's hometown), in April of 1931. The following letter, written on November 13, 1931, from the Family Welfare Association to the Governor Morehead School, reveals some of the difficulties that had begun to plague the blind street musician:

> We have recently become interested in Ernest Thompson who has been playing musical instruments on the streets of Baltimore. Mr. Thompson ... married a blind woman two years ago and together they have traveled from town to town begging. They have been in Baltimore since April and we have not been able to establish their residence in any state. Since we can not [sic] give them a license to beg here, some plan will have to be made for their care. Mr. Thompson tells us that he is a native of North Carolina, but is rather vague as to the towns in which he lived.

Ernest spent much of the 1930s traveling in a similar manner. Banjoist Glenn Davis reported playing with Ernest in Asheboro, on a street near the depot. He also journeyed to Asheville, North Carolina. In 1937, Ben Shahn visited the Asheville Mountain Dance and Folk Festival as a representative of the Farm Security Administration. There, he photographed some of the performers, including fiddler Bill Hensley with Ernest on guitar and harmonica. Unfortunately, none of the local newspaper coverage mentions Thompson by name, or what his role was in that year's event.

Thompson's niece Faye Thompson, Rufus's daughter, remembers fondly his visits during the period:

> Some of his friends from Winston would bring him down here. He used to come and stay with us for weeks or months at a time when we lived down in Lee County. And he played music for all of us around there and about all of my brothers played some type of music and they would play with him sometimes.... But we would have dances. What we call the living room now was the front room then, and we'd move everything out and set chairs all around in there and invite all the neighbors and all of 'em around that could play fiddles and stuff like that over and have square dances in our front room. And he was always the center of it. He played at schools down there and warehouses around Carthage, and Sanford and up here in Winston, especially when tobacco-selling time come in, he was always at Winston warehouses....

Thompson may also have sung on local radio during this time.

By the late 1930s, Ernest had begun to curtail some of his wanderings. His name appeared in the Winston-Salem city directories, and he and Cora were well enough off to have a telephone. Thompson must have been a familiar sight on Winston-Salem streets during the war years. Several musicians remember hearing Ernest in the 1930s and 1940s. Although the times had changed, Ernest Thompson's repertoire and performance style evidently had not. An article in the *Twin City Sentinel*, "Soldiers Help Blind Man Sing to Street Crowds," describes Thompson's performances on Trade Street much in the way that his sister Agnes discussed his World War I busking. The *Sentinel* even mentions some of the same pieces, "Life's Railway to Heaven," "Mexicali Rose," "You Are My Sunshine," and "Old-Time Religion," that he had recorded for Columbia almost twenty years earlier as part of his contemporary repertoire (May 7, 1943).

In 1949, Ernest and Cora moved to High Point, where he was to spend the remainder of his life. They took up residence at 1209 Dorris Street. The couple may have bought the house at that time; they are definitely listed as owning the property in 1954. Thompson began feeling the effects of his age, and his health deteriorated. These factors, along with new, tougher local ordinances governing street performers, led to a decrease in his performing. During the 1950s, Cora was often gone, leaving Ernest on his own. He alternated his solitary home life with visits to his remaining siblings and their families. Once a year, he would stay in Yadkin College, Davidson County, with his niece Mary Elizabeth Thompson Snider for a week or two. Mary's son Roy remembers that Ernest always wore a white shirt, bow tie, and suit coat: "It wouldn't be Sunday, but he always looked like a preacher."

In the late 1950s, fiddler Nolan Johnson recalls hearing Thompson, performing with banjoist John Meredith, on a High Point, North Carolina, street. By this time, Ernest was in poor physical shape. Suffering from hypertensive arteriosclerosis cardiovascular disease since his move to High Point, his health declined more precipitously in 1958. After a three-week illness, Ernest Thompson died of chronic congestive heart failure on December 7, 1961, at the Guilford County Home in Greensboro and was buried at the Fraternity Church of the Brethren on Fraternity Church Road outside of Clemmons. His tombstone quotes the song "Amazing Grace": "I once was blind, but now I see."

At the height of Thompson's recording career, the only performers who attempted to earn a living from their music were those with limited occupational choices. Primarily, these were blind street musicians who relied on the generosity of others to eke out an existence. By the time country music began to develop into a profession, Ernest Thompson was past his prime. An artist in his fifties rendering songs in a style from thirty years prior would not, and did not, fare well in the 1940s and 1950s. His Columbia recordings were a fluke, a brief moment of fame in the life of a performer who, if not for them, would have remained a local phenomenon.

Other Piedmont musicians followed Ernest Thompson's lead in recording for various labels. Sidney James Allgood Sr. (January 4, 1892–October 20, 1953) traveled to Asheville with fellow banjoist R.B. Smith to try out for Okeh's portable recording crew. Although his parents were from Yadkin County (where the family lived between

Ernest Thompson busks on Trade Street in downtown Winston-Salem during World War II. Joining him are (left to right) Miss Patsy Williams, PFC. Henry R. Troutt, Paul Troutt, and PFC. Asa W. Griffin. Forsyth County, May 1943.

1899 and 1908), Sid was born in Texas, where his father's work had taken the household. By 1893, the Allgood family was back farming in Yadkin County. Sidney spent the majority of his life around Winston-Salem, where the rest of his family eventually settled. S.J. worked for most of his professional life at the R. J. Reynolds Tobacco Company. Sid began at Reynolds in 1910 as a box maker, later holding positions as a machine operator, construction worker, and mechanic. Since the Tobacco Company employed Allgood at the time of his Okeh recording, it is possible that the firm also engaged his musical partner R. B. Smith.

Both Smith and Allgood were active in local fiddlers' conventions. Piedmont newspapers reported that Sid won the banjo prize at Skyland School Fiddlers' Convention April 17, 1924 (*Western Sentinel*, April 22, 1924: 3), and that R.B. Smith came in second at the Flat Rock Convention on May 15 of the same year (*Twin City Sentinel*, May 21, 1924: 14).

Sid Allgood's brother remembers that someone from Okeh approached the duo and asked to record their three-finger banjo playing. Fisher Hendley (see Chapter Nine) also appeared at the sessions, which were run by one of the pioneering Artist and Repertoire (A&R) men, Ralph Peer. Smith and Allgood took the train to Asheville and were paid for their trouble. Meant as an audition recording, "American and Spanish Fandango" was waxed on August 25, 1925. It showcased the duo's rippling banjo style on an instrumental standard from the previous century (Wolfe and Russell, "The Asheville Session"; Census; S.J. Allgood, Sr., obituary; Wishon; Winston-Salem City Directories).

"Got the Cotton Mill Blues": Musicians in the Mills

A large number of string musicians ended up in the Charlotte area, working for the various textile mills that surrounded the city. Many tried their hand at broadcasting, auditioning for spots at local stations and over the national powerhouse WBT. Victor Records brought portable recording equipment to the city throughout the 1920s and 1930s on the strength of the WBT roster. Harmonica virtuoso Gwen Foster of the well-known string band the Carolina Tarheels worked the mills in Gastonia and Belmont. Foster recorded in the late 1920s for Victor in Atlanta in 1927, six months later in Charlotte, and a year after that, again in Atlanta, with his friend Dave Fletcher as the Carolina Twins. Several other "lint heads" (as the mill workers were known) found their way onto records before Charlotte became a recording center.

Dave McCarn (March 23, 1905–November 7, 1964) wrote and recorded songs about working in the Belmont mills. The son of a Gaston County textile worker, David began his working life around 1917, at the same mill where his father was employed (Chronicle Mills in Belmont). David Cozzen, the grandfather for whom McCarn was named, was a fiddler who frequently took first place at the fiddlers' contests of his day.

In his early 20s, McCarn picked up the guitar (McCarn and Green and Kahn interview, 1–4, 6). Eventually, Dave McCarn joined with some friends in a local association called the "Yeller Jacket Band." The boys played a lot of dances and broadcast over the low-power Gastonia radio station, WRBU. (Homer Sherrill, later on WBT, also began his radio career at this smaller station; see Chapter Nine.) Additionally, McCarn had begun to make up songs of his own. Using traditional pieces as their basis, Dave McCarn told the plight of the mill worker from their own point of view. Dave didn't think much of these compositions, playing them locally as much for his own enjoyment as anything else (McCarn, 5, 7–9).

The great depression hit the cotton mills hard, and McCarn found himself out of work. As many did in his predicament, Dave McCarn took to the road in search of employment. While out traveling, Dave encountered one of Victor Records' portable studios. Dave McCarn told Archie Green and Norm Cohen how he came to record for Ralph Peer, then with Victor:

> I had a kid brother ... and I was carrying him around with me, and we happened to wind up in Memphis, Tennessee and we got down a little bit, you might say broke. And I had a little old guitar ... we was making the hock shops, try to hock it you know for a few bucks, but three bucks was the only thing we got offered and

I wouldn't take that so the last hock shop we stopped in, there were a couple of boys in wanting to get strings for the instruments there…. The manager asked the boys if they was going to make a record. Yes, if they could get some strings to stay on these instruments…. Well I perked up…. Went up to the auditorium and the room was full of people, Arkansas, Mississippian, Virginier and all of them there all around. And Mr. Ralph Peer was talking to Jimmie Davis…. And when they got through Mr. Peer, he said all you boys have to go home, we won't record anymore today. You can come back Monday. Everybody left. Me and my brother sat around awhile…. Well I told [Mr. Peer], "We can't be here Monday. We are just passing through." And he said "Well come on in here in this room…." So I played the two tunes and he said "we will give twenty-five dollars a piece for these." "You mean you gonna buy 'em?" "Yeah, well, how much money do you need to be here Monday?" "Advance me ten bucks."

So we stayed til Monday and the machine was broke down so we stayed over till Tuesday…. [On May 19, 1930, notes Archie Green, Dave recorded "Cotton Mill Colic" and "Everyday Dirt"] I forgot all about the record, didn't think no more about it. So finally I heard from him in six or eight months, or maybe even longer than that. One Sunday morning the telegraph boy knocked at the door and had a telegram for me. Mr. Peer sent me a letter and of course he knew that I would be broke, said how much money do you need to be in Memphis as long as he wanted [the session was November 19, 1930; Green, 2]…. So we went back the second time…. That time he told me, you can make as many [songs] as [you] want. But I didn't even have anything to put on…. But over night, I had two or three songs. Recorded them and I told him I would have some more the next day. Well I went back and that night, I knew I kept the roomers up all night. Well I had … three or four more by the next morning…. And that's all til the last time I recorded in Charlotte [in 1931]…. I don't think they called me anymore because the records I made didn't go like the first ones…. If I had one to go like the first one it would have been alright [McCarn, 9–12].

Another Gaston County resident, Wilmer Wesley Watts (ca. 1897–August 21, 1943), sang about millwork for the Paramount Company. Watts was born at Mount Tabor (now Tabor City) in southeastern Columbus County, where he began playing the banjo "by ear" as a small boy. Later, he added fiddle and guitar to his repertoire. Around 1918, Watts moved to Belmont outside of Charlotte to work in a textile mill. He was much in demand in the area as a dance fiddler. At the mill, he met guitarist Frank Wilson.

In January and April of 1927, the duo journeyed to Chicago to record for Paramount Records. Six sides were issued from these sessions, with Watts playing and singing to the Hawaiian guitar of Wilson. Test records also exist of an unissued song, along with an alternate of one issued piece, "The Sporting Cowboy." Frank was somewhat nomadic, and after he left the area, Wilmer teamed up with guitarists Palmer Rhyne and Charles Sweeten (nee: Freshour, August 29, 1900–May 1959), a Tennessean working at the Climax Mill. This group, first calling themselves the Gastonia Serenaders, became the Lonely Eagles when they traveled to New York City for a recording session in October of 1929. Again, the company was Paramount, and ten sides resulted for release.

In later years, Wilmer Watts turned to gospel music, performing with his children

Frank Wilson plays his Hawaiian guitar at an unknown location in the 1920s. Courtesy Mrs. Kathryn Sutton.

as the Watts Singers. Watts worked in the late 1930s at the Bessemer Cotton Mill in Bessemer City, and appeared on the radio with the group in Spartanburg, South Carolina, and over WBT-Charlotte. Their broadcasts were Monday thru Friday, in South Carolina in the mornings and in Charlotte at 5 P.M. (Nelson, 91–96).

Watts' first recording partner, Percy Alphonso "Frank" (or "Fonzy") Wilson, was born in the Rockingham County community of Chinquapin in 1900. Frank Wilson learned to play music as a boy, in the words of his daughter Kathryn, and surpassed his teachers at an early age. By 1920, Wilson was boarding in Alamance County and working in a cotton mill. That year, Frank met his future wife, Edna Josephine Totten (January 8, 1904–1989), at a dance. The couple married in August, and eventually had three children. At that time, Frank pursued music as a sideline, teaching piano, violin and guitar out of his home (a daughter was named for one of Wilson's students). He also held dances in his residence.

Although he had training as a barber, Frank Wilson mostly worked in one of the many textile mills dotting the Piedmont. In 1923, the Wilsons were renting in High Point. By 1924, Frank and Edna Wilson were living on McKinney Street, between Burlington and Graham, in the Midway school district, and running a dry cleaners ("pressing club") on Front Street near Worth in Burlington. In 1926, Frank and Edna lived in Thomasville. During 1927, as mentioned above, Frank Wilson was working in a Charlotte textile mill, when he met Wilmer Watts. Frank must have had it in his mind to spend more time making music, and these recordings helped him to make the move away from the mills. Unfortunately, the life of a professional musician also meant long absences from his family.

Because of the national craze for Hawaiian music, Wilson's Hawaiian guitar playing made him popular on the vaudeville programs of that time. Two groups which welcomed Frank Wilson as a member mixed traditional southern fiddle tunes with the popular songs of the period. The Blue Ridge Ramblers and the Hillbillies were ensembles that used southern musicians for theatrical programs, and Wilson played with both bands.

The Hillbillies were based around Al Hopkins (piano) and his brothers Elmer, John (banjo, harmonica and ukulele), and Joe (guitar). Originally from Ashe County in North Carolina, the Hopkinses grew up in Washington, D.C. The brothers mixed close barbershop harmony singing with rollicking fiddle tunes led by East Tennessean Charlie Bowman. While Frank Wilson was entering a recording studio for the first time, the Hopkins brothers were forming the first version of the band that helped give hillbilly music its name. Besides touring vaudeville, the group hosted a highly successful radio program for WMAL in Washington, D.C. It was there in 1928 that Frank joined the band, which at that time included Al and John Hopkins, Alonzo Elvis "Tony" Alderman (a fiddler originally from Galax, Virginia), and trick fiddler Frank Williams.

In December of 1928, Frank Wilson traveled with the Hillbillies to New York City, where they cut ten sides for Brunswick Records. Wilson's slide guitar can be heard on half of these selections. Frank also plays on two sides issued by Brunswick under the name Jack Reedy and His Walker Mountain String Band: "Chinese Breakdown" and "Groundhog." Wilson's voice can even be heard at the start of the former piece. Sometime in 1928, Frank and the Hillbillies also appeared in a short talking picture for Warner Brothers.

Wilson was back in Brunswick's New York studio at the beginning of 1929. As a member of H. M. Barnes Blue Ridge Ramblers, Frank Wilson can clearly be heard on eight sides recorded on January 28 and 29. However, Wilson still had an allegiance to the Hillbillies, for he jumped over to Columbia Records for their session during the next month. Under the name of Charlie Bowman and His Brothers, the group recorded four tunes for Columbia's country music series. Frank is reported to be on these sides, although he must be playing regular guitar, as his normal Hawaiian playing is not audible. Wilson also led the group on steel guitar for two additional pieces, "Katy-Did Waltz" and "Polly Ann." These were issued as by Frank Wilson and His Blue Ridge Mountain Trio.

Throughout this period, Wilson wrestled with life away from his family's home, which was back in Burlington by 1929. There are undated letters from Frank to his wife from the Metropolitan Hotel in Washington, D.C., where he expresses his homesickness and how much he misses his family. Unfortunately, Edna couldn't abide with Frank's long absences. In 1930, she sued for divorce on ground of abandonment, which was granted in February 1931. After that, his family lost touch with him and Wilson just disappeared. Frank Wilson was rumored to have been on the Grand Ole Opry in the 1930s, but there is no evidence to substantiate that claim. Nothing further is known about the musician who helped bring the Hawaiian guitar into country music (Birth certificate, Kathryn Wilson; Burlington City Directories; birth certificate, Odessa Mae Wilson; marriage certificate, Wilson and Totten; High Point City Directories; letters, Frank Wilson to Edna Wilson and Charles Wolfe to Carlin; Brunswick Recording Logs; Russell, *Old Time Music*, 11, 14; White House Correspondents' Association to Hopkins; "Hill Billies On Air Tonight"; "Hill-Billies Well Received"; "The Hillbillies"; Green, *Journal of American Folklore*, 212–214; Mare and Carlin interview; Bumgarner and Carlin interview; Census; divorce decree, Wilson vs. Wilson).

"Didn't He Ramble": Charlie Poole and the North Carolina Ramblers

A fiddle, a banjo, and a guitar are the archetypal Piedmont combination as personified by the North Carolina Ramblers string band. Led by banjoist Charlie Poole, the North Carolina Ramblers' classic recordings made between 1925 and 1930 for Columbia Records set the standard for many North Carolina musicians. Poole's records sold almost a quarter of a million copies before either Jimmie Rodgers or the Carter Family had entered a recording studio. Poole's influence on Carolina banjoists, and the North Carolina Ramblers' effect on string music, cannot be underestimated.

Fortunately, Charlie Poole's life and music have been well documented elsewhere. The majority of his classic recordings made primarily for Columbia Records have been reissued by County Records with annotations by historian Kinney Rorrer. In addition, Rorrer's groundbreaking biography of Poole was the first to depict the lives and times of many Piedmont musicians during the first part of the twentieth century.

Charles Cleveland Poole (March 22, 1892–1931) was born in Randolph County, the son of a mill worker. His parents, John Philip Poole and Bettie Ellen Johnson Poole, had lived in Iredell County before coming to Charlie's birthplace. After his birth, the family followed millwork to Haw River in Alamance County, residing there from 1900 to 1913. As Kinney Rorrer writes: "He took up the banjo as a child of about nine years old and displayed a gift for picking in a three-finger roll that bore a kinship to the classical banjo styles of the day. His first instrument was homemade from a gourd, with his first "real" banjo purchased for $1.50 with money earned at the mill" (Rorrer, *Rambling Blues*, 13, 18).

As an adult, Poole worked at Haw River's textile mills. During this period, Poole came under the musical influence of Daner Johnson. At the turn of the century, Daner was the preeminent Piedmont banjoist using the new three-finger picking technique. Local musicians held him in the highest regard and often chose not to compete rather than to face him in local banjo contests. However, since Daner never recorded, his fame stayed within the Piedmont and one can only imagine how he sounded. Daner Johnson and Poole were related through Daner's grandfather, Acquilla Johnson, who was a brother to Charlie's great-grandfather, Hiram Johnson (McAndrew to Carlin).

A young Daner Johnson sits for a studio photographer sometime around his twenty-first birthday. Unknown location, circa 1900. Courtesy Peggy McAndrew and Doris Thompson Stafford.

Daner Johnson

There are many legends about Johnson, among them that he won a banjo contest at the St. Louis Exposition of 1904, beating recording star Fred Van Eps, and played at the 1923 wedding of Gloria Vanderbuilt in New York City (McAndrew to Carlin). A great story told by banjoist Marcus Johnson (no relation) describes a Greensboro fiddlers' convention. Daner competed last "with his rusty banjo," and beat a man playing a brand new Gibson. The other contestant became so angry that "he busted the banjo over a chair and walked out." On another occasion, relates Sam Jr. Lowe, "up there in one of the big hotels in Greensboro, I believe it was the King Cotton Hotel or the O. Henry one, he played that 'Dixie' and said there's a bunch of Yankee tourists in there, and said they just threw bills on the stage." Many Randolph County musicians cite his influence, including Glenn Davis from Coleridge and Kelly Sears of Siler City. It is hard to prove or deny much about Daner's early life because of the lack of hard evidence from that period.

Daner Gordon Johnson was born in Randolph County, September 4, 1879, the son of Nancy Lou Johnson (November 25, 1838–January 1, 1903) and Thomas Ellis Troy (born September 11, 1859). His parents were never married and, when Daner was six years old, his father moved west.

Daner Johnson first married on May 31, 1909, tying the knot with Lillian Mae Foster (May 5, 1893–October 16, 1973). Daner was living at that time in "Fayetville" [sic]. After the wedding, the couple moved to Liberty, the residence of Lilly's parents. Johnson was working as a mechanic at the time of the birth of the couple's only child in 1914. Daner and Lillian separated sometime after 1919, and Daner remarried, this time to Pearl Richardson. The Johnsons were living on Mebane Street in Greensboro by 1923 and, until Pearl's death at the end of 1928, resided in the city, with Daner listed in the city directories as a "salesman" or "auto mechanic" (Greensboro City directories).

It was after the end of his first marriage that Daner taught Kelly Sears to play the banjo. Kelly Clay Sears (1907–1984) came from a musical Chatham County family. His mother, Mossie Fox, sang and played piano and a bit of banjo. William Moore Fox (August 27, 1886–1957), Mossie's brother, picked the banjo in a two finger style, as did his sons Joseph Eugene "Joe" (born June 11, 1922) and Hubert (circa 1915–December 1969). Mossie's sister Olivia played Autoharp, and an additional brother, June, was a fiddler. Kelly's brother Howard James (March 2, 1909–August 16, 1990) became a guitarist, and another sibling, Kenneth Benson (October 1, 1915–July 18, 1993) a dancer. When Kelly was nine, his father bought him his first banjo for $6. "My mother taught me to play 'Catfish,'" recalled Kelly (Kenion, "He Wants to Sell Talent," *Greensboro Daily News*, February 1, 1976 B9 via Joe Fox).

Kelly Sears took banjo lessons from Daner Johnson between 1919 and 1922. As Sears told Robert Winans:

> Dana [Kelly's pronunciation] and my father were friends; they used to do a minstrel show or two together. And he wouldn't show anybody his technique on a banjo, but my dad got after him and he finally decided that he would show me a few licks on it. He was the best I've ever heard. He'd play them old overtures.... And so I learned what I know by him.

The death of his second wife hit Daner hard and seems to have precipitated his downhill slide. Johnson took up a hobo-like existence, traveling from home to home in the company of his dog. He would appear at the backdoor of a residence, his banjo in a sack, take a meal with the household, and often play music into the evening with the head of the house. Daner would not sleep indoors, electing to stay in the barn. In the morning, Johnson would be gone, traveling on to his next destination. Daner Johnson died on April 17, 1955.

She's Only a Rose with a Broken Stem: Clay Everhart and the North Carolina Cooper Boys

Lexington's Clay Everhart and Poole's fellow Randolph County natives, cousins Tom and Dewey Cooper, had been playing together long before Charlie entered a recording studio. They paralleled his example by integrating turn-of-the-century popular music into the string band trio format. Up until this time, knowledge of Clay Everhart and the North Carolina Cooper Boys has been confined to a small cadre of collectors and scholars. That group's experience has been limited to the Cooper Boy's meager commercially recorded output and to fleeting references by elderly musicians. When I first encountered the band's name on a 78-rpm record label, I wondered if it was an obscure allusion to the barrel making profession. This is an attempt to clear up some of the misconceptions about Clay Everhart and the Coopers, and, to tell their story, of how they learned music and attempted a career as recording artists.

The North Carolina Cooper Boys consisted of two cousins: Tom Cooper, the guitarist and tenor singer, and Dewey Cooper, the fiddler and lead singer. Actually, calling one tenor and the other lead is somewhat misleading. Anyone familiar with their commercial recordings or that smaller number of people who have heard their numerous home recordings made in the early 1940s know that Tom and Dewey sang in unison as often as they sang in harmony. Be that as it may, Tom usually sang the high part and Dewey the low when they did diverge from the melody.

According to their cousin, Matthew Patrick Cooper (May 2, 1910–January 3, 2002), the patriarch of the Cooper clan, Robert Cooper (July 22, 1842–May 17, 1926), was a fiddler, confederate soldier, gold miner, trapper, and cobbler turned textile worker. The son of Riley "Wash" Cooper of Randolph County, Robert fathered four musicians: W. Cicero (April 14, 1868–January 30, 1952), James A. (September 29, 1869–March 31, 1936), Walter McCoy "Mack" (April 1, 1875–June 8, 1961) and Joseph Riley (September 11, 1882–December 6, 1942). Due to the abundance of musical talent and to the closeness of their family, the brothers naturally formed a band. That was later expanded to include those of their children who were musically inclined. Eventually, this embraced Cicero's son Robert Dewey (June 2, 1899–November 23, 1951) on fiddle, James' sons Thomas Franklin (July 15, 1894–June 20, 1983) and Clarence Theo on guitar, and Mack's son James Irving (April 2, 1911–July 10, 1967) on guitar. Anytime the family got together, they would sing and play. The family band also competed at area fiddlers' conventions.

Like many farm families at the turn of the twentieth century, the Coopers succumbed to the lure of millwork with its seemingly steady paycheck. And like many mill families in the Carolinas, when their employment proved tenuous, the Coopers moved to another town and another mill, searching for a permanent working situation. Tom Cooper was born in Randolph County, when the family lived between High Point and Randleman. The farming of Tom's youth quickly gave way to textile mill employment when Tom and his father moved to Greensboro to work as weavers at the White Oak Cotton Mills (Greensboro City Directories). Soon after that, their branch of the Cooper family moved to Lexington to work at the Winona Cotton Mill. Eventually, all the Cooper siblings and their families relocated for employment at the various Davidson County mills.

Tom and Dewey Cooper were married within a few years of each other. Dewey tied the knot first, taking Madie Fultz of Rowan County as his bride on September

The Patriotic Order Sons of America, a fraternal and mutual aid society active in the earlier part of the century, employed this family string band for one of their picnics. The Cooper clan made up the majority of the musicians. Left to right, they are, Mack (guitar), unknown driver, Cicero (fiddle), C. M. Miller (fiddle) Tom (guitar), Dewey (fiddle), Clay Everhart (banjo), James (guitar), Claude Fisher (banjo ukulele), Jimmy Raper and unknown drummer. Lexington, Davidson County, circa 1920. Courtesy Lawrence Cooper.

12, 1919. Tom followed soon after, marrying Beulah Mae Walser (January 11, 1903–June 30, 1983) of Yadkin College in Rowan County on October 21, 1921. Dewey and Madie remained childless, but Tom had two sons, Elmer Lee (born April 25, 1924) and Lawrence Monroe (born June 10, 1922), that followed him into string music.

By the 1920s, Clay Everhart was just one in the legion of two- and three-finger banjoists living in the Piedmont of North Carolina. However, his three-finger picking outshone the majority of his contemporaries. His son, Clayton Everhart, said "I've been to many fiddlers' conventions, and I've never seen him fail to win first prize, never!" Confining his playing to the background on commercial records with the Cooper Boys, his solo pieces recorded at home in the early 1940s reveal virtuostic turns on selections such as "Flop Eared Mule," "Listen to the Mockingbird," and his tour-de-force imitation of banjo star Fred Van Eps, a medley of "Arkansas Traveler" and "Old Black Joe."

Clay Everhart was born on June 3, 1889, in Lexington, North Carolina. Hilda Reid, Clay Everhart's daughter, believes that: "his [oldest] brother Hamilton Everhart [April 19, 1874–December 17, 1959] played banjo. And he also played the fiddle. [Clay] started [playing] when he was four years old, and [Hamilton] made my father a banjo out of a cigar box. And that's how he first started."

Everhart told his protégé Johnny Whisnant (born 1921) that he was taught to play a three-finger roll on the banjo "by a man named Cooper." Larry Beam, Everhart's grandson, thinks one of the Cooper clan may have helped to start Clay on the instrument.

By the age of sixteen, Clay Everhart was working for the Dixie Furniture Company at one of their related facilities. Several years later, on September 26, 1908, Everhart married for the first time. Notie Veora or Viola Lloyd, born August 19, 1894, was from nearby Davie County. Over the next twelve years, the couple had five children, four girls and one boy. Clay and Notie were living in Guilford County for the birth of their first two offspring. Perhaps Everhart was working in High Point, learning his trade as a beveller of glass mirrors for the furniture industry, as has been suggested by various family members and acquaintances. The Everharts were back in Lexington in 1911. By the birth of their third child, in May of 1915, the couple had relocated to a house across from Everhart's mother on the Greensboro Road.

Clay was playing with the Cooper family by the early 1920s. Hilda Reid also mentions a banjo and fiddle player named Cicero Foust and the Moncus family (see Chapter One) as keeping musical company with Clay Everhart around the same time.

Notie Everhart's health was never strong. Tragically, she died on January 15, 1921, from complications following the birth of her son Clayton Wesley (born December 13, 1920). The family came apart somewhat when Clay's first wife died. Clayton was sent to live with his grandmother for the first one and a half years of his life, and Clay's sister Lou raised Clayton's sibling Alma, two years old at the time of her mother's death.

Three years later, Everhart met and married Ila Belle May (born November 9, 1904) of Rowan County, eventually increasing the size of the family by five more children. Clay had probably become acquainted with Ila through her father, an amateur fiddler. "And after that," says daughter Hilda Reid, "he went to the [Piedmont] Mirror Company. And the mirror company closed down [in 1927] and he worked some at Lexington Chair. Daddy [then] was called to Mt. Airy to a mirror company there. In 1929, he moved to Lenoir." Clay got the job in Lenoir at the Union Mirror Company through his wife's brother, who worked in management. Daughter Ruth Coffey told me that "He boarded up here a long time, maybe a year or two. And, he would go backwards and forwards on the weekends. Mamma stayed [in the Lexington area] and took care of [her mother] Grandma May until she died and then we moved up here. But he would never buy a house [in Lenoir] because we were always going back home [to Lexington]."

In 1927, Okeh Records came to the city of Winston-Salem to make recordings. A portable studio just 21 miles from Lexington was too much for Everhart and the Cooper Boys to resist.

On September 21, 1927, the *Twin City Sentinel*, Winston-Salem's evening daily, ran an account of the sessions. It is surprising that only one article emerged about Okeh's presence in the twin cities, and that the writer fails to mention the locally-based Cooper Boys band. It is interesting to note that much of the hyperbole in the account came from the mouths of record company representatives. The old stereo-types about traditional music, including the one about string music exclusively coming from the mountain south, was repeated here:

> Mountain Folk Music Is Being Recorded Here: Talent from Three States Recording at Studio in Old West End School Building.
> That mountain ballad the old-fashioned gospel songs sung at the arbor camp meeting accompanied by the portable organ that is often carried many long and weary miles, the self-styled country fiddler, ye old-time musicians who made merry for the corn shuckin' and chicken stews at the tobacco barns, have their places in American music, is the opinion of the Okeh Record Company. This statement was made by a representative of the company who states that one desires records of music of this type, as dear to those living in the mountains or the rural districts, as the grand opera, jazz, popular or other types of music are to those living in the city or towns. He stated, too, that many persons living in the city find interest in this type of music peculiar to the mountain sections and are beginning to study its origin and background. The studio is in the Old West End school building.
> Realizing the need for preserving this type of music the company has sent its representatives into the hills of North Carolina, Virginia, Tennessee and Kentucky to search for persons who could best sing or play the mountain music. Several groups were first taken to New York City for recordings and then the firm decided to secure the best possible recording equipment and send it to Winston-Salem to record a large number of groupings. Winston-Salem was selected for the studio because of its accessibility to talent of the three states. The outfit is now working on the records and will be in Winston-Salem for at least another week.
> Tuesday [September 20] morning the Neal Sisters, Ruth and Wanda, of Old Fort, sang a number of duets, accompanied by Jewel [sic] Davis, Burt [sic] Layne and Mack Williams of Chattanooga, Tenn., who played two violins and a guitar. Monday morning [September 19] records were made of selections for the Aiken County String Band from Graniteville, S.C., and in the afternoon records were made by the Valdese Quartet of Valdese, N.C. *

Running September 19–28, 1927, Okeh's session drew groups from a five-state area. As the article states, the portable studio was inaugurated by the mandolin-led Aiken County String Band, waxing a version of "Soldier's Joy," followed by the Valdese Quartet. Ruth and Wanda Neal (previously recorded by Okeh in Atlanta on June 3) with Bert Layne of Skillet Lickers fame appeared the subsequent day, as did the Alcoa Quartet. Georgia's Jewell Davis and Danville's Four Virginians (Richard Bigger on fiddle, Fred Richards and Elvin Bigger on guitars and Leonard Jennings on tiple) filled Wednesday.

Sessions continued at a brisk pace, with two to three groups recording each day. September 22 featured Matt Simmons and Frank Miller (Simmons also recorded for

*Full text of article appears in the appendix.

Edison with Posey Rorer) from Stokes County; Howard Maxey of Franklin County, Virginia; and Vance's Tennessee Breakdowners. The Reid Brothers Band from Greene Mountain rounded out Friday. Recording on Saturday were [possibly Matt] Simmons Sacred Singers, the Balsam Gap Breakdowners, and the Hickory (NC) Nuts. After a day off, recording resumed on Monday with classic versions of "Sugar Hill" and "Train on the Island" by Crockett Ward and His Boys. The Ward family's Grayson County neighbors, the Pipers Gap Ramblers, were also recorded that day. Tuesday was devoted to the sacred music of L.V. Jones and His Virginia Singing Class and the Carolina Quartet. Fiddlin' Powers and Family, and, last on the final day, September 28, were Clay Everhart, Tom and Dewey Cooper. The sessions were supervised by Polk Brockman, the record dealer who had brought country recording pioneer Fiddlin' John Carson before Okeh's microphones in 1923.

The North Carolina Cooper Boys, as the trio was billed on their lone Okeh release of February 1928, waxed six pieces on that September day in 1927 (six seems to have been the magic number for Brockman, because most of the other groups also cut six titles). The cryptic names for most of the unissued selections, such as "Pictures Tonight" and "I Used to Wear A White Hat," yield little information as to the songs' identities, and family members have been unable to provide any additional data. One of the unreleased compositions, "Give My Love to Nell," is surely the William Benson Gray composition of 1894. The two tunes that made it onto a commercial disc include a version of "The Yellow Rose of Texas" (called "The Red Rose of Texas") and a comical song drawn from the Bible, "Daniel in the Den of Lions."

Surviving Everhart and Cooper family members fail to assign credit for the idea to audition for Okeh to any individual band member. And, no one has adequately explained the impetus behind the attempt to "make records." However, I am tempted to ascribe the effort to Clay Everhart. The fact is that his family attributes him with a desire to make a living from music. This, added to the possible termination of his employment by Piedmont Mirror, which seems to have occurred by 1927, would have given him good reason to push the recording session on the band.

For Polk Brockman, one can conjecture that recording the Cooper and Everhart band was an afterthought. The A&R man possibly added the Cooper Boys to his roster after a last-minute audition of the group. Or, because the trio was locally based, Okeh might have kept Everhart and the Coopers "on call" until an opening occurred in the recording schedule. Whether or not the Cooper Boys were an important part of Okeh's plans, a song the band was to record four years later for Okeh and Columbia Records was learned at these sessions. "I Ain't Nobody's Darling," as performed by the Pipers Gap Ramblers, became "Nobody's Darling On Earth" for the Coopers second recording date.

As no sales figures survive, it is hard to judge the success of the Cooper Boys Okeh release. They made only one additional attempt at recording, for Okeh's competitor and successor, Columbia Records. Paradoxically, by that time, in the fall of 1931, the group was, for all intents and purposes, defunct. Clay Everhart's family was in the process of completing its move to Lenoir. In addition, the Depression was

The North Carolina Cooper Boys prepare to drive to Atlanta and make records for Columbia. (Left to right) Clay Everhart, and cousins Dewey and Tom Cooper sit on the back fender of a Model A Ford. Tom holds his cousin Irving's metal-bodied guitar. Probably Lexington, Davidson County, circa 1931. Courtesy Madie Fultz Cooper.

about to temporarily finish off the country music industry, making a career as a recording artist, for the time being, an impossibility.

Another irony, considering the financial tenor of the times, was that Clay Everhart had just purchased his first high-quality banjo. Just the year before, he had bought a used, but nonetheless Gibson brand of instrument. Clayton Everhart remembers, "A man bought that banjo in Greensboro the best I can remember anybody ever sayin'. And, for some reason or other, gave it up. And Dad wanted it. And I think he got that banjo through Rumley [a music dealer in Lexington]. And then Dad paid Rumley on an installment plan, 50 cent here and a dollar there and whatever it was."

As with Okeh Records, family members were unable to supply a specific motivation behind the Cooper Boys' Columbia recordings. Lawrence Cooper sums up familial recollections when he says, "Well, let's just go to Atlanta to the Columbia people and see if we can record some of these songs and get something out of it." Clayton Everhart reminisces, "So, they hired somebody here in Lexington to take 'em to Atlanta that drove an old Essex automobile." Ruth Coffey adds, "I can remember [Clay] telling the tale that it took most of the day to get there."

Clay Everhart and the North Carolina Cooper Boys entered Columbia's Atlanta studio first thing on October 27, 1931. Bob Miller, assisted by Dan Hornsby, a Columbia studio musician, supervised the session. Four pieces were recorded that day. Although only two were released, all survive and so we are able to hear the full results of their labors. One side of their issued 78-rpm was "Standing by a Window." Many other recordings of the song preceded that of the Cooper Boys, although none under their title. This included one by Crockett Ward and His Boys from the Okeh Records Winston-Salem date. Listeners will recognize the tune for "Standing by a Window" as the one of the better-known song "Down Among the Budded Roses." Probably the most famous recording of "Budded Roses" was by Charlie Poole, whose version was released by Columbia Records in June of 1927. The flip side of the North Carolina Cooper Boys disc contained "The Rose with a Broken Stem." Copyrighted in 1901 by Everett J. Evans and Carroll Fleming, the Cooper and Everhart rendering was the only issued appearance of the song by a country artist in the prewar, 78-rpm era. The two unissued titles included "Down Among the Shady Woodlands," about which I have been unable to locate any information, and the aforementioned "Nobody's Darling on Earth." "Nobody's Darling" is the 1870 composition of Kentuckian William Shakespeare "Will B." Hays. Hays' songs captured America's imagination in the last quarter of the 19th century and were among the first country standards when the industry began recording rural talent. Indeed, among his best-known compositions was the first certified country "hit," "The Little Log Cabin in the Lane." (The Delmore Brothers also recorded their first sides for Columbia in 1931. Alton Delmore, in his autobiography, gives a good, albeit emotional, picture of the sessions and of the process of recording.)

The Clay Everhart and the North Carolina Cooper Boys lone Columbia coupling was issued in 1932. "Of course, they were hopin' that record would turn out to be a big hit," recalls Clayton Everhart, "which it didn't really turn out to be. It turned out to be average, and he didn't get a lot of money out of it." Lawrence Cooper adds, "All they got out of it was their expenses of going down and coming back. No royalty at all."

After moving away from the Coopers, Everhart looked to his progeny for musical companionship. Clayton recollects that "After he got through eatin' his supper, he'd say, 'Boys, get your instruments.' Now, that wasn't just a request ... that meant, 'Get 'em, buddy ... we are gonna practice.' And that happened four, five, six nights a week. And when I mean you practiced, you practiced that before you got your homework for school."

Ruth Coffey verifies this account "[Clay] didn't even want the boys to play baseball, because you might break your finger and then you couldn't note your guitar. And we all played music after supper at night. That was the entertainment. 'Get your instruments, boys. We're gonna play.'"

The Everhart Family Band. Patriarch Clay Everhart on banjo stands next to his sons Clayton on guitar and Jack on fiddle. Daughter Alma on guitar sits to the left of her mother Ila Belle. Probably Lenoir, circa 1937. Courtesy Larry Beam.

While most of the Everhart siblings played an instrument, it was Jack William (January 9, 1925–1978) on fiddle, and Clayton on guitar and mandolin that joined in establishing the new group. In all probability, this was because the boys were old enough to be musically accomplished, but still young enough to be living at home. Called the Sunset Travelers, or, alternately, Smiling Jack and his Sunset Travelers (or Sunset Rangers), the group was originally a quartet, including a neighbor, "Fate" Puett, on guitar. Lafayette Puett (November 13, 1910–August 1960) was a Caldwell County native who worked for a variety of the furniture factories around Lenoir. In late 1938 or early 1939, the Travelers added Tom Norman of Marion, North Carolina. Tom had finished second to the group at a talent contest held in Lenoir, after which

Clay recruited him into the band. Bill Spake, a bassist and comedian from Gastonia, rounded out the group for some engagements on an "as needed" basis.

Clarence Greene has written that "The Sunset Travelers were on hand for the inauguration of WHKY radio in Hickory [the station signed on in 1939; Clayton remembers their 6 A.M. radio program on weekday mornings], and also were regulars at the Lenoir branch of the same station (managed by a Mr. Shumway), located under the old Avon Theater on North Main Street."

Ruth Coffey recalls,

> We had a radio program up here at Lenoir on WJRI, for a year or more, that we sang and played midday every Saturday. My sister-in-law, Helen Everhart, Jack's wife, and I, sang. We come on the air with "I Want to be a Cowboy's Sweetheart," our theme song, and we yodeled it. I was about eleven or twelve at this time. And Shunway [sic], I forgot his wife's first name, he was the radio announcer. We didn't play slow, draggy stuff. We played fast music. And I mean, we whooped it up!
>
> [The Sunset Travelers] played like corn shuckings. Schoolhouses. They played Blowing Rock School I don't know how many times. Oak Hill School. They played for private parties and they'd go to play corn shuckings—anywhere they wanted music, they was there. They were paid a little something.

By the time Clay formed the Sunset Travelers with his two sons, country music was changing away from the sentimental Tin Pan Alley songs and fiddle tunes performed by the Cooper Boys to Western songs and "hepped up" fiddle tunes like "Alabama Jubilee." Clay seemed to easily adapt his style of playing to this newer format, backing Jack's longbow fiddle style on the instrumentals and the smooth, duet singing of the Travelers' vocal numbers. The Sunset Travelers existed into the early 1940s, until both Clayton and Jack entered the service. When they emerged, their own families and careers took them away from the family band. Clayton felt his father's desire to become a professional musician: "His ambition all the time was to make money with music, [but] Dad had too many mouths to feed and he couldn't give up feedin' his family to go out ... 'cause, sometimes you had to live hard if you made it."

"I don't think he ever dreamed that he could make a livin' at it," says Ruth Coffey.

> And my daddy was not an educated person. If the right person had got a-hold of him and our family, we would have been equal maybe to the Stonemans because we had a lot of talent. Now, they made some good music. And I mean, it was played good, it was right, it was on time. It wasn't sloppy music — they played good music. And maybe due to the fact that the depression hit about the time he recorded, maybe their records would have gone. Who knows?

Back in Lexington, banjoist Olin Berrier joined with Tom and Dewey Cooper in their music making, or, rather, the Coopers joined Berrier. An auto mechanic by day, Berrier filled his evenings playing for public dances and parties around the Western Piedmont. At one time, Olin's group also included Tom's sons Elmer and Lawrence Cooper (see Chapter Four).

The Berrier and Cooper clans get together for a picking session. Standing (left to right) are Leonard Berrier with tenor banjo, Cicero Cooper with fiddle, Dewey Cooper with fiddle, Olin Berrier with banjo and Tom Cooper with guitar. Tom's two sons, Lawrence with guitar and Elmer with mandolin, kneel in front of their father. Probably Davidson County, circa 1940. Courtesy Madie Fultz Cooper.

Clay Everhart was also friendly with Olin Berrier. From 1940 on, when Clay came to Lexington from Lenoir to visit, "he would always bring his banjo unless it was a funeral or sickness," recalls grandson Larry Beam. "He [was] liable to come down three, four, five times a year. A lot of times he would come down and he'd go to the old Lion's Club in Lexington, the Lion's Den, it used to be off Fairview Drive, and play with Olin Berrier. I think Tom Cooper played in that band at that time."

Two of the musicians he often played with during this period from Lexington were the brothers, Mead (born circa 1911) and Emery Everhart (no immediate relation to Clay). Emery played the washtub bass and Mead the guitar. "He'd get an audience, he'd play for anybody," continues Beam. "Where he had one or a crowd, he's kind of like a preacher, if he had one, he had a congregation. Now, a lot of times his boy would come with him or maybe his whole family would come with him. Bob, his youngest boy, would come along, and he played the fiddle and guitar."

Ruth Coffey remembers

> He liked to play with Olin Berrier. And, of course, he had people around Lenoir that came in and he played a lot with: Walt Hendrick (fiddle); Charlie Knight, a

fiddler who ran a grocery store; C. A. Stokes (fiddle); Jake Bowman (fiddle); Knox Ballew (guitar); Coot Walker, a ukulele player who was a foreman at the Hayes Cotton Mill; and let's see, I heard him speak a lot of Mack Crowe [January 5, 1897–November 8, 1966, banjo; see Clarence Greene's article for more information].

Ruth neglects to mention that her father also liked to play with Doyle Robert Coffey, a guitarist born April 10, 1921, in Cherokee County, whom she married in 1941.

Ruth also remembers:

> [Clay] played schoolhouses and dances and corn shuckings and all kind of stuff. And I remember once going to Oak Hill with him and playing the piano for a dance. And then he played a lot in what we used to call the Hog Waller. It was just an alley, you know, that people came to trade their cows and pigs and sell whatever they had. And people would get down there and pick and sing in the lot. And Doc Watson was there a lot and he played there. All the farmers come in on Saturday. Kinda what we call a farmer's market today is what it was.

By the late 1940s, Dewey Cooper had retired from active performing. His health, never good, deteriorated, and he died in 1951. By that time, Tom Cooper was also limiting his appearances in public, eventually dropping out of Olin Berrier's band. "They never got a nickel out of music," recollects Matthew Cooper. "They just played for the fun of it."

Clay Everhart worked as a glass beveller in Lenoir for 27 years. Upon retirement, Everhart moved to the Coquina Cove Trailer Park at Indian Rocks Beach, six miles outside of Clearwater, on the west coast of Florida. There, Clay played with the McMillan family and D. D. Yokeley, owner of the Banjo Ranch music store, as the West Coast Ramblers. Clay Everhart passed away on December 31, 1963, and was brought back to Lexington, where he always assumed he would return to live, for burial.

Larry Beam affectionately told me, "Grandpa, he was pretty smooth. He played with clarity. You could make out what his songs was, and they had pretty tunes to 'em, just like 'Flop Eared Mule,' was a pretty tune to me." Clayton Everhart noted, "People wanted to play with Dad because he was good. And he wanted to play with everybody else, too. My dad never turned down a chance to pick the banjo."

EIGHT

"He Was Looking for Those Who Lived Isolated Lives": Bascom Lamar Lunsford's Discoveries

"We just started riding. [Lunsford] seemed to hunt like a bird dog, just sniffin' them out. His instincts said go down [this] dirt road. He wouldn't stop on any paved road; he'd always go down a dirt road. He was looking for [those who were unspoiled by radio, the Grand Ole Opry, those who] lived isolated lives."

— Hoyle Bruton

In the spring of 1948, Hoyle Bruton, then a graduate student at the University of North Carolina at Chapel Hill and publicity director for the First Carolina Folk Festival, took an automobile trip with Bascom Lamar Lunsford. Lunsford was out scouting talent for the upcoming festival. Bascom — a folk song collector, festival organizer, and traditional musician himself — was always on the lookout for opportunities to extend his sphere of operations. On this occasion, he was hoping to expand his list of possible traditional performers.

Born and bred in Western North Carolina, Bascom Lunsford (March 21, 1882–September 4, 1973) was the most influential promoter of traditional music that the Tar Heel state has ever seen. He grew up with the old ballads sung by his mother, and had fiddled from a young age. As a teenager, Lunsford added the banjo to his musical skills, and began collecting the songs and tunes around him. Like A. P. Carter of the famous Carter Family, Lunsford used his various jobs — specifically selling fruit trees and honey — to spend time acquainting himself with the area's many music makers. Bascom Lamar Lunsford's crowning achievement was the recording of his "memory collection" (those songs and tunes gathered during his collecting years) for both the Library of Congress and Columbia University (Jones, *Bascom Lamar Lunsford: Ballads, Banjo Tunes, and Sacred Songs of Western North Carolina: 1–7*).

Clegg Garner's square dance band on stage at the First Carolina Folk Festival, held at Kenan Stadium, on the campus of the University of North Carolina at Chapel Hill in June 1948. Left to right are John Reid on fiddle, Roy Arnold (partially hidden) on steel guitar, Clegg Garner on fiddle, Sam Jr. Lowe on guitar, Carl Nance on banjo and George Pegram on banjo. This band was from Randolph County. Photograph by Charles H. Cooper; courtesy Mrs. Grace Thornburg.

Since the 1920s, when he had founded the Mountain Dance and Song Festival in his home area of Asheville and first made contact with northern "folk song" collectors, Lunsford had supported himself through the related activities of collecting, organizing, and performing. But, like many of his ilk before traditional music became a (minimal) profession, every year was a scramble for the Western North Carolina native.

And so Lunsford had entered into an agreement with Arthur Palmer Hudson, a professor at the University of Carolina, to run a folk festival on the Chapel Hill campus. Students like Bruton and other UNC staff would aid in the production of the event, sponsored by the Folklore Council of the Extension Division. Bascom would scout the talent, adding to his stock company of performers initially utilized by the Asheville Festival with Piedmont musicians and dancers, and also perform and mc at the event (*Durham Morning Herald*, March 21, 1948; letter from Lunsford to Grumman, December 24, 1946; 1949 Festival poster; Bulletin (press release) August 1948; Hudson, "Festival Review," *Southern Folklore Quarterly*, August 1948).

In the flurry of newspaper articles generated to promote the first and subsequent festivals, many of the details behind the event are revealed. These publications served the dual purpose of attracting an audience, as well as advertising to musicians that their talents were needed for the gathering. Jean Baskerville, in her article "Lunsford Finds Randolph County to Be Rich Field in Folklore Music" in the Greensboro *Daily News*, noted one of the finds from Lunsford and Bruton's wanderings:

> The first person the[y] encountered was Prof. E. H. Thompson of Farmer High School ... the caller ... of a square dancing team that will appear in the June festival. This team is composed of eight couples, most of them high school students, of the Uwharrie River and Carraway [*sic*] Creek sections of the county. The dancers have been holding big rehearsals in the gymnasium of Farmer High School. Music for the dances is furnished by the Garner string band [*Greensboro Daily News*, May 23, 1948].

As is mentioned in Chapter Four, Clegg Garner led the premier dance band of western Randolph and eastern Davidson counties, providing the music for square dances in the Denton and Farmer communities, as well as accompanying dance teams from both areas. Interestingly enough, square dance teams were somewhat the invention of Bascom Lamar Lunsford, as he suggested and nurtured their formation at the Mountain Dance festival, where the dance group competition was the "main event." All square dance teams, including those in Denton and Farmer (now more commonly referred to as "clogging teams" because of their use of the "clog" dance steps within their "routines" or presentations), are descendants of these western North Carolina aggregations.

Lunsford wanted to meet Garner and arrange to bring his band to the UNC Festival. Thompson sent them to Clegg's house, only to learn that the master of the house was off hunting crows (his profession was leading northern hunters). This was the first opportunity for Bruton to witness Bascom in action, which he saw repeated on numerous subsequent occasions. As he recalled:

> We would eat a meal with the people. Lunsford never once asked if anyone played music. We'd be sitting in the cane bottom chairs in the living room. Lunsford would go out to the car and get his banjo, bring it in and go to playing. Within five minutes, Garner went into the bedroom to get his banjo, which turned out to be the twin of the one Lunsford played. I was surprised, because Garner's hands were so gnarled, that he could play. Then, they'd sit for an hour, hour and a half and play. Before we left that day, the invitation would be extended and arrangements made for Garner to attend the Festival. We offered to pay his gas bill for travel to Chapel Hill.

Fredrick Clegg Garner was born July 22, 1888, on a farm located by the Uwharrie River in the county's New Hope township. His father died when Clegg was young, and so his grandparents raised him. Clegg supposedly learned music in his youth, in the company of Will Briles, who, like Clegg, played both the fiddle and the banjo. Somehow, Will had contact with African American musicians, and learned some pieces and techniques from them. Before World War II, Clegg also kept the musical company of Claude Winslow (see Chapter One and Chapter Three).

Around 1908, Clegg Garner left the area and traveled west to work in Boise, Idaho. Upon his return several years later, he was employed in a sawmill for a while, and then took up the training of hunting dogs for the parties he was to lead for the rest of his life. Clegg Garner died on February 12, 1962 (*Randolph County: 1779–1979*).

Although Clegg played the banjo and sang on stage at Lunsford's urging, his activities backing the Farmer dance team were confined to the fiddle. His band featured the second violin of John Reid, who ran a shooting club in Denton. Carl Nance of Farmer handled the banjo duties.

Carl Green Nance (see Chapter Six) was born in the Salem Church community of southwestern Randolph County. The Nances, like the Garners and the Briles, were long-time area residents and the families grew up playing music together. Carl also heard his mother's brother, Benjamin Watson Nance, who lived in the Piney Grove Church community, play the fiddle while growing up. His own older sibling, James Cicero (born 1878), was a banjo player in the clawhammer style. When Carl finally learned to play, he combined ideas from the older style with the up and coming "up picking" method. Nance fashioned a unique two-finger style that wedded an up and down motion with the index finger on the melody strings and his thumb on the fifth string. In 1911, Carl Nance married Nannie May Hill (August 14, 1886–January 22, 1935) of the Mechanic and Rachel areas. Their children who took up the banjo include John Branson (born May 17, 1913), Thomas Jvan (born September 26, 1914), and Ivey Wyatt (born July 6, 1922) (Denny, *Farmer-Yesterday and Today*; *Randolph County: 1779–1979*; *Courier-Tribune*, March 1, 1976: 9).

Carl's daughter Ruth Glee (born August 15, 1918) has fond memories of her father's music.

> School mornings— it was in the wintertime. He would get the fire in the fireplace going and then he'd warm his banjo and when the room got warm enough and it was time for the children to get up, why, he would come to the stairway and call us to get up and get ready to go to school. But, we'd wake up to "Home Sweet Home," "Sweet By and By," whatever he might be a picking.
>
> One time, he had a man hired to come and help him haul hay, and they had finished lunch and this man says, "Carl, we've got to get back to the field. There's coming up a cloud. The hay's gonna get wet." And Pop says, "We'll go, but I've got to pick a piece on the banjo." That's how much he loved his banjo. And he played what he wanted to play and got it out of his system, and he says, "We went on to the field and got up the hay and then it rained." [Laughter.]

The group's steel guitarist, James Roy Arnold (born November 6, 1921), began playing with Garner and Nance around 1944, the same year he married Nance's daughter, Glee. Arnold was born in the Cedar Springs community north of Denton. Gurney Peace (see Chapter One) was his guitar teacher after Arnold forsook his first love, the banjo. Roy remembers "When I was growing up, I wanted to play the banjo and I couldn't get up enough money to buy a banjo and I finally got a [steel] guitar. (Laughter) But that banjo was costing like fifteen dollars and I got my guitar for three and ninety-five, I think it was, from Sears and Roebuck. (Laughter.)"

Garner and company used Sam Jr. Lowe (born June 27, 1923) on guitar between 1948 and the mid–1950s. Around the age of seven, his father had started Sam on the

Clegg Garner String Band and the Denton Square Dance Team on stage at the Carolina Folk Festival in June 1948. Courtesy the Southern Folklife Collection.

instrument. Samuel Allen Lowe, Sr. (January 1, 1883–Decembr 6, 1989) played the fiddle and banjo at local house dances, school exhibitions, and fiddlers' conventions during the first part of the twentieth century, often in the company of Ernest Clark on banjo, Malcolm Routh on banjo and fiddle, and Tom Dugan on fiddle.

One of the band members who chose not to make the trips to Chapel Hill was fiddler Daniel Martin Luther (August 26, 1889–1971), a farmer and sawmill man. His son, Rex (born 1935), began playing guitar with his father at the age of ten. Both worked area dances with the Garner band.

The original Carolina Folk Festival was held at Kenan Stadium on the University of North Carolina campus June 18–19, 1948. Along with Thompson's dance team and the Garner band, the program included a dance group with string band brought by E. R. Echard of Guilford County, a collection of postal clerks and their "womanfolk" from Greensboro known as the Guilford Swingsters, and the Green Valley Boys from Randolph County. North Carolina groups presenting ballads, fiddling, folk dances, and "group singing of white and negro [sic] spirituals" included 500 to 700 actual participants ("Bingham Township Is 'Find' for Specialist of Folklore," *Durham Morning Herald* March 21, 1948; Lunsford and Grumman; 1949 Festival poster; bulletin (press release), March 29, 1948; Hudson, "Festival Review," *Southern Folklore Quarterly*, August 1948; Arnold to Carlin). The festival continued unabated through the 1950s, lasting in some form at least until 1961, although it is unclear if Lunsford was involved after the 1956 festival (Brewer and Hudson).

After 1955, the events became more standardized, with the same performers starring year after year. But there was still some good Piedmont talent recognized and presented. The Bowes Brothers string band of Woodsdale, Mrs. Hazel Byrd's string band from Greensboro, the Walt Sloan String band of Iredell County, Benny Smith and his Dixie Hot Shots from Asheboro, Randolph County's Deep River Boys, banjoist Paul Joines with "trick guitarist" Bill Short, the Montgomery County Band with Walser Morris on banjo and Corbett Bennett on fiddle, and square dance teams from Burlington and Orange County joined stars from the Asheville Folk Festival to share in the glory (Lowe to Carlin; "Carolina Folk Festival Scheduled," *Raleigh News-Observer*, June 1, 1952; "Folk Festival to Open at University Tonight," *Greensboro News*, June 11, 1953; "Carolina Folk Festival Ends Annual Performances at UNC," *Durham Herald*; "Ballad Singing, Dancing, Highlight Opening of Carolina Folk Festival," *Durham Herald*, June 11, 1954; "Folk Festival Scheduled at UNC," *Greensboro Daily News*, April 24, 1955).

At the same time Bascom Lamar Lunsford was managing the Carolina Folk Festival, he ran shorter-lived events in Winston-Salem and Burlington. These all employed a similar formula and many of the same performers. One "festival within a festival" that Bascom initiated has been held at the State Fair in Raleigh since 1948, the same year that Lunsford founded the Carolina Folk Festival. The Garner group played the first State Fair Folk Festival in October of that year, as did banjoist Glenn Davis and band. Unlike Garner, Davis continued his association with the State Fair past the first few years into the 1970s, bringing other Randolph County musicians to perform on stage (Womick, 1). After Lunsford's departure, Ruth Jewel, the supervisor of Music for the North Carolina Dept of Public Instruction, ran the Festival for fourteen years. It is presently organized by Annette Pulley (Jones, *Minstrel of the Appalachians* 76).

An important figure at Bascom Lunsford's folk festivals, as well as at North Carolina's fiddlers' conventions of the 1950s, '60s, and '70s, was banjoist, singer, and raconteur George Pegram. After he came to Lunsford's attention, Pegram and Lunsford became inseparable, and George became a mainstay for all of Bascom's events.

Ann Gilbert, quoted in the notes to Rounder Records' George Pegram recording, said "The first time I saw George Pegram he was holding forth in his own inimitable, gravity-defying manner. The usual crowd had gathered at his feet. He wore a smile of unadulterated bliss. Bobbing and weaving his head, he and a guitarist, accompanied by two female singers, were tearing along in high style on that great reliable, "'Old Time Religion.'"

To tell Pegram's story, I have drawn from many sources. George himself was the basis for much of the biographical information previously printed about him. However, he was known to greatly expand on the facts, especially when in front of a crowd. Whenever I could, I have used documents and details from other informants to validate George's stories. When information could not be verified, I have credited George as its source.

It is not hard to tell why Pegram was *the* favorite performer for almost thirty years at festivals and fiddlers' conventions throughout North Carolina. Banjoist and folklorist Art Rosenbaum describes Pegram's playing as a "raucous, hell-for-leather, driving style" (Jones, *Music from South Turkey Creek*). Robert Black further mentions, to achieve this effect, "George Pegram uses a technique much like the well known 'double-thumbing' style. It is a three-finger movement employing single notes; the melody is picked with the thumb and the drone is alternated between the first and second strings, using the index and the middle fingers."

George Franklin Pegram, Jr., was born August 5, 1911, and raised near Oak Ridge in Guilford County, the third child of George (circa December 20, 1881–November 5, 1955) and Phebe Daniel Henley Pegram (born 1892). This farming community was rich in string band music. Zack Whitaker (see Chapter Six) promoted fiddlers' conventions and dances throughout George Pegram's upbringing, and, probably, those were the events that George attended when growing up. One of Zack Whitaker's musical compatriots was George's "uncle" (they are actually second cousins once removed, according to Pegram genealogist Nola Duffy), fiddler Clyde Pegram. George claimed that Clyde helped start him in music and that the two played together once George became musically proficient. George also had a brother, Zeb (May 3, 1918–March 15, 1992), who played guitar and sang.

George Pegram tells several different stories of acquiring his earliest instrument. Either his first banjo, which he started playing around the age of nine, was one discarded by his grandfather, or a cigar box banjo, which George made. Pegram continues the story.

> My grandma drew a pension from the Civil War. I stayed with her, and she gave me a patch for tobacco. I said the first thing I was going to do when I sold my crop of tobacco, I'm going to buy me a banjo. I went down to Winston-Salem to a music store and paid $15 for a banjo—a Silvertone [Jones, *Music from South Turkey Creek*].
>
> I got to watching other banjo pickers. I'd pick it up. I'd go to school commencements, where there would be playing, and to fiddling conventions. I'd pick it up listening to others.
>
> The first money I ever made in my life was for pickin' a banjo all night. I was just a barefoot kid and they gave me 15 cents. I tied it up in the end of a handkerchief and took it and gave it to my Momma.

George evidently had fond memories of Oak Ridge. After his discovery by Lunsford, he would return there each year to perform at the horse show and fiddlers' convention that was began in 1946.

At the age of 26, George Pegram married Dorothy Louise Dick (1920–March 12, 2001) of Guilford County and moved to Statesville. The couple eventually had four children. Pegram claimed to have served in the Navy during World War II, and to losing an eye in the Japanese attack on Pearl Harbor (Sam Jr. Lowe states that Pegram was never in the military and that the eye injury was the result of childhood horseplay). To support his family, George worked in the tobacco fields, sawmills, and furniture factories of North Carolina and Virginia. "[Music] never paid enough to live on, and Pegram moved his family from job to job, from one small town to another, wherever he could find work and 'play a little music,'" reported the *Winston-Salem Journal/Sentinel*.

Pegram, possibly living in Denton at the time, recalled his first meeting with Lunsford.

> The old man discovered me. Oh, it was 1949, I believe it was. He came down there and he had car trouble. He wanted to spend the night. I said yes, I'd be glad for him to. He didn't know that I was a banjo picker—a musician. He had one of these recording things to make records. We eat supper and all. I asked him what his business was. He said folk music. I told him that I played the banjo a little bit once in a while. He said, "Go get your banjo then." I got my banjo and played "Cumberland Gap" and different ones. He said, "Why, that sounds just fine. Just fine. Let me record that." He did, and I was invited to the festival. (Jones, *Music from South Turkey Creek*)

This account seems likely, although some of its details are not correct. Since Pegram appeared at the first Festival, Lunsford must have visited George in 1948. Hoyle Bruton, publicity director for the 1948 festival, described talent-scouting trips with Lunsford in the spring, and thinks that Lunsford had heard about Pegram before he went to see him. Arthur Palmer Hudson, reviewing the 1948 Carolina Folk Festival in the August 1948 issue of *Southern Folklore Quarterly*, mentions Pegram:

> a broadaxe-finished mountaineer under a ten-gallon hat [vying] with Clegg Garner of Randolph for honors as banjo soloist. George's "Good Ol' Mountain Dew" [was] a "special request" number on every program after the first. A natural clown, with an excellent repertory of banjo songs and solo dance numbers, and with an inexhaustible fund of showmanship, George was the individual star of the Festival.

A reporter for the *Asheboro Courier-Tribune* added,

> One member of Garner's band, tall and lanky George Pegram, brought down the house with his rip-roaring rendition of "Good Ol' Mountain Dew," a number written by Lunsford in the style of the authentic folk songs. The large crowd, stacked up in the north side of Keenan stadium to the back wall, city folk and all, got the swing of folk music as George sang and whole assembly was soon clapping and swaying in rhythm.

This event seems to be, outside of local community events, one of Pegram's first appearances as a professional musician. Although George Pegram would continue to work at a variety of manual labor jobs, from this point on, he would attempt to make a part of his living at music.

Subsequent newspaper photos and recollections of area residents show Pegram playing with Clegg Garner's band for dances at Denton (Davidson County) and Farmer (Randolph County) into the 1950s. And, a recording of the Okie Mountain Boys made at the 1948 Carolina Folk Festival gives aural evidence that Pegram was also a member of that aggregation. The Okie Mountain Boys were Clifford "Grandpappy" Wright on fiddle and guitar and the brothers Bill and James Nelson on guitar, guitar and steel guitar, respectively. They were all furniture workers in Asheboro. In the late 1940s, George Pegram also performed with Corbett Bennett and His Mountain Dudes, both in public appearances and over radio station WTNC-Thomasville (see Chapter Nine). Throughout his musical career, no matter what Pegram's band affiliation, George was always straining to take the spotlight. Pegram was such a singular performer that it was hard to play and share the stage with him.

The Pegram family moved to Union Grove at Bascom Lunsford's instigation around 1951, to a small white house off NC 115 near the Wilkes County line. With some of Lunsford's relatives living close by, Bascom may have been trying to take care of George or to keep an eye on him. Pegram played at the State Fair, the Mountain Dance and Folk Festival, and the Burlington Centennial Festival (in 1949). He was a regular at the Carolina Folk Festival until 1956. Lunsford subsequently put Pegram together with harmonica player Red Parham.

Walter "Red" Parham ran Bascom Lunsford's farm and played at Bascom Lunsford's many events, including the Festival in Asheville. George Pegram and Red

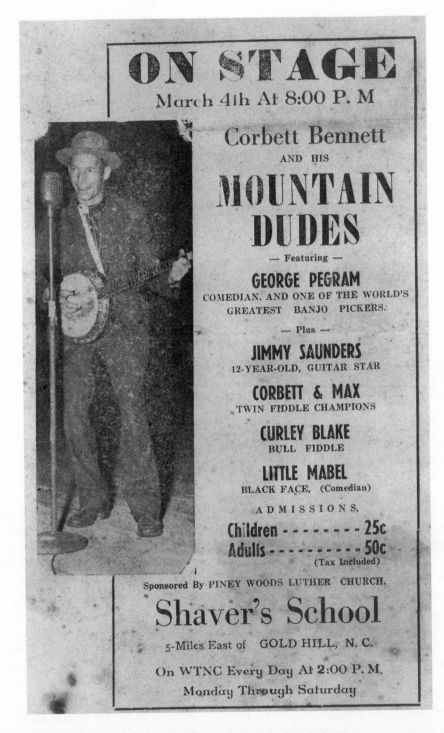

Late 1940s poster for fiddler Corbett Bennett's band, featuring the pictured George Pegram, when they were broadcasting via WTNC-Thomasville. Curley Blake also worked with Olin Berrier. Courtesy Obeira Walker.

Parham had begun performing together by 1955, when they appeared at the Carolina Folk Festival (Smithsonian Folkways recording FT1343). In 1957, Red and George were recorded by Kenneth Goldstein for Riverside Records at Lunsford's home on South Turkey Creek, in Leicester (*Pickin' and Blowin'*, Riverside LP, 12–650). Rounder Records released some other Goldstein recordings, probably from that same period, on the 1976 album *Music from South Turkey Creek*. George Pegram and Red Parham also appeared on several Riverside Records anthologies: *Banjo Songs of the Southern Mountains* and *Southern Mountain Folk Songs and Ballads*. The act ceased active performing when bookings decreased, and financial necessity forced the men to again appear on their own.

No matter how much Lunsford valued George as a performer, Pegram's lack of restraint caused friction between the two men. As Loyal Jones relates,

> For a while, [Bascom] would not have George Pegram on the [Asheville] festival. Pegram became so popular that the crowd would often break into chants of "We want George," and Pegram, somewhat heady over this popularity, might just come forward without Lunsford's nod. This was the sort of thing that Lunsford, creator and boss of the festival, would not tolerate. However, Pegram held an affection and respect for Lunsford [*Minstrel of the Appalachians*: 65].

By the late 1950s, George had become a fixture at the Galax, Virginia, and Union Grove, North Carolina, fiddlers' conventions (see Chapter Six for more about Pegram at Union Grove). At these events, he was often associated with Wayne Johnson's Brushy Mountain Boys of North Wilkesboro, featuring fiddler Jessy "Lost John" Ray (born 1917). Pegram's first award at the Galax came in 1959, when he won first prize in the "Novelty" category. He took second prize on banjo in 1960 and first in 1961, rendering the story of "John Henry" for his win. The Brushy Mountain Boys took third prize in the band competition for 1960 and 1963. In 1963, Pegram also played on the program, executing "John Henry," "Arkansas Traveler," and "Old Rattler." The band possibly attended the 1966 event, when George was "Outstanding Individual Performer," which he won again in 1969. George's Galax performance of "John Henry" from either 1961 or 1963 was recorded for the Folkways Records' 1964 release, *Galax, Virginia, Old Fiddler's Convention* (Smithsonian Folkways recording FA 2435).

The Brushy Mountain Boys appeared at the 1961 Union Grove Fiddler's Convention as a seven-member band. The band was included on the 1962 Folkways album *The 37th Old Time Fiddler's Convention At Union Grove, North Carolina* (Smithsonian Folkways recording FA 2434), and was mentioned as "one of the wilder bands and the winner of this year's [1961] band contest" in the album's notes. It is unclear if Pegram was with the Brushy Mountain Boys at this convention. Photos of the band show a different banjoist. However, the musician on the Folkways recording of "Hitchhiker's Blues" closely resembles George. George Pegram also appeared with fiddler Lost John Ray at the 1967 Union Grove Convention. Additionally, Wayne Johnson recorded a 45-rpm in the early to mid–1960s. Wade Walker (see Chapter Three) financed the record, featuring George and Lost John, for his "Wade" label. The issued tunes were "Mississippi Sawyer" on one side of the record, backed with "Cumberland Gap" and "Arkansas Traveler."

Beginning at this time, Wade's son, Mark Walker, reports

> Pegram worked for the Southern Railroad as an entertainer at their conferences and meetings, traveling all over the country and even to Hawaii. They bought him a banjo, one of the last ones that he had. But I think he pawned it off when he got hurting for money. It was one of the Earl Scruggs models [produced by the Vega company]. They'd buy him new clothes, you know, before they'd take him on those trips. And when he'd come home, he might come into work at the sawmill or somewhere with them good clothes on and they'd have to buy new ones again then.

By the late 1960s, the Pegram family had migrated once again, living for several years near Galax, Virginia. The following article appeared in the *Galax Gazette* July 24, 1969, and aptly describes Pegram's public appearances:

> A perennial favorite at the convention is George Pegram of nearby Fries, Virginia, located like Galax, near the line separating Carroll and Grayson Counties.
> Pegram, grizzled and balding and with only one good eye, is a virtuoso of the bluegrass banjo style. He is a showman, too, likely to put aside his instrument and dance into a loose-jointed shuffle.
> As he attacks the chorus of "Cumberland Gap," his lean old body tilts backward from the knees until his beaten black hat stands parallel to the ground and he is face to face with the August moon. He hoists his banjo high, fingers plucking louder and louder around the melody and a guttural hum hurtles from his throat into a piercing howl guaranteed to boil the blood: "Mmmmm … Yeoww! Way down yonder in Cumberland Gap!"

David Holt, the well-known banjoist and radio and television host, also witnessed his first Pegram performance that summer:

> I will never forget the first time I saw George Pegram play. It was 1969 at the Mountain Dance and Folk Festival in Asheville, North Carolina. He came out on stage grinning from ear to ear, eyes darting around the auditorium like he was getting ready to play a huge practical joke. He was bowlegged and slightly stooped from the weight of his banjo hanging around his neck. You sensed right away this guy was the "real thing."
> Harmonica player Red Parham blew a couple of high, piercing notes to start "Cindy." George grabbed at the strings of his banjo as though he were trying to catch up with Red. Then all of a sudden they hooked into each other's timing and were in perfect sync. It felt like an electric current went through the audience. Spontaneously the entire crowd began hollering and hooting. The music was so raw, so real and so damn good, you couldn't help it. They played through the tune like they were trying to hold onto an out of control freight train. It was one of the most exciting musical experiences I've ever had. And to this day, every time I play "Cindy" I think of how George Pegram made that song come alive.

In 1971, Rounder Records, now the largest independent record label dealing with string band and bluegrass music, released its first album, spotlighting George Pegram. Pegram, at Union Grove for one of the annual conventions in the late 1960s, had been recorded by Charles Faurot, well known for his albums of North Carolina and Virginia string band music made for County Records. Originally offered to Ken Davidson's

Kanawha label for release, it became Rounder's freshman long player when Davidson decided not issue the record. Fred Cockerham (November 3, 1905–July 8, 1980),
at the time living in Low Gap, North Carolina, is the best known of the musicians
accompanying George Pegram on this disc. A fiddler and banjoist famous through
his association with Tommy Jarrell and Kyle Creed, Fred can be heard on many
County releases.

Around the fall of 1969, the Pegrams relocated to Cedar Grove township outside of Asheboro, North Carolina. The move took George closer to his friend and
patron Wade Walker, and to a job with the State Dept of Transportation, overseeing
gravel-spreading crews for Randolph County. About this time, George Pegram
reunited with Red Parham, and the duo played the Mountain Dance and Folk Festival, Berea College, and the Union Grove Fiddlers' Convention. One of George's last
appearances was with Parham at the Asheville Folk Festival, in August of 1974. Mark
Walker describes a late 1973 or early 1974 show by Pegram at Gardner-Webb College:

> He played before the Mission Mountain Wood Band. But George just put on a
> real good show and I remember after the show there, he went down one side of the
> bleachers there and I believe he kissed or hugged every girl on that one side down
> there. And the crowd really did like him.
>
> But just, you know, sitting in the living room playing, I mean, he was a different
> person, almost, the way he'd play. But he would put on the dog in front of a crowd,
> especially if they got to hollerin' some for him and all. That just egged him on then.

George Pegram died September 12, 1974, of bone cancer. He is buried at the
Back Creek Church in Randolph County. According to Mark Walker

> Wade went to a lot of people that we would invite when [George] was at our
> place a playin' and asked them if they would give a little donation toward buying
> [George's] stone and some of Wade's family, they all give a donation and pretty soon,
> why, they had enough to buy it.
>
> He was just, you know, one of the best entertainers, I guess. About anywhere
> he would go, he would just make a crowd go wild. But, you know, he couldn't read
> or write and, you know, just didn't know how to manage money at all. But he could
> talk a good show, you know.

NINE

Broadcasting the Old North State: Stations, Programs and Personalities

"I think the radio coming in more or less enhanced [music], because you could listen to the radio and learn new tunes. Some of the tunes that stayed popular weren't usual around here. Those tunes took on pretty good."

— Howard Saunders (interview with Mac Whatley)

The airways crackled as the sun went down, daytime interference fading away as nighttime power boosts went into effect. Clear channel radio stations (those without any other broadcasters sharing their frequencies) from several states away came into clear focus, calling out on a Saturday night to listeners gathered around a neighbor or relative's receiver. A strange thing was happening: rural musicians throughout the country began hearing themselves over the airways.

Initially, versions of what the players had been performing at community functions emerged randomly between the somewhat alien sounds of classical, pop, jazz, grand opera, and the spoken word. Eventually, if you knew to listen during certain periods of the day — early morning wake up time, midday dinnertime, or Saturday evening time — you could be sure to catch the sounds of southern rural music.

Outside of America's large urban centers, which were home to this country's first radio broadcasters, an unlikely alliance of visionaries was coalescing. This group of tinkerers, civic boosters, and entrepreneurs came together based on their common interest in bringing radio into their communities. As a result of their efforts, small, low-power broadcasters sprang up throughout the 1920s and 1930s, featuring a haphazard and motley assortment of "talent." With no budget whatsoever with which to work, anything went. Whoever might wander into the studio would suddenly find himself "on the air." Almost overnight, southern community members could hear their neighbors over their radio sets.

The reflection of Southern music in the glare of radio was also a double-edged

Cover of WBT-Charlotte's promotional booklet. Undated.

sword. While it could show the South to itself, it also contained cultural distortions added by the broadcasters. To some degree, the "safe" stereotypes utilized in mass market images of "hillbillies and crackers" served to mold and to offset southern attitudes and music.

When Piedmont stations began to sign on, they looked to the preexisting powerhouses in Nashville, Chicago, and Cincinnati for inspiration. Management saw how successful the national Opry and Barn Dance programs had become, and so wanted their own local version for broadcast.

This chapter touches on some of the principal Piedmont North Carolina broadcasters of live country music in the heyday of the 1920s through the early 1950s. The focus here is on the stations and their schedules, including some short biographies of broadcasting musicians. In Chapter Ten, the lives of three string-band radio stars and their associates are given in-depth profiles, and the lifestyle of these musical broadcasters is discussed.

The Grand Ole Opry

Even after the advent of stations within the state, many Piedmont radios stayed tuned on Saturday nights to the Grand Ole Opry. This pioneering radio "barn dance" (variety) show originated (and still originates) from WSM in Nashville. The National Life and Accident Insurance Company had sponsored the station's construction in 1925, and brought in George D. Hay to manage the broadcaster. Fresh from his success with the WLS Barn Dance in Chicago, Hay began what was to become the Opry at the end of that year (Wolfe, *A Good-Natured Riot*, 4–11).

Originally, the show had to be received directly from Nashville. Eventually, it appeared over local radio stations like WSJS-Winston-Salem as a network broadcast. Other country music programs caught the attention of Piedmont listeners. But none captured their hearts in the 1920s and early 1930s like the Grand Ole Opry.

The popularity of the Opry is shown by the number of performers from the program that regularly performed in the Piedmont. Opry artists toured extensively through North Carolina, especially during the post–World War II era. These included Uncle Dave Macon (1938, 1939, 1940), Sarie and Sallie (1940), Ernest Tubb (1948), Eddy Arnold (1945), Hank Snow (1950, 1951), Bill Monroe (1939–1943, 1946–1947, 1949–1951, 1954, 1955–1956), Flatt and Scruggs (1952), and Roy Acuff (1938–1940, 1949–1950, 1954, 1957), as well as many of the Grand Ole Opry package (multiple act) shows (Hatch Print invoices, Country Music Foundation).

WBT: "Watch Buick Travel"

North Carolina's first radio station squealed to life during April of 1922 in the city of Charlotte. Amateur radio buff Fred Laxton carried the seeds for the original 100-watt station from his home to the Independence Building on the downtown square of the Queen City. When C. C. Coddington, the local dealer of Buick automobiles, purchased the broadcaster in 1926, he claimed its call letters, WBT, stood (not surprisingly) for "Watch Buick Travel." The station increased its power to 500 watts, and, by 1928, presented its first banjo and fiddle music on the air, in the performances of the Woodlawn String Band and Fisher Hendley's Carolina Tarheels (Coulter and Rumble, 4–5; WBT website).

Walter Fisher Hendley (born April 1891), a native of Anson County, learned to play on a banjo he made from a cheese box, a stick of chord wood, and a black cat's hide. Hendley attended Trinity College (now Duke University) during the 1914–15 school year and played two-finger style banjo with the College Glee Club. When Fisher joined the staff of WBT, it was still a 100-watt station. By that time, Hendley had already recorded for Okeh Records (see Chapter Seven). Fisher stayed with WBT into the 1930s, helping to start the Barn Dance program sponsored by Crazy Water Crystals (*Fisher Hendley Book*; Art Satherley ledgers; Ahrens-Striblin, *Old Time Country*, 8).

THE CRAZY WATER COMPANY RADIO PROGRAM: "CRAZY WATER AND CRAZY BANDS"

By 1929, WBT had a 50,000-watt signal that covered two-thirds of North Carolina, where one out of every seven families had a radio (Coulter and Rumble 7; WBT website). The Crazy Water Company, aware of the possible marketing opportunities for their products, sent their representatives into this region of radio listeners.

Crazy Water Crystals' association with string-band music in North Carolina began when James Wesley Fincher came to Charlotte to serve as president of the local office. Shortly after his arrival in August of 1933, Fincher arranged to sponsor a country music broadcast over WBT. The original Crazy Water program was carried over WBT on Tuesday and Thursday mornings at 8:15 AM and Mondays, Wednesdays, Fridays just after noon. This proved so successful that programming was expanded to include WSOC-Charlotte, WBIG-Greensboro, and WPTF-Raleigh, as well as other stations in North and South Carolina and Georgia. Ultimately, Crazy Water and WBT had an immensely effective partnership lasting until 1937, when a downturn in sales ended sponsorship by Crazy Water (Ahrens, "Crazy Water Crystals," 56–60; Coulter and Rumble, 7; Grundy 1591–1620).

In March 1934, Fincher added a barn dance to the schedule. Initially held in the station's studios, the Crazy Barn Dance eventually became a road show, spending the better part of a year-and-a-half touring and holding talent contests at various area auditoriums. A live audience paid to witness the performances by a dozen unpaid bands each Saturday night, talent eager for the opportunity to broadcast their music over the Charlotte powerhouse (Coulter and Rumble, 10).

One of the groups the laxative company brought to North Carolina went by the name of the Tennessee Ramblers. Led by Dick Hartmann, the band had worked in Pittsburgh and Rochester for the firm before relocating to Charlotte (Coulter and Rumble, 4–5). The Tennessee Ramblers first heard on WBT included Dick Hartman, William "Horse Thief Harry" Blair (born August 1912), Kenneth "Pappy" Wolfe, Jack

The assembled cast of WBT's Crazy Barn Dance, 1934–1937. Fisher Hendley, talent scout and master of ceremonies and a banjoist in his own right, stands to the left. The Broome Brothers String Band is standing to Fisher's left, with fiddler Ray, possibly mandolinist Homer, guitarist Lee Roy with father J. H. directly behind him. Next to them, probably, are guitarist Bob and mandolinist Joe. Crazy Water's local representatives, the father and son team of J. W. and Hubert T. Fincher, sit front and center. Fiddler Shell K. Allen's Kannapolis W.O.W. String Band is directly behind the Finchers. Holding his National brand guitar is Arthur "Kid" Goodman, followed by Haywood Suther (banjo-mandolin), Allen, Carl Dayvault (guitar) and Raymond L. Thornburg (string bass). J. E. Mainer's Mountaineers fill up the majority of the next to last row. Wade, J. E.'s younger brother, stands with his banjo at the left, followed by J. E. (fiddle), probably John Love (guitar) and the Dixon Brothers, Dorsey and Howard, guitar and Hawaiian guitar. Courtesy Rachel Wiles.

Gillette, and Cecil Campbell. Campbell was the only North Carolinian in the Ramblers. Born during 1911 in Stokes County, Cecil's first radio job was over WSJS-Winston-Salem. Campbell had been a member of the Tennessee Ramblers since 1932, when he joined the band in Pittsburgh (Coulter and Rumble, 30).

Another act that proved immensely popular with North Carolinians was the Monroe Brothers. At the end of 1935, the siblings, sponsored by Texas Crystals, were transferred to the Carolinas to appear on stations in Columbia, South Carolina, and Charlotte, North Carolina. A competitor of Crazy Water Crystals, the Texas variety, remembered older sibling Charlie Monroe, were "just exactly like Crazy Crystals only [with] a little larger box!" Unfortunately, Texas Crystals was no match for Crazy Water in the Carolinas, and Bill and Charlie ended up working at WBT for Crazy Water (Monroe and Green interview).

Most of the bands that appeared on the Crazy Water programs, however, were made up of area talent. Many were found through the local appearances of the Barn

Dance and retained their amateur status. The Broome Brothers Band from Wingate, J. A. Farrington's Carolina Melody Boys of Davidson, Salisbury's Hilo Hawaiians, Leroy Smith's Moonlight Serenaders of Mt. Gilead, the Wadesboro W.O.W. String Band led by banjoist DeWitt Wheless, harmonica specialist M. P. Medford, Shell K. Allen's String Band from Kannapolis and the Rambling Trio of Granite Falls, all made contact with Crazy Water and performed during the Barn Dance broadcasts.

Others made their own way to the station independent of the barn dance, anxious for the break into show business that would take them out of the area mills. Dewitt "Snuffy" Jenkins (October 27, 1908–April 30, 1990), a native of Harris, North Carolina, began playing the banjo professionally on WBT. His future partner, Homer Lee "Pappy" Sherrill (March 23, 1915–November 30, 2001), traveled the 25 miles from his home at Sherrills Ford south to Charlotte to fiddle over the station. Sherrill's East Hickory String Band became the Crazy Hickory Nuts under Fincher's guidance (Coulter and Rumble, 7, 21–22; *Crazy Barn Dance and Crazy Bands*).

Associates of the radio station discovered other musicians, like the brothers Mainer. Wade Mainer was born April 21, 1907, near Weaverville, just north of Asheville in the North Carolina mountains. After moving to Concord in the mid–1920s to work in a cotton mill, Wade joined his older brother J. E. (Joseph Emmett, July 20, 1898–June 12, 1971) in making music. In the early 1930s, the Mainers were popular at local dances and fiddlers' conventions. After adding John Love and Claude "Zeke" Morris (May 9, 1916–August 5, 1999) they named themselves "Mainer's Mountaineers," and broadcast over WSOC, Gastonia, North Carolina (which came on the air in 1933) (Coulter and Rumble, 26–7; *Spottswood* 53–55; Wallace). In 1934, they caught the attention of Fisher Hendley and Crazy Water Crystals, who sponsored the band on WBT-Charlotte and WPTF-Raleigh. Their WBT programs ran for 15 minutes, 5 days a week, and were broadcast each morning and afternoon. They also joined Hendley's group, the Tobacco Tags of Gastonia (George Wade, Luther Baucom, and Reid Summey) and the Dixon Brothers duo from Rockingham on Crazy Water's Saturday night barn dance show.

CONSOLIDATED ROYAL CHEMICAL CORPORATION: "IT'S BRIARHOPPER TIME"

An equally important sponsor on WBT was Consolidated Royal Chemical Corporation, best known for the tonic Peruna. Consolidated, along with station announcer Charlie Crutchfield, is responsible for the program most identified with Charlotte radio. From 1933 until 1951, it was "Briarhopper Time."

The Briarhoppers were more of a stock company than one specific band of musicians, and it seems that every member of the WBT staff were Briarhoppers at one time or another. This included Fred Kirby (born July 19, 1910), a native of Charlotte. It took a move to Columbia, South Carolina, for Kirby to meet Charles Crutchfield, at that time an announcer on WIS-radio. Fred Kirby left Crutchfield in Columbia, and beat a path back to Charlotte and WBT in 1928. For the next 11 years, Fred yodeled his way through many a radio program. Except for a short hiatus during World War II, Kirby stayed at WBT into the 1980s. He worked with the Briarhoppers and moved

The Woodmen of the World String Band of Kannapolis inside the WBT radio studio. Announcer and inventor of the Briarhoppers Charles Crutchfield sits front right by the microphone. Musicians left to right are guitarist Carl Dayvault, cellist Raymond Thornburg, banjo-mandolinist Haywood Suther, leader and fiddler Shell Allen and guitarist "Dolph" Dayvault. Charlotte, Mecklenburg County, 1930s. Courtesy Rachel Wiles.

into children's programming in 1951. His television show for kids was still on the air as late as 1985. Other members of the Hoppers during the 1940s and 1950s included Garnett "Fiddlin' Hank" Warren (born April 1, 1909) from Mount Airy, North Carolina, Don White (born September 1909; real name: Walden Whytsell) from West Virginia, and Shannon Grayson (September 30, 1916–1993). Warren had come to WBT in 1936 as a member of the Tennessee Ramblers; he became a Briarhopper in the early 1940s (Colter, 18). Don White arrived in Charlotte as a member of the Crazy Bucklebusters. Roy "Whitey" Grant (born April 7, 1916), of Shelby, North Carolina, and Arval Hogan (born July 24, 1911, in Robbinsville, died September 12, 2003 in Charlotte), left their jobs at the Firestone Cotton Mill in Gastonia to become a part of WBT history (WBT website; Coulter and Rumble, *The Charlotte Country Music Story*, p4–5, 10–11, 17–18, 23).

During the 1940s, the Briarhoppers expanded their influence through three other regionally or nationally distributed radio shows. The Dixie Jamboree was Claude Casey's Saturday morning workout. Casey, a South Carolinian, (born September 13, 1912), was in Charlotte from 1941 until 1953 (Coulter and Rumble, 20). The Carolina Hayride took over the Charlotte Armory on Saturday nights for a barn dance. Carolina Calling ended the weekend on Sunday mornings with a mix of country and popular talent.

WBT radio star Fred Kirby at left, with Bob Phillips at right, broadcasting for Philco, circa 1940.

Carolina Calling's most famous performer was Arthur "Guitar Boogie" Smith (not to be confused with the Grand Ole Opry fiddler). Smith joined the WBT cast of musicians in 1943, moving to a featured slot on the Carolina Hayride, which broadcast nationally on Saturday afternoons.

Born April 1, 1921, Arthur Smith grew up south of Charlotte in South Carolina. His father led the local brass band, and Arthur was pressed into service as a trumpeter at an early age. He soon picked up various stringed instruments, including the fiddle and guitar. In a famous story, Arthur relates how his first professional group, a Dixieland jazz band, became a string band:

> We nearly starved to death until one day we changed our style: we had been doing a daily radio show ... as the Arthur Smith Quartet. One Friday we threw down our trumpet, clarinet and trombone and picked up the fiddle, accordion and guitar.... The next Monday we came back on the radio program as Arthur Smith and the Carolina Crackerjacks [Coulter and Rumble, 29].

In September 1938, Smith and his Crackerjacks made their first recordings, for an RCA field session held in Rock Hill, South Carolina, about thirty miles to the south of Charlotte. Recording proved to be Arthur's forte. In 1945, after purchasing an early electric guitar, Smith cut the guitar instrumental "Guitar Boogie," which brought him to national prominence at the top of the country and pop charts. When banjoist Don Reno was a member of the band, "Feuding Banjos" was released on Monument Records. This 1955 recording was used as the basis for "Dueling Banjos" in the 1973 movie *Deliverance*.

Arthur Smith was also an area recording studio and record label pioneer. As Smith stated to Mike Collins in an interview for public radio in Charlotte, he got tired of traveling out of town to record, and so built his own studio in an out building on his property. When business flourished, the studio moved to its own building on Monroe Road. Among the famous recordings made there were James Brown's hit single "Papa's Got a Brand New Bag."

By the 1950s, Arthur's brothers Sonny and Ralph had joined Smith for "The Corner Store" on WBT radio, which mixed music with rube humor. During the same time period, WBTV went on the air, and the Arthur Smith group was a common sight on local telecasts. One of the best-known musicians working with Smith during this period was guitarist Tommy Faille. Born in September 1928 in Lancaster,

The Arthur Smith Show troupe broadcasting over WBTV, Charlotte. Left to right, Arthur's brother Ralph (accordion), Carl Hunt (banjo), Carlene Howell, Wayne Haas (electric bass), Arthur Smith (electric guitar), Kay Murray, Jim Buchanan (fiddle) and Tommy Faile (guitar). Circa 1965. Courtesy Glee Aronld.

South Carolina, Faille had been a member of Fisher Hendley's Aristocratic Pigs, as well as Jenkins and Sherrill's Hired Hands before joining Arthur Smith's Cracker-jacks in 1951. Faille also hosted his own program from 1969 until 1975 (Coulter and Rumble, 20–21).

Today, Arthur Smith remains active. He has been producing releases of southern gospel for his own record label, as well as hosting and performing on several series for the North Carolina Public Television network.

WPTF: "We Protect the Family"

North Carolina's and the Piedmont's second radio station originated in the state capital of Raleigh. The broadcaster, which came on line October 25, 1924, began as a 50-watter with the call letters WFBQ. Power was doubled within a year and the station was renamed WRCO, for the Wynne Radio Company. Several more years passed, and WRCO was acquired by the Durham Life Insurance Company. Their motto, "We Protect the Family," was abbreviated for the new moniker, WPTF. The station's power was boosted to 500 watts and its location moved into the basement of the Durham Life building (Baron; "Story of WPTF," Raleigh *News and Observer*, April 26, 1942).

In the early days, WPTF programmed country music in the same haphazard way as did other broadcasters. But it was Crazy Water Crystals that, once again, put the station on the map. As was the case at WBT, Saturday nights featured the Crazy Barn Dance broadcasts. J. W. Fincher's son, Hubert Thomas, known as "Uncle Tom," played host to a mixture of local and professional groups as the show toured auditoriums in the eastern Piedmont. If anything, the Crazy Barn Dance appearances were more popular in the Raleigh area than in Charlotte. For example, a show held in Burlington on June 20, 1936, drew 3,000 people; unfortunately, the auditorium only held 1500 and half the attendees had to be turned away!

Not surprisingly, the amateur bands that populated the WPTF Crazy Barn Dance roster mostly came from eastern North Carolina. These included the Alamance Ramblers (Dewey Kimbro, Frank Mann, Buster Mills, and Hulan Norris) from Burlington, Roxboro's Allensville Stringband, The Lonesome Trailers and C. R. Pittman's Night Owl Band, both from Raleigh, Benson's Johnston County Ramblers, the Midnight Ramblers from Henderson, and harmonica player J. H. Bledsoe and his Melon Growers from near Lumberton.

The Crazy Mountaineers—J. E. and Wade Mainer, Boyden Carpenter, and Zeke Morris—had come over from WBT and served as the "host" band for the Saturday night broadcasts (*Souvenir of the Crazy Barn Dance and the Crazy Bands*). In mid–1936, after about a year at WPTF, Wade and J.E. decided to each lead their own groups (Spottswood, 53–55). J. E. Mainer formed a band with Zeke's brother George Morris and Leonard Stokes, calling themselves "Handsome and Samba." Eventually, J. E. hooked up with Gurney Thomas and his group for broadcasts in Greensboro (see Chapter Ten). Wade, in the company of Zeke and Wiley Morris, left for Asheville radio station WWNC.

In the later part of 1937, Wade Mainer and the Morris brothers returned to WPTF. They landed the spot from 7:15–7:30 AM immediately following the Monroe Brothers. Sponsored by the Zebulon Supply Company, the band, now called the Smiling Rangers, gained fiddler Homer "Pappy" Sherrill and lost Wade. Sherrill had spent the intervening years working for Crazy Water in Charlotte and as a member of the Blue Sky Boys act in Atlanta, Georgia. Sherrill and the Morrises lasted until April 1938, when they moved to Danville, Virginia, and WBTM-radio (Erbsen). In 1939, Wiley and Zeke Morris, along with fiddler Walter "Tiny" Dodson, left Danville to appear over Salisbury radio for around six to eight months (*Wiley, Zeke and Homer*).

Other professionals working for Crazy Water at WPTF included recording artists such as the Dixon Brothers and Norwood Tew; Leonard Stokes and Mitchell Parker, known as the Dixie Melody Boys, who also broadcast over their home station of WMFR (see Chapter Ten for more about Parker); the Leatherman Sisters from Hickory; and James B. Grady, "Champion Fiddler from Eastern North Carolina," who

The Monroe Brothers, Bill on mandolin and Charlie on guitar, flank their announcer and manager Byron Parker while appearing over WBT-Charlotte, circa 1935.

brought his Huckleberry Pickers over from WBT (*Souvenir of the Crazy Barn Dance and the Crazy Bands*; *Crazy Barn Dance and the Crazy Bands*).

If live appearances by the Crazy Water Barn Dance got Piedmont dwellers to turn on their radio sets, it was the Monroe Brothers that made them sit up and listen. Like the Mainers, Charlie and Bill Monroe migrated from Charlotte to Raleigh. Their long-time announcer, Byron Parker, had split off from the duo in order to host his own radio program over WIS in Columbia, South Carolina. By the end of May 1937, Charlie and Bill were broadcasting their tight harmony singing and lightening fast instrumentals for Seiberling Tires from 7–7:15 A.M. weekday mornings over WPTF (Smith, 43–46; Monroe/Green; *Worthville: a Lost Mill Village*, 158). However, without Parker's moderating influence, the tempers of the two Monroes got the best of them. In the spring of 1938, in the heat of an argument based more on a personality clash than any real disagreement, the hottest country act in the Carolinas broke up (Smith: 44–46). Each assembled his own group. Bill, although remaining popular in North Carolina, chose to eventually to make Nashville his base of operations. After a short break, Charlie would return and make the Piedmont his home for the best years of his career (see Chapter Ten).

"TOBACCO TAGS" AND "SWINGBILLIES"

Before the Monroe Brothers were tearing up the airwaves, the bands most associated with WPTF were the Tobacco Tags and the Swingbillies. These groups with overlapping personnel were two of the most popular in the Raleigh area. The Tobacco Tags were formed in Western North Carolina by Henry Luther "Luke" Baucom (born December 18, 1902) of McDowell County on mandolin and guitarist Edgar Reid Summey (born June 9, 1903) from Gaston County. Samuel Lee Pridgen (born February 13, 1910 in Henderson, North Carolina), guitarist and bass player, joined the group in May of 1931. After the addition of Pridgen, the group began broadcasting their mix of sentimental and novelty songs over WPTF (*Songs of the Tobacco Tags*).

Sam Pridgen had begun playing at the age of fourteen, when Sam's father took five dollars from his wages at the Durham Hosiery Mill to purchase his son a Stella brand guitar. Pridgen was more influenced by crooners like Gene Austin of "My Blue Heaven" fame (Sam even sang this song at dances) than by the old square dance music. Sam learned the modern, closed chord guitar style rather than the older, open chord back up used for house dances and the like. After figuring out that he could make as much money for one night's work in a dance hall as he would for one week's labor in the cotton mill, Sam Pridgen went professional (Ponder, 1C; *Durham Morning*, date unknown, 1c).

By 1936, the Tobacco Tags, with Hubert Fincher as their announcer, were on WPTF at noon and 5:45 P.M. daily and at 1 P.M. every Sunday. By that time, mandolinist George Wade had joined the group, replacing Pridgen, who had moved on to the Swingbillies (*Crazy Barn Dance and Crazy Bands*).

The original Swingbillies were the quartet of vocalist James Clay "Charlie Dunk" Poole, Jr. (December 2, 1912–July 15, 1968), Garfield Hammonds on banjo, Harvey Lloyd "Hash House" Ellington (born November 9, 1910 in Warren County) on fiddle and guitar, and Ray Williams playing the guitar. The group mixed the hillbilly songs of Dunk's father Charlie Poole, Sr., the famous recording artist and performer of the previous decade (see Chapter Seven), and the modern swing and jazz pieces performed by Williams (Rorrer, 17, 61–2). Dunk Poole had been schooled in performing as a member of his father's stage shows. He later fell in with Harvey Ellington, and the two had many adventures while out playing music.

Harvey told this oft-repeated tale to writers Bill Phillips and David Newton:

> Looking for steadier work, [he and Dunk] became the musicians for Doc Haithcock's medicine show that amounted to a small circus complete with acrobatics, ventriloquists, and a flaming knife throwing act. Ellington's job was to play a tune and draw a crowd. Then Dunk Poole would warm up the audience with one of his father's old songs. By that time the audience was ready to buy the medicine that Doc Haithcock peddled and Ellington had just mixed up back stage.

In the spring of 1932, Doc Haithcock abandoned Poole and Ellington in the hamlet of Wallace. The musicians drew upon all of their skills, playing wherever they could and passing the hat to survive (Phillips, 3–4).

In 1933, the unnamed group worked for another medicine show, this one owned by Doc Lee. Three years later, the band, by this time including Williams and Hammonds, hooked up with WPTF. Under the sponsorship of Blackwood Filling Station, they took over the noontime slot from the Tobacco Tags, moving the Tags back to 12:15 P.M. Graham Poyner, an announcer for the station, named the band "the Swingbillies," and they were in business. Sam Pridgen joined sometime during their year on WPTF, and J. B. Clark, another of the station's announcers, helped them to make contact with Eli Oberstein of Victor Records. Oberstein liked what he heard, and recorded them in Charlotte for Victor's Bluebird subsidiary. The Swingbillies waxed ten sides, including the pop tunes "St. Louis Blues," "Melancholy Baby," and "I Can't Give You Anything But Love," along with covering Charlie Poole, Sr.'s, hit, "Leavin' Home."

But, by 1939, the Swingbillies were no more. According to writer Dixie B. O'Connor, Graham Poyner dismissed the band from WPTF because he disapproved of Dunk Poole's drinking. Sam Pridgen remembers that they weren't making money, just surviving, and this contributed to their demise as well (Rorrer, 17, 61–2; "Playin' the South," *Leader Magazine*, 1, 3, 5).

Harvey Ellington left the Swingbillies to join the Tobacco Tags in September of 1938, then sponsored over WPTF by the Robertson Chemical Company (*Songs of the Tobacco Tags*). The Tags migrated to Richmond, Virginia, where Sam Pridgen was then working with the Caroginians. Pridgen rejoined his old group, which returned briefly to Raleigh radio in 1942 and 1943, before breaking up as the various members joined the military. *(Songs of the Tobacco Tags*; Ponder, p1C; *Durham Morning ?*, p1c+)

BLUEGRASS IS ON THE AIR

After World War II, live music continued unabated over WPTF. Some performers active before the war, like Harvey Ellington, continued to work the station

(Ponder, 1C; *Durham Morning* ?, p1c). The *Raleigh News and Observer* began operating a competing radio station in 1948, bringing in the brothers Bill and Earl Bolick, known professionally as the Blue Sky Boys, to initiate the new enterprise. Although the Bolicks were given two slots daily, it was hard to draw listeners away from the established WPTF. In addition, a polio epidemic closed theaters, causing the cancellation for many of their live appearances. These and other factors caused the Blue Sky Boys to leave Raleigh in March of 1949 (Bolick).

Back at WPTF, management was leaning more toward the new bluegrass sound pioneered by Bill Monroe, Lester Flatt, and Earl Scruggs. The first of the groups known to bring this new music to Raleigh were Danny and Charles, the Bailey Brothers. In 1949, after working for WSM, and at WNOX and WROL in Knoxville, this brother duo brought their band — Willis Hogsed on banjo, L. E. White on fiddle, Junior Tullock on bass, and Carl Butler on guitar — to WPTF. Soon afterwards, Hoke Jenkins came in on banjo and Clarence "Tater" Tate replaced White on the fiddle. In 1950, this band recorded two 78-rpm singles (four songs) at the WPTF studios, which the Baileys released on their own label, Canary Records. By late in 1951, Johnnie Whisnant was the banjoist and Chubby Collier the fiddler with Dan and Charles. Slim and Wilma Martin (see Chapter Ten) also worked with the Bailey Brothers during their stint in Raleigh (Rounder Collective).

Throughout the time the Bailey Brothers were in Raleigh, Mac Wiseman and Clyde Moody, both former sideman of Bill Monroe, worked at WPTF. Lester Flatt and Earl Scruggs (born January 6, 1924 near Shelby), in the company of Everett Lilly on mandolin, Chuck Johnson on bass, and Art Wooten or Benny Martin playing fiddle, overlapped some of the Bailey's stay, which ended in early 1952 (Ewing, 4; Godbey, 56–67).

WBIG: "Where Business is Good"

Residents of Greensboro were blessed with North Carolina's third radio broadcaster when, in 1926, the Wayne Nelson Radio Company initiated programming over the ten-watt WNRC. Actually, the city had an earlier failed radio experiment, WQAZ, which existed in 1921 and 1922 under the sponsorship of the *Greensboro Daily News*. During the WNRC's early years, the usual procession of aspiring guitarists, fiddlers, banjoists, and singers paraded in front of the studio microphones.

In 1934, the Jefferson Standard Life Insurance Company purchased WNRC and it became a network affiliate of CBS ("Anniversary of WBIG Planned," Greensboro *Daily News*, August 20, 1951). WNRC was renamed WBIG ("Where Business Is Good"), but the station continued to host string band music.

"PRESENTING THE 'WORST MOMENTS IN MUSIC' EACH WEEKDAY AFTERNOON"

During the War years of the 1940s, Johnny Harris led a popular string band, the Carolina Ramblers, which appeared on WBIG, by this time located in the basement of the O. Henry Hotel. Johnny, a fiddler and comedian, worked at Cone Mills in

Greensboro. At that time, a sharply critical newspaper reviewer, who obviously was not a fan of country music, mentioned Harris: "In direct contrast with Michael's [Dance] band is the hillbilly aggregation, Johnny Harris and His Ramblers, presenting the 'worst moments in music' each weekday afternoon at 4:30, under the sponsorship of Regal Jewelers" (*Democrat*, 9).

Around the same period, one of Johnny's fans was a schoolgirl in the Siler City area. After hurrying home every day after class in order to hear Harris's afternoon broadcasts, she ran away to Greensboro to meet her heartthrob. Interestingly enough, everything worked out, and the couple was married at the end of the 1940s.

"EASY" JONES

Many listeners and musicians that I interviewed about the golden age of live radio in the Piedmont spoke just as affectionately about the announcers as they did the musicians. While an in-depth discussion of station announcers is beyond the range of this book, one does warrant a mention here. "Easy" Jones (approx. 1903–July 11, 1969) worked for most of the stations mentioned in this chapter throughout his long career. Elbert Z. Jones, Jr., was born in Lakeland, Florida, and studied journalism at the University of Florida in Gainesville. Jones was on the staff of the University of Florida station, WRUF, hosting live country music during the same year (1930) as "Red" Barber began his sports casting career there. His laid-back on air presence led to the nickname "Easy" (which was obviously suggested by his first two initials) and to a string of radio jobs in North Carolina and Georgia. From WBIG-Greensboro to Atlanta for the Crazy Water Company and then to ownership of WMFR (*Souvenir of the Crazy Barn Dance and the Crazy Bands*), Easy spent ten years moving from job to job before landing in Burlington. In 1941, Jones signed on WBBB, remaining with the station until 1968, one year before his death (*Daily Times-News*, July 12, 1969: 1, 3).

WSJS: *Winston-Salem Journal Sentinel*

North Carolina's fifth radio station and the fourth broadcaster in the Piedmont was sponsored by the *Winston-Salem Journal-Sentinel* newspaper. Abbreviated to WSJS, it signed on Good Friday 1930, five years after initial plans were formulated to give the twin cities a radio station (*Twin City Sentinel*, February 19, 1925: 1, 19).

To begin with, the 100-watt station occupied two rooms in the rear of the periodical's newsroom on North Marshall Street, filling the fourth floor of the Journal building with fiddles, banjos, and guitars. As Worth Bacon wrote in the *Journal-Sentinel*'s April 17, 1960, edition, the string bands would use the newspaper's offices to warm up before going on the air, often making it impossible for the staff to work!

Commencing April 17, when a minister signed on the station with a prayer and the Mocksville Stringed Band played "Whistling Rufus," "Bully of the Town," "Leave Me With A Smile," and "In the Evening By the Moonlight" (*Twin City Sentinel*, April 17, 1930: 1), the *Sentinel* reported on the daily schedule for WSJS. Not surprisingly,

Boyden Carpenter had worked for Winston-Salem broadcaster WSJS and as a member of the Crazy Water-sponsored Crazy Mountaineers at WPTF. Carpenter joined upstart WAIR when the station first signed on the air. Sponsored by Wagon Wheel Tobacco, his early morning radio program as "the Hillbilly Kid" included Curly Proctor (left) and Bob Harp (right). Winston-Salem, Forsyth County, late 1930s.

it was a broadcast day filled mostly with popular music and features such as Dr. E. J. Moore discussing "Your Dog and His Hot Weather Problems" (*Twin City Sentinel*, August 11, 1930: 12). But string bands were well represented. A total of 99 appearances by 30 separate country musicians or groups occurred during the first half year of operations. Twenty-one string bands and five Hawaiian guitar aggregations performed, along with a handful of harp blowers, banjoists, and solo singers. Most appeared only once or twice, although two of the Hawaiian guitar duos were regulars, with ten to twelve spots over the course of a similar number of weeks. With a few exceptions, the musicians all played at night and mostly on Thursday and Friday evenings, in sharp contrast to the later standard of early morning and mid-day time slots for weekday country music broadcasts. The station was possibly trying to draw some of the audience away from the Grand Ole Opry as well, as some forty Saturday night slots were filled with string bands and their ilk during this initial time period of broadcasting.

Most of those groups were amateur bands from the locales around the Twin Cities. However, at least two of the bands that performed in the early day of WSJS had made records and made some attempt at making money from their music. The Red Fox Chasers from the mountains northwest of Winston-Salem included the talents of a mechanic, a farmer, a truck driver, and a tobacco factory worker. Fiddler Guy Brooks, harmonica player and vocalist Bob Cranford, guitarist and singer A. P. Thompson, and banjoist Paul Miles featured a mixture of dance tunes and the folk and popular sentimental songs of the day. The quartet recorded for Gennett Records of Richmond, Indiana, performed at local schoolhouses and fiddlers' conventions, and broadcast on the radio (Nevins).

The trio of Simmons, Miller, and Lewis came down from Stokes County to appear on WSJS. Charles Matt Simmons (July 19, 1894–October 22, 1959), a guitarist and singer, and vocalist Frank Miller, both from Lawsonville, had recorded at the Okeh Records 1927 Winston-Salem session and for Edison in New Jersey during September of 1928 (see Chapter Seven). Simmons, a rural mail carrier and World War I veteran, and Miller, who ran a factory making ax handles, were joined by local farmer John Lewis (August 27, 1894–August 9, 1969) of Danbury on fiddle for several radio broadcasts (Rorrer, 45; Simmons Discharge papers).

By 1937, the noise from the crowds of performers got to be too much for the reporters at the *Journal* and so the station moved its studios to the Robert E. Lee Hotel (*Twin City Sentinel*, January 21, 1967, "Station is Moved"). During the same year, George Walker, an engineer at WSJS, jumped ship to start the rival broadcaster WAIR. With studios also located in the Robert E. Lee Hotel (Barron), the upstart went head to head with WSJS by utilizing some of the same talent as the older station. Musicians on WAIR included Boyden Carpenter broadcasting for Wagon Wheel Smoking Tobacco (songbook) and Charlie Bowman's (August 17, 1912–April 2, 2000) Blue Ridge Ramblers from Patrick County, Virginia.

Roy Hall and His Blue Ridge Entertainers, one of the best-known groups between Roanoke and Charlotte, also chose WAIR as their base of operations. From the fall of 1938 through sometime in 1939, the Entertainers hosted a half-hour program at 6:30 A.M. sponsored by Dr. Pepper. Guitarist and singer Roy Davis Hall (January 6, 1907–May 16, 1943) came from Haywood County, North Carolina, and led a group

Page from souvenir booklet for Roy Hall and his Blue Ridge Entertainers. Sponsored by Dr Pepper on WAIR Radio in Winston-Salem, this nationally known group included Roy Hall (vocals and guitar), Tommy "Magnus" [sic] (fiddle), Buck Buchanan (banjo), Bill Brown and Wayne Watson (guitars). Circa 1938.

that included Georgian Tommy Magness on fiddle, who later played with Bill Monroe and Roy Acuff (Tribe, *Roy Hall and His Blue Ridge Entertainers*).

WMFR: "We Make Furniture Right"

In 1935, High Point radio station WMFR signed on the air. Wayne Nelson, who had built the first Greensboro broadcaster, entered into a partnership with a local drugstore owner to construct the facility ("Approval Given," High Point Enterprise, May 5, 1935: 1). While it was not a high-powered station, string bands flocked to the radio studios located at 156½ South Main Street (High Point City Directories).

Robert Moses Workman (September 19, 1907–March 25, 1980) was among the group of musicians broadcasting over WMFR in the nascent days of the station's history. After hearing his uncle Oder Workman play the fiddle, Bob used an old violin neck and scraps of wood to assemble an instrument. It was during his youth that Bob convened his first band. The Silver Hill Buddies, as they were named, played concerts at local high school auditoriums. After a stint at WSJS, the Buddies moved over to WMFR. In 1936, Workman, under his performing name of "Uncle Henry" (not to be confused with the others who used this nickname, see Chapter Ten), was fiddling with the Arizona Wild Cats, a local western band that included the brothers Vernon "Fuzzy" and Walter Eckomer "Eck" Dorset[t]. By 1938, these groups had

The "Happy Hillbillies" pose inside the studios of WMFR Radio. Notice that this was not a room dedicated to live music as was found at the larger stations, but the studio from which all the broadcaster's programs emanated. Left to right are Hal Harrison (announcer), Bob Workman (fiddle), Virgie and Vivan, Raymond Waisner (guitar) and Vern Dorset (guitar). High Point, Guilford County, circa 1938. Courtesy Bryce Workman.

evolved into the Happy Hillbillies, and included Raymond Waisner and Vern Dorset on guitar (see Chapter Four). Bob Workman was known during this time as a "trick" fiddler, because he played the instrument behind his back, under his legs, and also held the bow with his lower extremities and moved the violin across it — although it is hard to gauge how WMFR's listeners reacted to stunts that they could not see! Throughout all these years, Bob Workman was unable to support a family with his earnings from music, so, he held jobs either in hosiery mills or furniture factories (Workman and Green interview).

Besides broadcasts by individual groups, a WMFR barn dance program was another feature of those early years. Titled the Dixie Jamboree, the show was presented before a live audience in an auditorium over the Belks store downtown.

PHOTOGRAPHER PAUL L. SMITH:
"WE PHOTOGRAPH ANYTHING-ANYWHERE-ANYTIME"

The guardian angel of string musicians on WMFR was a local merchant named Paul L. Smith (January 21, 1889–April 10, 1958). Before Smith got the idea to sponsor musicians in order to promote his photography business, most groups appeared on WMFR without financial support (and without financial benefit to either the station or the performers). Smith had come to High Point from his birthplace in Davie County (*High Point Enterprise*, April 11, 1958: 6B), opening his studio over Woolworth's at 115½ South Main Street in 1935. During most of WMFR's first decade on the air, Smith's Studio was located close to the radio station (High Point City Directories), and Paul Smith, a fan of string band music, must have been aware of the advertising possibilities through the sponsorship of airtime. And so when the Barnyard String Band entered Smith's Studio to get their picture made, the photographer saw opportunity knocking.

When WMFR radio went on the air in 1936, their roster included Shorty Barnes and the Barnyard String Band. In fact, band member John Allred remembers that they were the first country band to appear on the new station, although the Duncan Brothers were also broadcasting their religious songs during the same period. Bob Henderson, another member of the Barnyard Band, had approached the new station, which, probably hungry for talent, allowed the group to appear gratis. The band that "just wanted to play on the radio" would troupe down every Saturday morning to perform for a half an hour, eventually adding a weekday 5:30 A.M. slot as well. Listeners would hear Gene McMahan sing "Old Pal of Mine" or Allred do "The Talking Blues" and the "Knoxville Girl." Then, McMahan and his fellow musicians would turn back into factory and mill workers and attend to their regular jobs.

John Reuben "Red" Allred was born October 9, 1917, in the Guilford County community of Jamestown. His grandfather, John C. Allred (1869–1938), played the banjo in the clawhammer style, although no one else in the family were musical. "All they played," says Red, "was ... talking machines." Inside of a year after Red's birth, the family moved to Rankin Street in High Point, within shouting distance of banjoist Dave Walden's home. It wasn't until 1924, however, that Red first remembers hearing the music of John David Walden (February 27, 1880–November 9, 69), a life-long employee of the Snow Lumber Company (1913–1955), and his musical partner, fiddler Charlie H. Whitlow (February 29, 1880–October 1963), who was working at the time as a machinist for the Stelhi Silk Mills (High Point City Directories). Walden was a permanent resident of High Point, while Whitlow had come to the city from the Yadkin College Community of Davidson County at the age of eighteen (*High Point Enterprise*, November 10, 1969: 11A and October 10, 1963: 8D). By 1924, the Allreds had moved, but so had the Walden family, and they remained neighbors on South Wrenn Avenue for several more years (High Point City Directories).

Another big influence on Red Allred's music was the Grand Ole Opry radio program. When Allred was nine years old, Red's family would listen to the Opry on a radio owned by his uncle Joe. Red eventually had the opportunity to attend local performances by Opry artists, including Uncle Dave Macon. Allred heard Macon at Allen Jay High School in High Point, possibly in October of 1938, which made a big impression on the aspiring musician.

Red first tried to play the harmonica, obtaining instruments by selling salve. In addition to following Walden and Whitlow, he'd play along with 78-rpm records by adjusting their speed and, therefore, pitch to match the key of his harmonica. By the time Allred was a teenager, he was learning guitar and banjo. As Red remembers:

> My dad bought me an old guitar back in about '32, ... I forget what he paid for it, four or five dollars, it was a [Galleno], it was a good guitar, made down in Mexico. Before that [before he had the guitar], I'd go listen to them fellars play, they'd go and play at a dance, or a cornshuckin'. Willie Walden picked the guitar then, but he'd get loaded and he'd get to where he couldn't pick and I'd get a hold of his old guitar. Til I got mine, and then I'd watch him play, and I'd chord, you know ... that's the way I learned.... Same way with the banjo. I watched Dave [Walden] pick his banjo and that's the way I learned to pick a banjo.

As Allred worked on his music, he remained in contact with Dave Walden and Charlie Whitlow. By 1933, Whitlow was working at the Globe Parlor Furniture Company, where he was joined by both Red's father Reuban Allred and Red himself during the later part of the 1930s (High Point City Directories).

Around 1933, Red and some friends formed a band that became known as the Barnyard String Band. This included Red handling the guitar and lead vocals; mandolinist Robert William Henderson (born February 1, 1911), a boarder at Crown, Adams and Silver Knit Hosiery Mill; guitarist and lead singer Gene McMahan (May 11, 1914–March 28, 1982); and textile worker Farris Slay on the tenor banjo.

Bob Henderson was from Union County, South Carolina, the son of a cotton mill worker. At the age of nineteen, Henderson came to High Point, seeking employment in an area textile mill. Several years later, Bob and Red had become acquainted and began playing music together. Occasionally, they were joined on the fiddle by one of the area's best, Corbett Bennett (April 23, 1912–May 1984; see Chapter Eight).

Eugene McMahan, like Henderson, had been born in Union County, South Carolina. He first shows up in High Point in the same year as Henderson; perhaps the two knew each other before coming to the city. After an abortive attempt at furni-

Paul Smith outfitted this band vehicle with advertising and a public address system for promoting his business and his band. He also used his photographic skills to assemble this collage in the pre-computer days. Left to right are Bob Henderson (mandolin), Lib Lawson (vocals), Gene McMahan (guitar), Paul Smith, Jack Allred (banjo), Red Allred (guitar), "Doc" Truitt (mandolin) and Irvin Williams (fiddle). High Point, Guilford County, circa 1938. Courtesy Red Allred.

ture work, Gene followed his father into the various area textile mills (High Point City Directories).

Within the first couple of years of WMFR's existence, Allred, Henderson and company met photographer Paul Smith. Although he didn't pay the group, Smith sponsored their WMFR program, now just on Saturday mornings, as well as produced their publicity pictures free of charge and helped Bob Henderson book the group on personal appearances. Paul purchased a Buick automobile in order to transport the band to show dates. Smith covered the car with advertising for his studio and outfitted it with a sound system. The band could then play live from inside the car (as long as the battery held out!) and alert the locals to their upcoming concert. The Barnyard String Band became the Happy Ramblers, and then Paul Smith and his Snap Shots (sometimes called "His Nighthawks"). Along with the name change came a slight shift in personnel. Paul's son Lon, a pianist, was added to the ensemble. Red moved over to the banjo, replacing the departing Slay (who also departed High Point; High Point City Directories), with Irvin Eugene "Zipper" Williams (July 26, 1911–May 17, 1962), a worker at Tate Furniture Company, covering guitar and fiddle. As the band began adding performances, Paul Smith's ambitions for his charges grew, and the group fluctuated from a quintet up to a septet. A second mandolinist, knitter Bob "Doc" Truitt, was added. A female vocalist, Lib Lawson, or a blackface comedian would sometimes perform as a part of Smith's troupe. Furniture workers Leon (September 10, 1916–February 25, 1995) and J. W., the Woolard Brothers, recently

The Happy Ramblers, an earlier incarnation of the Snapshots, in a publicity postcard from Smith's Studio. Left to right are Lon Smith, Paul's son (guitar), Bob Henderson (mandolin), Red Allred (banjo), Gary Davis (announcer), Irvin Williams and Gene McMahan (guitar). High Point, Guilford County, circa 1937. Courtesy Red Allred.

arrived from Goldsboro, were another addition. Red moved back to the guitar, with banjo chores handled from that time by either hosiery mill worker Herman Poole (September 13, 1919–December 8, 1969), Red's brother Robert Jackson "Jack" Allred (born 1920), or Hubert Lohr. Hubert Daniel Lohr was a furniture worker who had been playing the banjo since 1920. He was later a compatriot of Olin Berrier's, who liked what he heard over WMFR and sought out Lohr (see Chapter Four).

The Snap Shots played schoolhouse shows in Paul Smith's hometown of Smith's Grove (outside of Mocksville on Route 158), Denton, and Thomasville. They also shared both the stage and their radio programs with touring musicians, including the Monroe Brothers. Public dance halls were another venue where Smith brought the band. Red Allred remembers that they could be wild places, with drinking by attendees leading to fighting and shooting.

By 1942, Red Allred had stopped playing with the Snapshots because of the conflict between their performing calendar and his work schedule. By 1950, when Allred returned to High Point, WMFR had eliminated their live music programming and gone to an all-record format.

Another group who came under Paul Smith's patronage was Odell Smith and the Rhythm Buddies. Francis Odell Smith (July 7, 1908–May 25, 1959) was born at the family homestead near Germanton in Stokes County, North Carolina. Wesley Smith (died 1924), Odell's grandfather, played the fiddle, and taught his son Roscoe the instrument. Odell's father, mill worker Robert Forest Smith (July 5, 1889–November 15, 1970), played the autoharp, and took the notion to learn the fiddle. In 1918, when Odell Smith was ten years old, as Odell's younger brother Amos later recalled:

> My daddy was sittin' there tryin' to play the fiddle, he bought it to learn hisself on. And me and Odell was standin' in front of him. And he seen Odell was so interested in it, he says, "You want to play this?" And he held the fiddle out. He said, "Yes, sir." And he took it and sawed across it a few times and started playin' "Nearer My God to Thee," and played it through, the first time he ever had the fiddle in his hand. And he played from then on.

By the early 1920s, Odell was accompanying local dances, and working, as did his father, at a cotton mill in the Spray, Leakesville and Draper area. Smith was still too young to drive, so his father had to take him to and from musical engagements. But life for the Smith family was not easy. In 1919, Odell lost a brother to the flu epidemic. Five years later, his last sibling, the youngest sister, was born mentally handicapped. Finally, in 1930, Forest abandoned the family. By that time, Odell was living on his own, and playing music as a professional.

In 1929 and 1930, Odell Smith became a member of Charlie Poole's (see Chapter Seven) last band. He accompanied Poole to New York City to make recordings, and also toured on occasion with the banjoist. Because the Lily Mill, where Odell worked, would not give Smith time off to make records, Odell quit his textile job. During 1931, he recorded as a member of Walter "Kid" Smith's (no relation) Carolina Buddies. As Amos Smith relates, "They never did make much money" because there wasn't much to be made (Rorrer: 48–60).

Family legend has Odell Smith meeting his future wife at a dance hall in High Point called either the Half or Blue Moon. Odell's fiddling uncle Roscoe worked in High Point from the late 1920s until World War II, and may have been another reason for Odell's moving to the city.

While living in High Point (from approximately 1933 to 1943), Smith worked at various area textile mills (High Point City Directories). Odell also began performing over WMFR, and, like the Barnyard String Band, began without a sponsor. Odell Smith's program was a half-hour daily broadcast carried live in the early morning. One of the members of Smith's band at that time was banjoist John W. Swaim (born November 1911), who describes Odell as "the best I [ever] seen. He had perfect timing and he just didn't miss nothin'!"

In 1936, Smith met guitarist Clifton Kinney "Cliff" Clinard (September 30, 1915–October 19, 2001) at the Trinity Fiddlers' Convention. The two musicians hit it off immediately, and Clinard ended up playing with Odell until Cliff entered the military in 1941. Cliff Clinard had first heard music when he was growing up on a farm on the Old Greensboro Road north of Thomasville. His father, George Curtis Clinard (April 22, 1880–June 9, 1953) played guitar in a group which included Francis Everhart, Joseph Daniel "Joe" Wagner (November 10, 1877–May 23, 1951), and William L. "Will" McGee, all multi-instrumentalists. This band was typical of the time in that George Clinard and company provided the music for all the gatherings in their neighborhood. It was his mother's brother, Fleet Erastus Darr (November 8, 1900–August 18, 1958), who played a bit on a multitude of musical instruments, that started Cliff on the guitar around 1930. From then through the start of World War II, Cliff played for dances "from South Carolina to Virginia." Clinard worked in a glass factory in Thomasville during the early 1930s; he also was employed by the Shroup Mill Company while playing with Odell Smith.

Other musicians who worked with Odell during his partnership with Cliff Clinard were four-string banjoist Tommy Jones, a long-time employee of the Highland Cotton Mill; fiddler James Oscar Prather (September 22, 1898–July 11, 1979), a High Point furniture worker; pianist Kermit "Bunk" Bowles; guitarist Grady Bowles; and two of Odell's acquaintances from his stay in Spray, banjoists Pete Stone and Smith's brother-in-law Ed Rogers.

In 1939, Odell Smith found a benefactor in Ted Frienschner, an engineer for the Wayne Trademark Company. Like Paul Smith, Frienschner was a music fan. Unlike Smith, Ted Frienschner did not use his association with Odell to further the fortunes of his business. Ted gave Odell a job at Wayne Trademark, which made the patterns used by the textile industry for printed (versus woven) socks. Frienschner bought a Hopf-made violin for Smith and a Martin brand guitar for Cliff Clinard. He also gave Odell time off when he had performing engagements. The Odell Smith group stayed busy playing a mixture of concerts in school auditoriums and fiddlers' conventions on Saturday nights, and for dances on other nights of the week. Cliff Clinard commented that he made more from music then he did at his day job, sometimes as much as $25 a night from playing at a public dance. Because of Smith's background, the

Another group sponsored by photographer Paul Smith over WMFR were the Rythm (sic) Buddies. This band included fiddler Odell Smith, Lynn (guitar), George (announcer), Woodie Mashburn (string bass) and Tommie Jones (banjo). High Point, Guilford County, circa 1941.

group worked a lot on the North Carolina and Virginia border, in communities such as Martinsville, Galax, and Bassett, Virginia.

Toward the end of Odell Smith's stay in High Point Paul Smith became his sponsor over WMFR. The Rhythm Buddies, as the group was then called, broadcast every Thursday evening from 8:05 until 8:30 P.M. By that point, Cliff Clinard had entered the service. Odell Smith and Tommy Jones were joined by Woodrow Wilson "Woody" Mashburn (April 15, 1913–February 11, 1994) on string bass, and a guitarist only known by his first name, "Lynn."

By the time Clinard returned home from the military, Odell Smith and his family had already been gone from High Point for two years. The lure of wartime employment was too great for Odell. After training as a sheet metal worker in 1941, he moved first to Elizabeth City and finally, after the war ended, to Cherry Point for work at the Marine air station. Odell continued to earn extra income playing for dances. At the start of the 1950s, he began to slow down his music making, which was all but over by the middle of the decade (High Point City Directories).

After the departure of Odell Smith, live music continued on WMFR. The Dixie Jamboree remained on Saturday mornings, usually without a live audience. Music was also broadcast from a studio in Thomasville.

WGWR: "The Friendly Voice from the Center of North Carolina"

The boom years following World War Two were a growth time for radio stations as well. In the period before television took over, many new broadcasters went on the air. The military had trained large numbers of young men in radio technology, and these returning veterans often put their skills to work by building and running small, local broadcasters.

WGWR ("We Grow With Randolph"), located in the Randolph County seat of Asheboro, was one of these radio stations. It began programming in 1947 from studios located on Salisbury Street (*Randolph County,1779–1979*, 35).

One early band on WGWR was the Green Valley Boys. Their leader was guitarist, singer, and raconteur John Henry Brewer (August 24, 1918–April 13, 1979). The fifth child of eight born on the Randolph and Chatham county line to John Quincy (1882–1948) and Elizabeth Augusta Fields (1886–1965) of Lee County, John Henry grew up surrounded by music on both sides of his family. All of his mother's people sang and played instruments, especially Elizabeth's brother, Lynn Fields, who picked the guitar and the banjo. John Quincy Brewer farmed and fiddled, leading a neighborhood group that included Petty Brown on fiddle and banjo, Swanee Brown on banjo, and Miss Iner Brown on autoharp. When John Henry was a boy, his father's band would supply the music for house dances, where John Quincy's second son, Clarence (known as "Whittie," December 14, 1908–June 10, 1992) called the figures.

In 1930, John Henry earned enough money by delivering *Grit* magazine to purchase his first guitar. After serving in the Army during World War II, Brewer assembled his first Green Valley Boys. Besides playing on the radio, the group worked a

Woods Chatham Foods sponsored the television broadcasts over WFMY of John Henry Brewer and the "Chatham Ranch Boys," renamed for their sponsor. The band — John Henry on guitar (wearing the white hat), Boyd "Sleepy" Marley on fiddle, Everett Moffitt on string bass and "Zeke" Reitzel on banjo — posed with announcer Al Cooper at the company's Siler City warehouse for this publicity still. Not only are the company's products proudly displayed, but an audience, hay and even a horse were brought in to go along with the band's western finery. Chatham County, 1953–1954. Courtesy Everett Moffitt.

goodly number of square dances. This included a regular Saturday night dance, some years in Greensboro tobacco warehouse called by Mr. Brooks, and around 1953–1954 at a venue in Randleman. When Everett Moffitt (see Chapter Ten) went to work for John Henry, his group included guitarist Saly Newman (see Chapter Ten), Joseph Bernard "Zeke" Reitzel (June 22, 1922–February 19, 2000) on the banjo, upholsterer Calvin Fred "Speedy" Marley (born 1925) on fiddle, James "Jimmy" Kivett on guitar, and Brewer's older brother G. Carl (January 18, 1911–March 17, 1978) on the mandolin (*Courier-Tribune*, July 3, 1947: 4 and October 23, 1947: 2). Since Brewer's band didn't travel out of the immediate area, the band's personnel remained relatively stable. Saly Newman and Carl Brewer did not leave the Green Valley Boys until after 1951, and Fred Marley stayed with John Henry at least until 1953. Joe Reitzel lasted a minimum of two more years, and Moffitt played with Brewer for three years afterwards. Zeke Reitzel was not always available to play with the Green Valley Boys, so Oscar Hutchison, the banjoist with Tommy Floyd (also on WGWR) substituted for Reitzel.

Perhaps the high point of Brewer's career in music came in 1953. Television became available in the early years of the 1950s, and John Henry was recruited by Woods Chatham Foods of Siler City to push their products over the new medium.

For 1953 and 1954, Brewer and company would make the trek up to Greensboro for their telecasts over WFMY. On Friday nights from 7:15–7:30, John Henry and band, now called the Chatham Ranch Boys, were beamed into homes around the Triad. "Speedy" Marley left after about a year, and his spot was taken by his brother, Boyd Matthew "Sleepy" Marley (born March 4, 1918), a furniture worker in Liberty. Guitarist Woody Greeson also worked for about a year on the telecasts with Brewer.

By the later part of the 1950s, Brewer's desire to perform had slowed down. He married and eventually entered into a partnership with "Sleepy" Marley at the Carolina Stockyards in Siler City and ran auctions. The days of live radio were waning, and most of the members of the Green Valley Boys had to come to terms with the drop in demand for public performances.

Tommy Floyd

One man that broadcast back in the early 1950s is still well remembered by area listeners. Although Tommy Floyd was born in the mountains, this charismatic performer who came to Asheboro over 50 years ago was thereafter treated in the area like a native son.

The story of Tommy Floyd is one of many successes, but also of heartbreak over the big break that never occurred. On one hand, Tommy was a good promoter who raised a family with the income from his music. On the other hand, Floyd longed to graduate from local markets onto a larger stage like the Grand Ole Opry. But, like the majority of regional stars, Tommy never got his chance in the national spotlight. In that regard, he is a suitable representative for the majority of musicians trying to make it in the country-music business before it became the multi-million dollar industry of today.

Thomas Calvin Floyd was born October 10, 1912, in the Francisco community of Stokes County. His father, Julius Terrel Floyd (born 1887), was a tobacco farmer, whose sons all exhibited an interest in music. These included Tommy on guitar and Jessie, who preferred the mandolin and fiddle. In Francisco, Tommy organized his first band, including Jessie, Ed Wilson on banjo, and Os Hill on fiddle, to play at local functions such as cornshuckings, tobacco curings, and house dances. Floyd also began working in a Martinsville, Virginia, furniture factory, to support his music making.

In 1930, Tommy started using the name the Blue Ridge Buddies for his bands. Ten years later, the Buddies moved their base of operations to High Point. Floyd possibly broadcast for WMFR during the war years, but mostly he and his brother Jesse supported themselves working for the Marsh and Strickland Furniture Companies. Tommy was definitely broadcasting over WHPE, owned by the *High Point Enterprise* newspaper, in 1948, when the station signed on for the first time. The Blue Ridge Buddies appeared six days a week (except Sunday), from 11:30–noon and 5–5:30 in the afternoon over WHPE. The Buddies at that time were Tommy and Jesse, Harold Miller on guitar, Dempsey McBride or John Robson Ham Jr. (May 24, 1919–September 18, 1990) on the fiddle, and Tommy Goad on banjo. A variation on this band

Tommy Floyd in the studios of WHPE Radio in High Point. Standing, left to right are Tommy on guitar, Dempsey McBride on fiddle and Jessie Floyd on mandolin. Kneeling are Harold Miller on guitar and "Zeke" Reitzel on banjo. Guilford County, 1948. Courtesy Tommy Floyd.

worked in Thomasville for radio station WTNC in the early 1950s. The Floyd Brothers and Goad were joined by Fred Hunt on guitar, Red Nichols playing electric steel guitar, Paige Hepler on fiddle, and Max Lanning on bass. In 1948, Tommy Floyd was able to finally list himself as "musician" in the city directory (High Point City Directories).

It was during this same time period that Tommy's children also began to be incorporated into his act. The first to perform was the oldest boy, Thomas Calvin, Jr., known as "Buster" (born 1940) on guitar, followed by Glenn Ray "Buddy" (March 23, 1943–November 3, 1996) on bass, Patsy (born August 2, 1945) on vocals, and Terrel Monroe (November 10, 1948–1992) on keyboards. Eventually, all worked with their father's groups.

In 1949, the Floyd family moved once more, this time to Asheboro in Randolph County. Sometime in 1950 or 1951 (Songbook #2), Tommy began hosting programs over WGWR. There was a live broadcast Saturdays from 10:30 until noon, which originated from the radio station and was open to the public. Floyd welcomed the

Tommy Floyd, with his expanded band on WGWR, sponsored by Holsum Bread. Left to right, standing, John Tilley, the driver, Oscar Hutchinson (banjo), Tommy Floyd (guitar), Buster Floyd, and Jessie Floyd (mandolin). Kneeling are Fred Hunt (guitar), Red Greer (steel guitar) and Bobby Hicks (fiddle). Asheboro, Randolph County, 1951. Courtesy Tommy Floyd.

audience with the words, "Howdy all you friends and neighbors / Pull up your old rockin' chair / The time has come, we'll all have fun / The Blue Ridge Buddies is on the air!" In addition, for at least part of the time Floyd was associated with WGWR, the Buddies broadcast weekdays from 4:30–5:30 P.M. (Songbook #2). Their sponsor was Holsum Bread of Greensboro. Red Greer replaced Red Nichols on steel guitar, Oscar Hutchison came in on banjo, Tommy's son Buster was added on guitar and bass, and a young Bobby Hicks, later with Bill Monroe and Ricky Skaggs, joined on fiddle. Fiddlers and banjoists seemed to come and go, but through the early 1950s, the core of the band stayed the same.

What appeared to be Tommy Floyd's "big break" came in 1952. Luck's Beans, a local food service company, decided to sponsor the Blue Ridge Buddies as hosts for a series of fifteen minute syndicated country music spots carried by television stations in the Southeast, including Greensboro's WFMY. In return for their patronage, Floyd gave away cases of Luck's products at his live performances. Somehow, as Tommy tells it, he had arranged for Luck's to sponsor him in a television program syndicated by WSM, Nashville's country music giant. Floyd had all the preparations made, but, at the last minute, the management at Luck's decided that the deal was too expensive and backed out. By 1953, Luck's sponsorship of Floyd ended and Tommy remained in North Carolina (Songbook #2; Banks, "Tommy Floyd," *Greensboro News and Record*, July 30, 2002: *B-2*).

Dwight Barker

Television was still in its infancy when Tommy Floyd and Luck's Beans attempted telecasting country music. Their efforts were followed by Dwight Barker, who achieved success in the Triad (Winston-Salem, Greensboro, High Point) during the 1950s and 1960s.

Dwight Thomas Barker was born May 14, 1918, in the Rocky Creek community of northern Iredell County. His father, Carter Erastus Barker (April 10, 1884–May 4, 1973) played clawhammer-style banjo. "We'd work in the fields and farm during the daytime and sit on the porch and pick the guitar at night," Dwight recalls. "Back when I was born, we didn't go places, we stayed on the farm and we knew not to leave!" Besides his father, his musical partners were his three younger brothers, George Washington (born August 17, 1922), Jack Daniel (born May 23, 1925), and E.C. (Erastus Carter, February 8, 1927–May 1, 1978). Three of the Barker boys went semi-professional in the 1930s, and performed with a variety of musicians, including fiddler Clarence Poole, at functions within the community.

In 1939, the Barkers made their radio debut in Winston-Salem sponsored by R. C.

WSIC's Saturday Night Jamboree, Mulberry Street School, Statesville, with the whole cast posed on stage. They include, standing left to right, L.W. Lambert on banjo, Zeb Speece on guitar, Harold Tomlin, La Vaughn Lambert Tomlin, Dwight Barker announcer and host, Williams, Jim Shumate on fiddle, Ray Porter, Jack Barker and E. C. Barker. Sitting are Jason Lambert on guitar, Johnny Compton on guitar, Willie Black, comedian, Ray Josie on guitar and Ralph Grose on fiddle, Eloise Sparks, Pal Arlen and Wanda Speece Arlen. Late 1940s. Photograph by Bob Pyler; courtesy L.W. Lambert.

Cola. In addition to Dwight's brothers, fiddler Ralph Grose (born July 6, 1914), Ralph's brothers Blaine Harrison (born May 13, 1922) and Thomas Dale (born March 5, 1927) were band members. Ralph Grose also became Dwight's brother-in-law that year, after Barker married Grose's sister Ruby. Between 1939 and 1941, Dwight Barker played music as a sideline, earning his living by working in a cotton mill. Barker spent World War II in the signal corps, where he kept a band going that played for the troops.

In 1947, Dwight started the WSIC Saturday Nite Jamboree. The Jamboree was underwritten by the Statesville PTA and held at the old Mulberry Street School from 8:00–10:30 P.M. during the winter months. It marked Barker's first engagement as a full-time professional musician, as he managed to support himself with the combined income from the radio program, other broadcasting work, and personal appearances on weekend nights. His band during this time, called the Melody Boys, included Ralph Grose, Dwight's brothers E.C. on guitar and Jack on steel guitar, and Ray Porter on bass. After about three years, the Jamboree moved to Friday nights and the Playhouse Theater. In early 1953, the Melody Boys began a new radio program called the Old Mountain Opry. Fiddler Jim Shumate, who had performed with both Bill Monroe and Flatt and Scruggs, joined the Barker brothers and Grose, who moved over to the bass, during this period, an association that would last through the 1960s (January 8, 1953, p113; see Chapter Eleven for more about the Jamboree and Shumate). But the new medium of television was beckoning, and Dwight jumped at the opportunity.

One of the new telecasters was WTOB ("World's Tobacco Capitol"). Channel 26 television, located in Winston-Salem, had come on the air in 1953. Glenn Thompson and Gurney Thomas, broadcasting from 8:30–9:30 (see Chapter Ten), spent thirteen weeks on the air. But, when the station balked at their salaries, Thompson and Thomas soon acceded the airwaves to Dwight (undated newspaper ad; Thompson and Weiss and Davis interview). Barker brought his band from Statesville, adding guitarist Ray Josie and comedian Willie Black. Dwight remembers: "We went to WTOB first, they was UHF, you know. And, so, one night, I got a call at the station from Channel 2, WFMY. Said, 'Dwight, would you like to come where everybody could see you?' And I said, 'We might!'"

Billed as "the first telecast of a hillbilly jamboree program in the South," Barker and his Melody Boys premiered over WFMY-Greensboro on April 4, 1953. Broadcasting from 11 until midnight, the Saturday Night Jamboree, as it was known, featured Dwight, along with a variety of regional talent. That first broadcast included Boyden Carpenter (see this chapter and Chapter Seven), the Melody Sweethearts from Montgomery County, and Dee Stone and the Virginia Mountain Boys ("Televised Jamboree," *The Greensboro Record*, April 4, 1953: 6). Dee Collins Stone (March 2, 1919–July 17, 1969) of Franklin County, Virginia, played regularly during the first four or five months of the Jamboree's existence (*Bluegrass Unlimited*, January 1998, 20).

During his first year at WFMY-TV, Barker began supplementing his musical income by hosting radio disc programs and area fiddlers' conventions. His radio associations have included WDBM-Statesville (1957–1970), WHIP-Mooresville (1953–1976), WRKB-Kannapolis (1977–1981), WFMX-Statesville (1976–77), WDRV (1986–1992), and WDSL-Mocksville (1992–present). In 1965, Dwight Barker was honored as DJ USA in Nashville by WSM. He and Ruby also produced three musi-

Dwight Barker in the studios of WSJS-television. Standing (left to right) is E. C. Barker (electric guitar), Jack Barker, Rena Reynolds (vocals), Jim Shumate (fiddle), Dwight Barker (guitar), Gar Bowers (banjo) and Ralph Grose (electric bass). Seated are Ray Josie (guitar) and Willie Black, comedian and guitarist. Winston-Salem, Forsyth County, circa 1963–1970. Courtesy Dwight Barker.

cal sons. Rather then following their father and uncles into country music, Gary (born 1941), John Dwight (born September 8, 1945), and Robert Lynn (born August 16, 1951) all are well known in beach music circles.

After ten years on WFMY, Barker moved over to WSJS-TV, Channel 8, in Winston-Salem. Matt Howell Motors and Blackwelder Furniture sponsored the Saturday program. While using several banjoists, James Ora "Garr" Bowers (a former associate of Bill Monroe) seems to have been Dwight's instrumentalist of choice.

Guests such as George Hamilton IV made their television debut on Barker's program. A typical television program for Barker and his Melody Boys included country songs like "Pick Me Up on Your Way Down," fiddle and banjo instrumentals such as "Lonesome Road Blues," comedy numbers including "Step It Up and Go," and hymns like "Lord, I'm Coming Home." Dwight recollects that: "Back then, you needed more than just bluegrass. And so we did country, and some gospel duets, trios and quartets. Bluegrass wasn't all of it then, it was part of it. Fiddle tunes and banjo tunes, we had to have it all then, but, later, it went separate ways."

Barker ended his affiliation with WSJS in 1970. Dwight also quit full-time performing at this time, partially because it became too difficult to maintain a band. Barker concludes: "We had a lot of good years. Not many people had a better life than I have, [maybe] made a lot more money, but, I've enjoyed my life."

TEN

The Professionals

"I bet over the whole years I've played music, I've went in the hole."

— Elgin Boyd

The 1930s and 1940s were the decades during which the country music industry was created. A system developed where radio stations provided entertainers with a home base, and these musicians then worked the station's coverage area. Groups broadcast for little or no pay, and used their radio programs to publicize personal appearances. Because most locales lacked established country music promoters, performers relied on their listeners to sponsor events. Mostly, parent organizations used schoolhouses to present concerts as fundraisers for their schools. As this system became more sophisticated, performers were able to make their living exclusively from "personals." When an area became "played out," musicians would change their base of operations to another station. If a new area didn't work out — there weren't enough playing opportunities or too much competition from other bands— groups might move after only a month or two.

Wartime gave a number of young musicians opportunities they may have never gotten. As in baseball and defense work, all able-bodied males were in the armed forces, leaving openings for the underage, the infirm, and the novice. Interestingly, this also gave female musicians a break. At the same time, the entertainment business was booming. Workers had money to spend and people were looking for diversions from their jobs and the news of the war.

Music, not surprisingly, was a difficult business at best. Before construction began on the interstate highway system in the 1950s, travel over the old two-lane roads was slow and difficult, and often done late at night. Some musicians spoke of how they wouldn't see a bed for weeks, but this was less the case with North Carolina-based groups who only toured within a hundred-mile radius of their homes. However, recollections from regional players are still peppered with stories of late-night breakdowns, sleeplessness, car wrecks, and blowouts. Woody Greeson tells of the night the car he was traveling in had seven flat tires! Another time, flats caused Greeson to walk the final fifteen miles home. The lack of tires and fuel during World War II was an additional headache that drove many from the music business.

Bud Osborne described the life of a traveling musician to journalist John Lowe: "In 1950, you traveled by automobile, ... You might be in Louisville, Kentucky, one night, Birmingham, Alabama, the next. That's why I didn't have any trouble losing weight. You didn't eat and you didn't sleep regular. It was just a bunch of traveling" (Lowe, "Country Music's Lure Is Strong," *High Point Enterprise*, June 23, 1985: 4d).

The lack of sleep was doubly difficult for those musicians still working day jobs. Zeke Reitzel often wouldn't get home until 5 A.M. "I wouldn't go to bed," says Reitzel, "I just changed clothes and go to work." Sometimes, the lack of sleep was the cause of serious accidents. John Henry Brewer fell asleep as he rounded a curve late one night at Coleridge, wrecking his car and destroying his high-priced Martin guitar.

The money was another matter. Sam Pridgen commented that, during the 1930s, if you made $30 a week, you were doing well (Pridgen and Poss interview). When Mainers Mountaineers joined the Crazy Water cast at WBT, rather than broadcasting for free and collecting money for personal appearances, the band was paid a flat weekly salary of $26 per person. The band soon tired of receiving what they viewed as a substandard amount for their services. When it became apparent that they could make much more under the traditional arrangement, they threatened to leave WBT. Crazy Water then let the Mountaineers collect the money from their concerts (Erbsen). Many musicians, such as Dwight Barker, figured out early that to make it as a professional musician, you needed to administer the funding for your own radio programs. As Barker says, "That's the secret, of controlling your sponsorship, when you do that, you control your show."

Leading a band and keeping musicians presented a constant challenge. Charlie Monroe, one of the most popular entertainers in the Piedmont during the 1930s and 1940s, saw many musicians come and go. And this was in a group where its members received a Christmas bonus of $100! Many band members thought they could lead their own ensemble. Monroe told Doug Green just how hard it was:

> When you're working on the side [as a sideman] you wonder to yourself ... why he don't do so and so? There's three or four reasons why you don't! First thing, you got a handful to start with, to run a show and keep in entertaining and take care of the business. And a lot of them think well how can I do that, I can be a millionaire in no time, but the thing they forget: it doesn't operate that way. You have to get with it, you have to plan it, you have to figure it out, you got to go in the right direction and keep on crowding ... keep on working hard and don't give up [Monroe and Green interview].

If it was hard being a male musician, it was doubly hard being a female musician. Gurney Thomas, leader of the Hill Billy Pals, employed Jimmy "Slim" Martin, who happened to be married to the musician known as "Little Wilma." Not surprisingly, the Martins liked to work together on the same show. Gurney discusses how that created problems, clashing with the audience's moral standards:

Slim Martin, with his bride Wilma around 1940.

Now I would have used Wilma a lot more than I did except I couldn't let her ride in a carload of men. There weren't nobody believe she was Jimmy Martin's wife. So, when the shows wasn't too far, she rode with him in their car. And that is to keep down talk. "You see 'em Hill Billy Pals, one woman in a car load of hillbillies." Now you couldn't make nobody believe she's his wife, it's just like Rachel and Oswald with Roy Acuff. They weren't no more kin than you and I. But, Roy Acuff claimed her to be Oswald's sister to get down bad publicity.

And country music was a profession best left to the young and single men. One of the pitfalls was the tendency toward the "wild side of life," and the attraction of the bottle. Lester Porter eloquently discussed the problem:

A lot of guys, and I think that was the trouble with the music business in the '30s, '40s and early '50s for county musicians, everybody thought they had to drink to play. I can show you and tell you musician after musician, they'd get to playin' and they'd get to drinkin'. It just seemed like they couldn't play unless they were half drunk. And then they couldn't play at all! Course they thought they were. It happened all the time. That was the most discouragin' thing to me. Even the professional musicians.... It just seemed like drinkin' was part of the life. But, it never was with me. I didn't like it; I stayed away from it if I could.

Ultimately, marriage usually signaled the end to the professional life of a Piedmont player. Although many pros relied on their wives to take care of the day-to-day running of a household, and many spouses were invaluable when it came to booking and promotion, the separation brought about by travel strained a marriage. "After I got married, my family was my life," says Lester Porter. "It was more important than the music was. Many a young musicians from North Carolina ... that are really good and could make it with a little hard work and preserverance [sic], they would let the family come first and it would always hold 'em back." Woody Greeson had hit the big time when Charlie Monroe hired him at the end of World War II. Woody was all ready to go, but when the time came to leave, he realized that he couldn't be away from his wife. And Bud Osborne summed it up best, when he commented, "I have a family that I wouldn't trade for the whole city of Nashville" (Lowe, "Country Music's Lure Is Strong," *High Point Enterprise*, June 23, 1985: 4d).

For many instrumentalists and singers, playing music in public was a young man's folly. They performed for a few years while single and didn't have any financial responsibilities. Then, when life on the road proved tiring, they gave it up for a family and a job in a factory or a mill. Bud Osborne had an answer for all those who couldn't understand why a talented musician like himself would give up the life of a professional musician: "Yeah, I might could have made it big. But for every big name you can think of, I can name another fellow who didn't make it" (Lowe, 4d).

The few who hung in with public music making all their lives faced a different question. Why hadn't they gone to Nashville and the Grand Ole Opry when the offer came? Gurney Thomas told me

They talk about bein' on the Grand Ole Opry and this thrill.... It didn't do me no worse then I would go out to a good crowd on the stage at some schoolhouse out in the country. It ain't nothin' but another stage and people, that's all it is. And nothin' but more folks, if you just look at it right. I had a chance to go on the Opry along about the time after them records. [Gurney recorded for King] … I give the Solemn Ole Judge [George D. Hay] an audition in his office with my guitar and De Ford Bailey was there. And he said, "Well, we pay DeFord [the Opry's African American harmonica performer] $12 a week, that's union scale, for a Saturday night performance and that's all I can get by paying a single." And, I went back home, I said I'd think about it, and that's all'd ever happened to it.

Lance Spencer seconds Gurney's sentiments:

Playing at a [local] radio station and going out just far enough to still be able to come back in a night was a lot easier than being on the Grand Ole Opry. Because the Opry was a tough deal and we made a great deal more money than they did. It was customary then at the Grand Ole Opry, if you played Friday night in Dallas, Texas, Saturday night you had to be at the Opry. No matter where you were, you had to come in. And those guys stayed on the road. Anybody who was making money with a local, small station were a lot better off and knew it.

Charlie Monroe: "We Were Hot-headed and Mean as Snakes"

In the spring of 1938, one of the most popular country acts in the Carolinas, the Monroe Brothers, broke up. It's hard to tell, so many years after the fact, what initiated their final disagreement. Charles Pendleton Monroe (July 4, 1903–September 27, 1975) would have probably been happy to continue with the status quo, but also had less to lose if the duo split. After all, the older Monroe brother sang lead and was comfortable with audiences, handling the public in an easygoing, friendly manner. Charlie's wife Betty was good at managing the requests for Monroe's public appearances, as was shown after the brothers split up. So Charlie was confident that he could be a successful act, with or without his brother. Bill, however, was growing tired of his supporting role as a harmony singer and mandolin soloist. Old feelings of jealousy and old wounds over his perceived mistreatment by his sibling, triggered by some slight or difference of opinion, bubbled to the surface and ended the Monroes' partnership. Bill went west to Asheville, then to Atlanta, and eventually to Nashville and the Grand Ole Opry.

Charlie tried to continue as if nothing had happened. Even though he assembled a band rather than forming another duo, it always featured a mandolinist and tenor singer named "Bill." If the musician had not been christened Bill, then Charlie renamed the player. (Strangely enough, Bill Monroe would not have a band member that *shared* his first name, and so would christen the employee with a new name.) Charlie hired Zeke Morris (see Chapter Nine) to fill the spot vacated by his brother, along with another mandolinist and singer, Bill Calhoun, to fulfill the Monroe Brothers' recording obligations, working in September 1938 and February 1939 for Bluebird (Rosenberg, 40; *Bluegrass Unlimited*, 14). Charlie first moved to WDBJ, in Roanoke, Virginia, where he broadcast from early October until mid–December at

In Person

CHARLIE MONROE
and his Kentucky Partners
Saturday, May 5th, 8:00 P.M.
Fayetteville St. School, Asheboro, N. C.
Admission 25c & 75c (Over 12 Yrs.)
Sponsored by Ladies of Brower's Chapel Church

Charlie Monroe in the late 1940s. Courtesy Fred Olson.

8:15 A.M. every Tuesday, Thursday, and Saturday (Poster; *Roanoke World News*, September 1938–February 1939). By his 1939 recording session, Monroe had relocated to WNOX-Knoxville, where he stayed just a short time (*Bluegrass Unlimited*, 14). Charlie then decided to forge a full band, which he named the Kentucky Pardners. (*Bluegrass Unlimited*, 12–19; Monroe and Green interview). Monroe moved to WWVA in Wheeling, West Virginia (*Bluegrass Unlimited*, 15), bringing with him Zeke Morris's replacement, Curley "Bill" Seckler. His WWVA group also included Dale Cole, a champion fiddler from West Virginia and a blackface comedian; Tommy Edwards on mandolin; and guitarist and comedian Tommy Scott.

"THEY WAS A-SELLIN' EVERYTHING FROM
JEWS HARPS TO GOURDS"—TOMMY SCOTT

Tommy Scott, born in Toccoa, Georgia, on June 24, 1916, met the Monroes when both were broadcasting over WPTF. Tommy's spot was heard over the Raleigh station before the brothers, around 6 A.M. At the age of sixteen, Scott had left home with Doc Chamberlain's medicine show. Since that time, Tommy had worked at WPTF Tuesday and Thursdays at 11:15 with Uncle Pete and Minervey's Old Hometown Show, a "hill billy comedy." Scott provided the incidental music to introduce their performances on the radio and to cover set changes at schoolhouse appearances. Tommy Scott moved with Uncle Pete to rival broadcaster WRAL, but their program only lasted about a month. After another thirty days spent back in Georgia, Tommy got the call to join Charlie's Kentucky Pardners.

By mid–November of 1939, the Kentucky Pardners had moved once again, this time to WHAS in Louisville, Kentucky (*Louisville Courier-Journal*, November 9–15, 1939). Dale Cole stayed behind in West Virginia, and Monroe brought Paul Prince in to fiddle for the Pardners. When Curley Seckler departed Charlie's band, Lavelle "Bill" Coy replaced him (Monroe and Green interview). Besides hosting an early morning show broadcast from the station's studios, Charlie also appeared as a part of the Renfro Valley Barn Dance (*Bluegrass Unlimited*, 15).

While Charlie Monroe was living in Louisville, he "discovered" the banjoist Dave Akeman. Better known under the moniker of "String Bean," Akeman later joined Bill Monroe's Bluegrass Boys and was a member of the Grand Ole Opry. Dave Akeman first made the acquaintance of Charlie's band at their early morning radio broadcast. As Tommy Scott tells the story:

> WHAS in Louisville at the time was upstairs over a store building. You go in, open a door, walk right in and then the steps started up and that was a lockable door. We was on at six in the morning for an hour. Charlie required us boys to be there fifteen minutes before they had unlocked that door.... And then he'd come in about two to three minutes before. And on this particular morning we walked in there and it was cold down to ten degrees. And when we opened that front door, there stood this long lanky guy with a banjo not in a case. And he said, "My name's Dave Akeman, and I've been listenin' to y'all, and I'm a lookin' for a job in hillbilly music." And I said, "Well, we ain't the boss. Charlie Monroe'll be here in a short time, but he's the most unusual human you've ever met. And he's liable to throw you out, and

he might just talk to you, I don't know." About that time, Charlie walked in, and I said, "This man plays and sings." String had told me that he done a little blackface comedy and then the type thing he was doin' as String Bean. And I said, "Charlie, I need somebody to do a double with me on black." And Charlie said, "We don't need nobody!" And up the steps he went. String followed, he says, "Could I go up and sit in?" And I said, "Yeah, if he don't throw you out." So, he just went in and watched the show. And I said to Charlie, "Don't you want to give the guy the courtesy to play you a song?" He says, "I don't want to hear that, can't pay it! I'm payin' y'all now too much — twelve dollars and a half's a lot of money." I told String I was sorry. Next morning, String was back again, like Felix's cat. And I told Charlie, "Well, he come back a wantin' to know if he could just sing one song." And he said, "Well, sing one." String went into it and [Charlie] said, "You're the worst banjo player I ever seen!" And I said, "Well, he don't play that much banjo but he's a comedian and I need him. We've got together and each one of us is gonna pitch in two dollars out of our twelve and give to him. And if you'll do that it won't cost you nothing for a week and see what me and him can come up with." Well, he said, "Long as it don't cost me nothing, ok." And at the end of that week, he said, "Ok, y'all quit fooling around with it. I'm gonna give him twelve dollars and a half a week, too." And that's how String started.

But, as with his other residencies since leaving the Monroe Brothers partnership, Charlie's sojourn in Louisville was short lived. Monroe bought a circus tent and embarked on the first of his successful tours under canvas, which continued in the warm months throughout the 1940s (*Bluegrass Unlimited*, p15).

"WE'RE THE GAY KENTUCKY PARDNERS, WE'RE THE GAY KENTUCKY PARDNERS, SINGING THE SONGS YOU LOVE TO HEAR, AND HOPING YOU'LL TUNE YOUR RADIO OUR WAY" — THEME SONG FOR CHARLIE MONROE

By the fall of the year, Charlie was again ready to try another radio market. After an abortive attempt to work out of WFBC, in Greenville, South Carolina, Monroe landed at WBIG in Greensboro (*Bluegrass Unlimited*, p12–19). This time, back where the Monroe Brothers had their biggest success, Charlie finally found a home. Bill Coy, String Bean, Paul Prince, and Tommy Scott arrived in North Carolina, and began filling the airwaves with song for one hour daily on the "The Noonday Jamboree" (*Bluegrass Unlimited*, p16). Many listeners fondly remembered Charlie from his days with his brother Bill, and the mail poured in requesting performances by the Kentucky Pardners. Betty Monroe, Charlie's wife, would choose which venues to pursue, sometimes having to pick from as many as twenty separate requests for the same date. Jokingly, Betty would often ask the band, "Which one do you think would fix us the best dinner?" remembers Tommy Scott.

Each day following their mid-day radio broadcasts, Monroe and band would pile into his two Lincoln Zephyrs, one towing a trailer. The automobiles or trailer had loudspeakers mounted on top, with plywood sign boards attached to each side of the trailer. Both the PA and signs were used to publicize that evening's appearance. Gene Britt, a youngster in the 1940s, told of the impression Charlie made when he drove by the Britt family home in Walkertown. Sixty years later, Gene

Maynard Spencer outside of Charlie Monroe's home on North Edgeworth Street in Greensboro in 1941, with Monroe's automobile and trailer to the left. Notice Charlie's logo on both, as well as the loud speakers on top of the auto. Courtesy Lance Spencer.

could still clearly remember the car and trailer, and at how he admired Monroe for his fancy cars and snappy clothes. Once the show was over, the money taken in at the gate was split, 25 percent for the sponsoring organization and 75 percent to Monroe.

One of the ongoing concerns for performers was finding sponsors willing to pay for their spot in the radio schedule. An unsponsored program meant that the station would be giving away time in their broadcast day, rather than making money from the show. The broadcaster might have already sold the sponsorship and would then find the talent to perform in that slot. Or a business would approach a well-known musician and negotiate a fee for representing its product. Some talent figured out the importance of controlling their own airtime, and would sell their services themselves and then buy a time slot with some of the proceeds.

Charlie Monroe took the idea of selling his own time a step further. When he learned that band member Tommy Scott had been given the Herb-O-Lac formula by his former employer, Doc Chamberlain, Charlie struck a deal with Scott. Monroe would supply the money to manufacture the product and Tommy would deliver the medicine to retail outlets. The Kentucky Pardners would then sponsor themselves over WBIG with the proceeds from Herb-O-Lac, which Monroe renamed Man-o-ree. (The name appears to be meaningless. Tommy Scott told me, "I have no idea what it means, it's just somethin' somebody [in the band] thought up.") As Tommy Scott remembers:

> The deal was that I would furnish the medicine under his name [Man-o-ree], he'd buy the [radio] time, I would go and put it in the drugstores, he bought me a brand new car, I guess it was a '40 ... model Ford.... "And I'll be back two weeks from now. If you haven't sold a bottle, and you want to give it back to me, we'll still be friends." Once it got up to a profit, we'd split 50-50.... So it went for a year and a half. I think we got to sixteen stations one time. And then Charlie would pay the long distance telephone line from here to there [in order to send the program out to different stations], and then pay them [for the radio time]. In the meantime, we got up to ten thousand bottles a week at a dollar apiece.... We was selling through the drugstores....

Originally, Tommy had the tonic made and packaged for them by General Products Laboratories, located in Columbus, Ohio. For some reason, he and Charlie eventually decided to bottle the concoction themselves. General Products would mix the medicine and send it to North Carolina in large containers. Charlie then set up the transfer operation above a downtown Greensboro drugstore, where Monroe's band members could earn extra money by transferring the Herb-O-Lac into bottles.

Tommy described a typical program over WBIG. The Pardners would start with the Man-o-ree theme song, which Scott claims to have written. The announcer would then come on: "Now, it's the noontime program the one you've been a waitin' for. And here they are, Charlie Monroe and his Kentucky Pardners, brought to you by Man-o-ree, the makers of that tonic laxative, keeps everybody hail, hearty and healthy." The first musical selection would be a Monroe Brothers-style duet, such as "What Would You Give in Exchange for Your Soul?" Another advertisement for Man-o-ree would follow, and Scott would have a solo spot. The band would mention where they were going to be performing that evening. After another advertisement for Man-o-ree, the Pardners would play an up tempo song, such as "Rollin' in My Sweet Baby's Arms." Then it was then hymn time, "for the shut-in friends." Yet another commercial for Man-o-ree was followed by the closing, up-tempo selection.

What was supposedly a great financial deal for Scott never came to fruition. "I never got a penny of the 50-50," claims Tommy, and, frustrated with what he perceived as Monroe's attempt at swindling him out of his share, he left the band and took Herb-O-Lac with him. Charlie kept on with Man-o-ree, changing the formula and hiring a duo from West Virginia to replace Tommy Scott.

The Spencer Brothers and Charlie Monroe

It was the end of 1940, and the Spencer Brothers were unhappy. Several months earlier, Lance (born May 7, 1923) and Maynard Spencer (born October 13, 1925) had followed a number of other musicians from West Virginia to perform at the Dinnertime Frolic on WBTM ("World's Best Tobacco Market"), in Danville, Virginia. Their shows just weren't drawing audiences, and they were about to be starved out. Strangely, this is just when fate landed them a spot with Charlie Monroe. As Lance reminisces:

> We were playing somewhere one night and a lady came up to me. And she said, "You know, you guys are wasting your time with this group." That's exactly what she said. And I thought — you know, a lot of ladies come up to you in that business. She said, "Why don't you go with Charlie Monroe." And I said, "Well, I hadn't even thought anything about it." She said, "Well, I'll tell you what I can do, I can line up an appointment for you." And she did. The next time she called me, she said to come to Greensboro. We went to Charlie's house, he was on North Edgeworth Street, downtown. And he hired us.

"WE WERE PACKING THE AUDITORIUMS" — THE SPENCER BROTHERS

At the end of 1940, the Spencer Brothers joined Charlie Monroe's troupe, working the WBIG Noonday Jamboree, now a half an hour long, from the O. Henry Hotel six days a week, and road shows six evenings a week for a salary of $50 each. By the end of their tenure with Monroe, the brothers were on a percentage, and would often make $200 a week apiece.

Monroe contended that there was "not a school house in the radius of 200 miles around Greensboro we didn't play." The group was so popular that they often booked return engagements with no loss of audience. In addition to Charlie and the Spencers, at various times, the show included brother Birch Monroe on fiddle and bass, Bill Coy on guitar and tenor vocals, Tommy Edwards on mandolin, Ray and Adelle ("The Two Nuts from Georgia") as blackface comedians, Roy Perky on fiddle, and several others.

On a typical road show, the hour and fifteen minute performance would be repeated until all attendees got to see the band, or until midnight, as Lance relates:

> We played in West Jefferson at the courthouse one Saturday. And it was policy on Saturday to get to wherever we were going a little bit early and ballyhoo the area. And so we got up there about three, four o'clock in the afternoon. We had two big speakers on top of the car, and Birch would drive and I'd ballyhoo with a microphone inside the car. So we went over to Jefferson. We were gone for forty-five minutes. When we came back, the line was around down the street. So, Charlie said, "Guys, lets get in and get started showin'." And that night we put on six shows. We quit at midnight; back then you had to quit, you couldn't show in North Carolina on Sunday, in those places at least. A lot of those people came out and went right back in and just saw the show over. But [Charlie] definitely had the biggest thing in show business in those days.

When Lance and Maynard started with Charlie Monroe, Dave "Stringbean" Akeman was still working with the Kentucky Pardners. "String" and the brothers immediately hit it off. In addition to Charlie's noontime radio program, the trio had an

Charlie Monroe and the Kentucky Pardners, as they appeared on WSJS-Radio in Winston-Salem. Notice the difference in size of the studio exclusively used for live musical broadcasts versus that pictured earlier at WMFR. Left to right are Maynard Spencer on mandolin, Bill Coy on guitar, Charlie Monroe on guitar, Birch Monroe on fiddle, Tommy Edwards on mandolin and Lance Spencer on guitar. Forsyth County, 1942. Courtesy Lance Spencer.

early morning show sponsored by Black Draught. At the beginning of 1942, Monroe moved his program to Winston-Salem and WSJS.

The Kentucky Pardners made another step toward country music stardom by auditioning for the Grand Ole Opry. As Lance recollects:

> In 1942, we were home on [summer] vacation and got a letter from Charlie and he said that he wanted to take the group to Nashville and do an audition for the Grand Ole Opry. And so we took a train from my home down to Nashville. We auditioned on Saturday morning at ten o'clock in the studios of WSM. And the solemn old judge, George Hay, was on the golf course when we went to the studio, so they called him to come in. And, he wasn't too happy, of course. Anyway, Charlie and the Kentucky Pardners did their thing and the Spencer Brothers did theirs. So the old judge said, "Let's have the Spencer Brothers do another number." I knew then that something was happening. So, we did another number. And he said, "Charlie, you've got the best outfit in the country. No question about it. But you know who we've got. We've got Roy Acuff, who plays the same brand of music, and we've got your brother, Bill. Really, our catalogue just won't hold another outfit. But we'll take the brothers." I said, "Well, I'm gonna be going in the service and my brother'll be going to service." He said, "Well, then come back after the service or, if you want to, sign a contract now." Those days, you weren't thinking about the music business, you were thinking about everything else.

With the Spencers of draft age, their musical careers were put on hold. Just one year after the bombing of Pearl Harbor, Lance enlisted in the Marines. Maynard was drafted when he turned eighteen, and he elected to join the Marines as well.

Once again, Charlie Monroe was on the lookout for talent. Since the war was taking all able-bodied men, he either had to hire women, men too young or old for the draft, or those with deferments. Lester Flatt, who probably had been excused from service, returned to North Carolina to play mandolin and sing tenor to Charlie's lead. He brought along his wife Gladys, and she too became a part of Monroe's show (Smith, 82–3).

Teenager Bud Osborne, too young yet for the military, probably became a Kentucky Pardner while the Spencer Brothers were still in the troupe. Orne Harrison Osborne (June 16, 1926–November 1999) was from East Tennessee. Bud began playing music at an early age, starting with guitar at the age of seven or eight, and picking up the fiddle soon afterwards. Since there were no local musicians to teach Osborne, he modeled his fiddling after musicians he heard on records and on the radio. At the age of 14, Bud auditioned for Eddie Hill and landed a spot on WNOX-Knoxville. For three years, Bud Osborne was a part of Hill's band for appearances on WNOX's live jamboree program, the Midday Merry-Go-Round, broadcast on Saturdays. Hill's band also played show dates in Tennessee and Kentucky. In 1943, while Bud Osborne was visiting his father, then living in High Point, he met Edna Smith, who was to become his wife.

Osborne decided to stay in the Piedmont. He worked for a number of bands, including those of Woody Mashburn and Charlie Monroe. His tenure with Charlie Monroe did not last long, as Osborne entered the service by early 1944.

Although live performances over the radio were the preferred method of broadcasting, Monroe had decided to make transcriptions to disseminate his programs to other radio stations, and to cover for the band when a show date prohibited their presence at the station. The Kentucky Pardners either recorded their live weekday broadcasts for later replay or prerecorded their programs at WSJS in Winston-Salem. Charlie purchased air time over seven radio stations in North Carolina and Virginia, including WBIG and WSJS, in order to broadcast these shows. A number of these transcription discs from the first half of 1944 survive, and County Records of Floyd, Virginia, issued excerpts on LP in 1974. At that time, the Kentucky Pardners included Lester and Gladys Flatt (known as Bobbie Jean), Paul Prince as primary fiddler, Birch Monroe on fiddle and bass vocals, Larry "Tex" Isley of Reidsville on electric guitar and baritone vocals, and Helen "Katy Hill" Osborne on banjo and vocals. Listeners heard Lester leading songs he would later record with Flatt and Scruggs ("We'll Meet Again Sweetheart") and Bill Monroe ("Will You Be Loving Another Man"), as well as dueting with Charlie on "When It's Time for the Whippoorwill to Sing" (Freeman; Vernon).

During early 1946, Charlie with his Kentucky Pardners returned to WBT for a 5:45 A.M. program aimed at farmers. (Coulter and Rumble, 26) By the time that Bud Osborne mustered out of the military, Monroe had moved his band to the place of Osborne's first employment, WNOX. Bud soon joined him there, where Charlie stayed until 1948. Through the early 1950s, Charlie Monroe kept North Carolina as his base of operations, although he was spending more and more time at his farm in Beaver Dam, Kentucky. In 1952, Charlie and Betty decided to move back to Kentucky, to a farm purchased with their earnings from a highly successful ten-plus years in North Carolina. (*Bluegrass Unlimited*, 15 and 17).

Gurney Thomas

If Charlie Monroe was among the most popular performers in Piedmont during the 1930s and 1940s, then Gurney Thomas was its most tenacious. From the late 1920s through 1980, for a remarkable fifty-plus years, Thomas made at least part of his living from broadcasting and performing. And, as Gurney said, he had the opportunity to leave North Carolina, but preferred to stay in his home state.

James Gurney Thomas, Sr. (born September 25, 1913) is from near Candor on the Montgomery and Moore county line. Before she married in 1905, his mother, Dovie Anne Luck (September 16, 1880–February 16, 1936), a cousin to the owners of Luck's Beans that sponsored Tommy Floyd (see Chapter Nine), played banjo in a family band that included her brother Colon on guitar. When Thomas was twelve years old, his father William Donaldson Thomas (August 27, 1864–July 24, 1934) moved the family off their farm into the city of High Point. Some of Gurney's brothers and sisters were working at the Hillcrest Silk Mills, and Gurney soon joined them, lying about his age in order to obtain his work card. It was during this period that Gurney Thomas, who had fooled with the guitar back on the farm, became serious about the instrument. William Thomas had employed an African American who sold Gurney his guitar and showed him the basic chords. Now in High Point, Thomas began to accumulate 78-rpm records by the Carter Family and the Skillet Lickers with guitarist Riley Puckett, among others. Jimmie Rodgers was his special favorite. Gurney also began playing out in public, often in the company of another guitarist, David Hicks. Hicks provided Thomas his first real knowledge of chords and technique when the duo took their music to local square dances and parties.

Sometime in the late 1920s, Fred Kirby, who was broadcasting on WBT (see Chapter Nine), was playing a series of weekend shows at High Point's Rialto Theater. Thomas began to think about performing on his own: "[He] inspired me to think, 'I could do that good.' Now, whether I was or not, I don't know.... But other people told me, too ... 'You're as good as he is.'" So, Thomas screwed up his nerve and approached the manager of the Broadhurst Theater, one of High Point's most prestigious movie houses:

> I didn't even know three songs, I had to learn 'em when I played the [Broadhurst] theater the first time.... I never had knowed him to use nothin' like a hillbilly. But, I thought I'd at least go ask him.... [Pat McSwain, the manager] told me, "You have to start somewhere.... You bring your guitar up about eleven o'clock Saturday mornin' and let me hear you." And he put me down there right in the middle of the stage, went up there in the control room, turned on the spotlight. He sat down in the middle of the theater and I sung a couple of songs. And he asked me about the "St Louis Blues" and I told him, I might know a verse of it. I did it, and

Gurney Thomas (then spelling his name "Gurnie") at the start of his career, looking very much the part of "The Original Troubadour of the South." Possibly Burlington, Alamance County, circa 1932. Courtesy Gurney Thomas.

The Southern Pioneers, Gurney Thomas's first band. Standing are "Red" Smith (guitar), announcer Bob Poole and Jack (guitar). Sitting are Gurney holding a mandolin and "Mac" McClure (banjo). The Pioneers were appearing over WBIG Radio in Greensboro. Guilford County, circa 1935. Courtesy Gurney Thomas.

then he told me that was enough. So I just thinked, "Well, so much for this." Come on back to the office and he booked me, was about five or six weeks.

Now, I put on five shows on Friday evenin' and four Saturday evenin.' He told me to deal with twelve minutes, not go more than thirteen and don't get under eleven, it'd get him off schedule. And then if I'd miss, why, he'd want me to kill a little bit more time to keep the movie on schedule.... He wrote me a letter that I could play any theater in the whole "Wilbur Kinsey" theater chain that used somethin' similar to what I done. And I played their big theaters, nothin' but me and a guitar.

Gurney was on his way. As "The Singing Kid," he worked as a solo act in movie theaters throughout the Piedmont. At the same time, Gurney was broadcasting on Saturdays from 1 to 1:15 P.M. over Greensboro radio station WBIG (*Gastonia Gazette*, p3D; undated newspaper article).

However, Gurney was still relying on his day job to pay his bills. So in 1932, when the Hillcrest Mill closed, the Thomas family relocated to Burlington, where Gurney's brother Carlton had gotten him another textile job (High Point City Directories). Thomas worked in the mill for six months and then formed a band with banjoist Mack McClure. Mack and Gurney eventually joined forces with Red Smith, calling themselves the Southern Pioneers. Red later led the Carolina Jug Band over WBIG and WBBB.

However, the Southern Pioneers were still strictly a local band. So when Fred Kirby came to Randleman in 1934, Gurney signed on with Kirby's ensemble. Unfortunately, just as it appeared that Gurney had gotten the break he needed to move into music full-time, his father suffered a stroke and died. Gurney left Kirby and moved back with his family.

Thomas then took up where he left off. In the mid–1930s, the Southern Pioneers procured an early morning slot on the Greensboro radio station, WBIG (*Gastonia Gazette*, p3D). Thomas also worked at WBIG as a member of Bill Lasley and His Ridge Runners. In November 1936, Gurney began corresponding with Eli Oberstein, the artists and repertoire manager for RCA Records. Oberstein was interested in recording the Southern Pioneers for RCA's Bluebird subsidiary, and spent the following months trying to work out the details for Thomas and band to attend a recording session (Oberstein to Thomas). Unfortunately, unforeseen circumstances once again intervened. On Christmas Eve, Gurney Thomas was involved in a serious car accident. He broke his leg, and spent most of 1938 in bed.

After this string of unfortunate events that blocked Gurney from going pro in the early 1930s, 1939 proved to be a banner year for him. J. E. Mainer, fresh from a stint in Columbia, South Carolina, had been contracted by Consolidated Royal Chemical Corporation (also called Consolidated Drug Products), the makers of Peruna and Kolorbak. Peruna (pronounced "Pee-roo-na") was a cold remedy, while Kolorbak, not surprisingly, got rid of gray hair (*Border Radio*, 173; see Chapter Nine). Unfortunately for J. E., but, luckily for Gurney, Mainer's band had just walked out on him. In September of 1939, J. E. Mainer and Gurney Thomas, after joining forces earlier in the year, headed for Texas. Gurney's band at that time included Coy Cheek (December 24, 1914–September 7, 1998) and Price Saunders on banjo. Sterling Price Saunders (September 4, 1916–April 14, 1983) was from Troy, the county

Taking it easy in the land of the cactus and the longhorn, Gurney Thomas was in Texas recording radio programs for Consolidated Drug. Left to right are "Cowboy" Slim Reinhart, an unknown companion and Gurney Thomas. San Antonio, Texas, 1939.

seat of Montgomery County. He began playing banjo around 1930, like others, performing informally around his area at community functions.

But, from the start, things didn't go as planned. Cheek's upcoming nuptials prevented him from leaving North Carolina, and so he was replaced with Bill McCallum from Randleman, who later worked with John Henry Brewer. Then, McCallum and Mainer didn't take to each other, and Gurney and Bill split off from J. E., making their own transcriptions for Kolorback as the Southern Troubadours. Mitchell Parker, who had worked for Crazy Water in Raleigh and on the radio in High Point, and Reid Whitley, both from Stanly County, came in to replace Thomas and McCallum in Mainer's band.

When the musicians finally got down to business, they joined an all-star cast of country stars who had made the pilgrimage to the Lone Star State. The Carter Family, the Pickard Family (formerly of WSM-Nashville and WLW-Cincinnati) and cowgirl singer Patsy Montana all were sponsored by Consolidated. The scam was a simple one. Because Mexican radio stations were not subject to the same regulations as their American counterparts, they could broadcast at any power they wanted. So American groups with American sponsors could be beamed at American audiences from Mexico with far greater coverage than could be attained over an American station.

Mainer, Thomas, and others arrived in San Antonio to make transcribed (pre-recorded) programs at a garage studio run by Don Baxter and his wife Dode. These would be brought across the border at Del Rio, and broadcast over XERA in Villa Acuna, Coahuila (*Border Radio*, p172 and 174). Mainer's group made enough shows to cover 26 weeks of programming. Gurney and Bill then made their own shows. By the time they were done, 192 fifteen-minute programs for transcribed broadcast were in the can.

In 1940, all the musicians were back in Greensboro, working over WBIG. J. E., using the name of Mainer's Mountaineers, was still working with Price, Mitchell, and Reid. Gurney and Bill also had a slot, appearing at noon. But the current Mountaineers were unhappy working for J. E., and jumped ship to join up with Gurney.

GURNEY THOMAS ON WBIG

In the later part of 1940 or early in 1941, Gurney Thomas assembled his first edition of the Hill Billy Pals. Price Saunders on banjo, Mitchell Parker on guitar, Bill McCallum on guitar, and Reid Whitley on guitar and mandolin backed Gurney on guitar and vocals. The group began on WBIG, but soon moved over to WPTF in Raleigh for the better part of 1941 (*Gastonia Gazette*, p3D). However, circumstances again forced Gurney out of the music business. Gas and tires became impossible to obtain. At the end of his tenure in Raleigh, Gurney had been able to wrangle a weekly salary of $75 out of WPTF, but it wasn't enough to support a band. "Even with them

Opposite: Same band, similar outfits, different leader. The Hill Billy Pals — Price Saunders standing with his banjo, Reid Whitley on guitar and mandolin kneeling left and Mitchell Parker on guitar on the right. Fiddler J. E. Mainer "borrowed" the Pals from Gurney Thomas, the later pictured with his band at the WBIG microphone. Circa 1940 or 1941. Courtesy Gurney Thomas.

... we weren't doin' nothin but just existin' almost," remembers Gurney. Price Saunders entered the military. Bill McCallum moved to Florida in order to perform in clubs. Gurney, who had lost a foot in a motorcycle accident some years before, was exempt from the draft, and returned to textile work. During 1942, he lived in Asheboro and worked as a loom fixer for Burlington Mills.

Music, however, exerted too strong a pull on Thomas. He met steel guitarist Wilbern Cranford at Burlington Mills and the duo began playing together. Wilbern Alexander Cranford (born July 17, 1921) was born in Asheboro, although he grew up in High Point. Cranford began noticing music in the 1930s, listening to the Monroe Brothers, the Blue Sky Boys, and the Tobacco Tags on WPTF, and, to a lesser extent, the Briarhoppers on WBT. As a young teenager, Wilbern spent his summers in Randolph County with his uncle Charlie Cranford. "It just so happened the area where we was livin'," remembers Wilbern, "there was two or three guys that strummed the guitar a little bit and got me started." Wilbern quit school in the ninth grade to work running a knitting machine in a textile mill. Cranford was turned away from the military, and so was free to perform. Everett Moffitt joined the duo on bass and Saly Newman came in on lead guitar, then Glenn Davis added his banjo and comedy. The group was now complete.

The Moffitts are an old Randolph County family who were land granted property outside of Coleridge before the Civil War, where they still live today. Everett Robert Moffitt (born June 12, 1920) was raised working at his father Robert Harris Moffitt's (July 13, 1893–1969) farm and saw mill. Robert played the harmonica a bit, and Ev's mother Minnie Craven (ca. 1885–1965) the organ, even though instrumental music was not prominent during Everett's youth. His parents did attend singing schools and brought young Moffitt along, but it never held much appeal for him.

Everett traces his love of music to the schoolhouse fiddlers' conventions he began attending around the age of twelve or thirteen. "I know [the fiddle] had pretty sounds to it," tells Moffitt. "I fell in love with that." He also heard Glenn Davis play in the 1930s. Luther Glenn Davis (March 28, 1909–February 4, 1986), the third child of Claude Franklin Davis (July 12, 1885–May 22, 1934) and Nannie Jane Phillips (June 5, 1879–May 20, 1977) of Chatham County, was born into the same Coleridge community as Everett Moffitt. Glenn's maternal grandfather was a fiddler, and Glenn's maternal uncle "knocked" the banjo, showing Glenn how to tune it. When Ev first heard Davis, Glenn was living in Asheboro, where he was to spend the 1930s. Says Ev: "If [Glenn Davis] went to a fiddlers' convention, you'd about figure he'd come away with a prize.... If he didn't get first, he'd get second or third."

The young Moffitt was also inspired by the music he heard on the Grand Ole Opry. "The first [radio] I ever heard," says Ev, "was in 1927. I was seven year old when my mama's brother had one that had wires stretched for a quarter of a mile each way, you know, and run it off a car battery. I believe Daddy had a 1920 model Chevrolet and they'd run the wire out to that for the power." By 1932, the Moffitt family had a radio of their own. They also owned a phonograph, but Everett's parents preferred the sounds of brass bands to the string band music of Charlie Poole or the yodeling of Jimmie Rodgers.

In the mid–1930s, Ev ordered a fiddle via a mail order catalogue. Moffitt would hear tunes at a convention, keep them in his head, and then try them on his own instrument when he got home. "I didn't play in the house," tells Moffitt.

> There was a … field growed [sic] up in pines that was taller than my head. And I'd go way off out of hearin' from the house while I squeaked and squawked, til I got brave enough to bring it out in the public, you know, and show my parents what I had come up with…. And I never had any intention of playing in front of anybody, I just wanted to do it for my own entertainment. I said, "If a man over yander can play a fiddle, I can play one." I just felt like I could…. If I can play for my own pleasure, just sittin' around somewhere under a shade tree, I'd be happy. But the people wouldn't let you rest, here they come with guitars and mandolins and so forth.

Even though Everett fiddled for the usual community functions, his attention was soon diverted to another instrument, the string bass that he heard at the fiddlers' events: "I just loved that sound. We went to a fiddlers' convention at Bennett, and the man I [eventually] bought it from, Dwight Reece, was playin' it. And you could just feel the windowpanes a swellin' out and in. I said, 'I got to have one of them things.' It was the just the best sound I'd ever heard in my life, I fell in love with it."

But there were few string basses around his area at that time, and the instruments were hard to come by. In 1942, at his induction physical for the military, he again saw Reece. Since Dwight was going into the service, he agreed to sell his instrument to Moffitt, who still had six months to go until his formal conscription. During his stint in the military, Everett earned plenty of experience playing the bass with a special services unit in Oregon. The band was made up of professional musicians: Jack Wood from Roy Hall's band on steel guitar; Arthur Glick on guitar, who came from WJJD-Chicago and the Suppertime Frolic; Chick Sanderson of the Golden West Cowboys and "Smokey" Kish on fiddle. The playing experience Ev gained prepared him to join up with Thomas upon Moffitt's discharge.

In 1944, Gurney approached WGBG ("Watch Greensboro Become Greater"), the new radio station controlled by the owners of WMFR. He was given a spot on Saturdays at noon, first for fifteen minutes and then for thirty minutes. During that first year on the air, Newman went into the Navy and was replaced by Hubert Carl "Woody" Greeson (born January 23, 1927). Greeson had worked throughout the War years with Johnny Harris on WBIG (see Chapter Nine). He decided to play with Gurney rather than go with Charlie Monroe and be away from home. Glenn Davis, tired of trying to balance performing with his job as a textile worker, left the music business after a year with Thomas.

Despite the difficulties of keeping a band together during wartime, Gurney's efforts were a success. By the war's end, the Hill Billy Pals were broadcasting twice daily, from 6 until 6:25 A.M. and from 12:45 until 1 P.M., in addition to their Saturday slot. The Pals also made transcriptions late at night after returning from show dates. These aired in their early morning, when they were away on show dates, and on the Sanford, North Carolina, radio station. Uncle Henry (William Taylor), an announcer on WGBG, had joined their troupe as a comedian, and guitarist Mitchell Parker, recently released from the service, came back into the fold. Most importantly, Gurney was able to quit his day job during the school season to make personal appearances.

Gurney Thomas and the Hill Billy Pals as they appeared over WGBG Radio. Standing, left to right, are Gurney Thomas (guitar), Glenn Davis (banjo), Everett Moffitt (string bass) and Woody Greeson (lead guitar). Sitting are "Uncle Henry" Taylor (announcer and comedian) and Wilbern Cranford (steel guitar). Possibly Greensboro, Guilford County, 1944. Courtesy Gurney Thomas.

"WE HAD A CLEAN SHOW, WE DIDN'T HAVE NO DIRTY JOKES
OR UNCLEAN, SUGGESTIVE SONGS…. WE ALWAYS ENDED OUR
PROGRAM WITH A HYMN"—WILBERN CRANFORD

A typical radio broadcast for Gurney and the Pals would always open and close with the theme song "Rocky Mountain Sweetheart." Then the announcer would tell the listeners, as Wilbern Cranford relates:

> You're listening to Gurney Thomas and his Hill Billy Pals coming to you from station WGBG in Greensboro, North Carolina, sponsored by either a tobacco company, Mann's Drugstore or Dr. Foster's LK, from High Point. And now we turn the program over to Gurney."
> [Gurney would say] "Howdy friends it's another pleasant opportunity that we have to be here to play and sing for you today. And I hope you'll enjoy the program."

From that point on, the program's musical selections were determined by listener requests. As Everett Moffitt tells it:

> Your mail determined what you put on [your shows]…. If a new tune come out [by] some of these people that we liked or imitated like Jimmie Rodgers, Ernest Tubb … we'd get that record and learn it, and then put it on the air. Well, if we got mail

for it, we'd put it on quite often, and we'd also put it on when we made our personal appearances.

Gurney's songbooks reflected what was popular with the public, and therefore included in his shows. *Gurney Thomas' Folio of Favorite Song Hits As Sung by the Hill Billy Pals Book Three*, published during Thomas's tenure at WGBG, includes the Merle Travis and Cliffie Stone composition "No Vacancy," "You're Breaking My Heart ('Cause You Don't Care)" and "Just Because of You, Little Girl" recorded by Jimmie Davis, Ernest Tubb's "Rainbow at Midnight," and others from Gene Autry, Bob Wills, and Ted Daffan. All except the hymns were contemporary hits on the country charts. Before the show ended, each member of the band would be featured on a specialty number. Cranford might play Leon McAuliffe's "Steel Guitar Rag," Moffitt a tune on the fiddle, and Greeson a hot piece on the guitar. Then, the band would sing a hymn and bid farewell with, "Well, the clock on the wall says it's time to go. So, until this time tomorrow we'll say 'so long.'" Occasionally, Thomas shared his radio program as well as the stage of the National Theater in Greensboro with touring performers such as Smiley Burnett, Sunset Carson, Tex Ritter, Fiddling Arthur Smith, and Bill Monroe's classic band with Lester Flatt, Earl Scruggs, and Chubby Wise.

"If I'd get home by about four o'clock I was in good shape"—Everett Moffitt

As with other country performers working during the 1940s, Gurney Thomas's radio programs were used to publicize and promote his band. Listeners would write in and request a date for Thomas and his band to come give a concert. It was up to the group to handle all the advertising, including the printing of posters or hand-bills, which could then be sent home with the students at whatever school or venue where they were scheduled to appear. The band traveled in one automobile and towed a trailer containing their equipment. When they arrived at the venue, every member of the Pals had a job outside of playing the concert. One group member sold tickets, another would set up their public address system, which used a single microphone, and so on.

Gurney Thomas and the Hill Billy Pals ended up playing six nights a week all over southern and western Virginia, and North and South Carolina, at courthouses, theaters, and school auditoriums. At a schoolhouse, the Pals would split the fifty-cent admission charge, giving the local school organization forty percent of the money taken in at the door. The band would also make money off of songbook and photo sales. And they usually drew a good crowd.

Gurney Thomas and King Records, "The 'King' of Them All"

For the radio artist, the income that recordings yielded was rather limited, the "real" money being in personal appearances. So it was almost an afterthought for Gurney to send a recorded audition to King Records of Cincinnati, one of the new independent labels that sprung up after World War II. Sid Nathan, the owner of King, sent back a five-year contract. In June of 1946, the Pals loaded up their automobile, tied the bass to the roof, and started out for Ohio.

There is some disagreement among the band members about the length of the sessions. Two of the former Pals remember finishing all the recording in one block of time, whereas Gurney claims that the songs were cut in two night sessions of four songs each, with an additional day session where one of the tunes was redone. Half of the recorded songs were hymns. Of the four secular compositions waxed, two were by Mitchell Parker, one by Woody Greeson's sister Ruth and the fourth by Gurney himself. Regardless of the details, after a tour of the King facilities, the Hill Billy Pals drove back to North Carolina. In total, the band was gone for seven days, therefore losing the income from a week's worth of shows.

Gurney was not happy with the results. He felt that Nathan and his engineer did not take the sessions seriously. Thomas also had problems with the publishing royalties from the sessions, a common problem that still persists between artists and record labels. When King released the first 78-rpm record from the sessions, "To Love Until I Die," the company issued a rejected take rather than the one redone by the Pals. This was the final straw, and Thomas decided not to record for King again.

After his return from Cincinnati, Gurney expanded the band, adding Slim Martin on fiddle. Fiddler and comedian James "Slim" Martin (born September 10, 1919) was from Murphy, in the western mountains of North Carolina. He had been one of Charlie Monroe's Kentucky Pardners for a short time in Louisville, and had rejoined Monroe right before the Pardners returned to Charlotte (*Bluegrass Unlimited*, p17; *Charlie Monroe's Souvenir Songbook*). Thomas also decided it was time to move on. He made an agreement with a bigger radio station in Danville, Virginia, WDVA, and by the summer of 1947 had temporarily moved his band to a new broadcaster in Asheboro, WGWR, while awaiting the WDVA contract (*Courier-Tribune*, p4; see Chapter Nine). When Gurney was involved in yet another automobile accident, which sadly seemed to be endemic in the musical profession, "Uncle Henry" Taylor jokingly remarked that the station was really called "Watch Gurney Wreck Randolph [County]." More changes occurred, as Everett Moffitt, the only unmarried band member, tied the knot and decided to stay behind in North Carolina. John "Red" Sneed replaced Ev, and Cub McGee joined Slim Martin on the fiddle.

PERSONNEL CHANGES

As often occurred with these itinerant performers, Gurney's move to Danville was an unsuccessful one. After a year, Thomas and the Hill Billy Pals switched their allegiance to WPTF. Wilbern Cranford was replaced by George Mitchell of High Point, Red Sneed left and Cecil Hedgecock came in on string bass. Jim Hall, "The Radio Ranger," who had appeared with Gurney in the past, came in as a full-fledged band member. After a year in Raleigh, Gurney could tell that the market was changing. Although it was getting harder to draw an audience, he accepted the invitation of "Uncle Henry" Taylor to bring a band to WPAQ in Mount Airy. In 1951, the group included H. O. "Sleepy" Jenkins on fiddle, Sonny Tabor on bass, multi-instrumentalist Bill Franklin, and George Mitchell on steel guitar. Unfortunately, the era for

Gurney Thomas broadcasting in Raleigh over WPTF in 1948. Mitchell Parker, George Mitchell, Cub McGee, Gurney Thomas, Jim Hall and Cecil Hedgecock (left to right). Courtesy Gurney Thomas.

live music on the radio was ending (undated newspaper ad; *WPAQ: The Voice of the Blue Ridge Mountains*).

Thomas had moved his family to Belmont, south of Charlotte, in 1949. Southern Attractions, based in Charlotte, agreed to represent Gurney as a solo act, pairing Thomas up for appearances with western movie stars. Besides touring with movie cowboys such as Sunset Carson and Fuzzy St. John, Thomas appeared in western towns such as Dodge City. Gurney would work shows with other singers, appear on bills with bands that he could utilize for back-up, or assemble groups if and when he needed one. There was the television program on WTOB and area dances with Glenn Thompson (see Chapter Nine). Gurney played a regular Saturday night dance and the Gaston County Fair, and ran the Carolina Jamboree at the Gem Theater in Belmont. Thomas helped to book Flatt and Scruggs, and would appear on their shows. This led to the bluegrass duo covering Gurney's song "Some One Took My Place with You," which the team recorded in 1953. Some of the bands employed by Thomas included the Lincoln County Partners, Hoyt Herbert and the Strings of Five, and the Country Partners.

Radio work was another opportunity that presented itself in the 1950s. However, rather than play live music, this time, the job was in that new occupation of "disc jockey." Gurney remembered that

Gurney Thomas and Glenn Thompson, on their television set in the studios of WTOB. Winston-Salem, Forsyth County, 1953. Courtesy Gurney Thomas.

> Show business weren't that bad, but it was goin' down. The Opry stars started goin' around two or three or more together, playin' schools.... That television comin' in and changin' trends.... It weren't goin' down where we weren't gettin' by, but it was lookin' worse all the time. And we'd have went around and around in the same territory and was gettin' the shows so far away.

Thomas began a long-term association with Belmont broadcaster WCGC. For the better part of 26 years, Gurney held forth over the local station. He was DJ of the Year in 1954 and brought to Nashville to announce a portion of the Grand Ole Opry. The management of WCGC was generous in allowing Thomas the time off to make personal appearances. He attempted to move up to the more powerful WAYS radio in Charlotte, but their format changed, and, after 16 months, he returned to WCGC.

Until 1980, when he retired from the country music business, Gurney was a fixture on WCGC. He became the early morning man, winning over listeners with his easy, down-home manner. He used his radio program as a springboard to promote shows for touring country stars at the Charlotte Coliseum in 1961 and 1962. Gurney even authored a "mock" advice column for the *East Gaston Suburban*, entitled "Dear Gurney" (Flyer; Newspaper clipping).

Glenn Thompson

The career of Glenn Thompson is inextricably connected to that of Gurney Thomas. Gurney and Glenn come from the same area of Moore County. When approached by the younger man for his first radio job, Gurney referred Thompson to the new broadcaster in Burlington. The two musicians shared the airways for telecasts, as well as stages for square dances. Their stories are related, yet different personalities caused each man to take a distinct approach in pursuing a musical profession.

Glenn Thompson always had his eye on business and on the bottom line. He was determined to figure out ways to make a living from music. Thompson was also aggressive about controlling his own destiny. He fought for a radio salary when it was an unheard of expense, promoted his own shows under canvas, and invested his earnings in broadcast stations and real estate.

The son of farmers Lonnie and Ethel Britt Thompson, Glenn Thompson (born October 16, 1921) grew up on the border of Montgomery and Moore counties. As a youngster, Glenn listened to the Opry and imitated the Delmore Brothers with his cousin Henderson Britt. Around the age of ten, Dorsey and Howard Dixon, recording artists and radio stars (see Chapter Nine), paid the neighbors a visit. Glenn said he was spellbound by the duo, which gave a performance Sunday afternoon on the porch of a local home. Thompson also idolized Jimmie Rodgers, Victor Record's first country music star. House dances were common around Moore County and touring groups often appeared at the Eagle Springs School. When Charlie and Bill Monroe, then on WPTF-Raleigh, gave a personal at Eagle Springs, Glenn was front and center. Thompson's first public appearance was at the same schoolhouse where he saw the Monroes. He performed at a Bible school commencement with Britt as "Glenn and Slim" (Thompson and Weiss and Davis interview).

When Glenn was about seventeen, he left the farm to seek his fortune. He held jobs in a laundry, a service station, and a textile mill before following a cousin to Newport News, Virginia. There, just after Pearl Harbor, Glenn landed a defense job in a shipyard.

All along, it was Thompson's intention to make his living from music. He played over WGHP radio while in Virginia, and, when he moved to Panama City, Florida, ostensibly to work in a service station with a friend from North Carolina, a local country band snapped him up. John King and the Drifting Cowboys, as the group was named, played western swing music over the local radio station WDLP (Thompson and Weiss and Davis interview) and at dances for shipyard workers. Glenn was paid the kingly sum of $175 a week! However, the draft finally caught up with Thompson, who was no longer exempt because he had left his deferred job behind in Virginia.

Thompson was discharged in the fall of 1944, and he made a beeline back to North Carolina. First, he approached Gurney Thomas, then at WGBG, for a job, but Gurney didn't have any openings. Thomas sent Glenn Thompson over to WBBB, where Smokey Graves was looking for a partner.

Thompson on WBBB: "We're Building Better Burlington"

WBBB, Burlington's first radio station, went on the air in 1941. The one thousand watt broadcaster could be heard in parts of North Carolina, Kentucky, Tennessee, Virginia, and South Carolina. Following its sign on, an assortment of string bands and hillbilly crooners traipsed through the doors of the station at 310½ South Main Street. The performer from those early days that later achieved the most fame was Tennessean Lester Flatt. Best known as a member of Bill Monroe's band that defined bluegrass music, and as half of the duo of Flatt and Scruggs that took bluegrass to a wider audience in the 1960s, Lester Flatt (June 14, 1914–May 11, 1979) came to Burlington soon after WBBB went on the air. Clyde Moody, a member of Monroe's band before Flatt, worked the station with Lester for a few months before returning to Monroe's fold. A number of the musicians I interviewed remembered Flatt from the station, and claimed to have worked with him. Lester's time in Burlington, however, was short-lived. In 1943, Lester Flatt was hired by Charlie Monroe, then based in Greensboro, which began his rapid rise to country music stardom (Rosenberg, 68).

Flatt was succeeded at WBBB by Jim Hall, a singer and a worker in the Swepsonville mill; Smilin' Brownie; fiddler and singer Virgil William "Smokey" Graves (August 24, 1918–January 13, 1988), and Red Smith. Hall's band, which played the radio station, square dances, and personal appearances, included Zeke Reitzel on banjo and Robert Hudson on guitar and mandolin. Reitzel was 4-F, and so had lots of work playing music on the home front. Clyde Robert Hudson (born October 27, 1923) was the son of Chatham County banjoist and auto mechanic George Clyde Hudson (May 4, 1887–July 6, 1970). A knitter at Standard Hosiery, Robert and his brother Howard Alfonso "Pee Wee" Hudson (born December 11, 1927), a banjoist still in high school, played with Red Smith in the Carolina Jug Band.

When Glenn arrived in Burlington during October 1944, Jim Hall had just left WBBB to work in Richmond. Another entertainer on the station had just entered the army. Smoky Graves decided to hire Thompson and Glenn had landed his first full-time radio job. Their act, called Smokey and Glenn's Blue Ridge Entertainers, only lasted fifteen months. In January 1946, Graves decided to move to WSJS in Winston-Salem. He named his new band the Blue Star Boys, and brought along the Blue Ridge Entertainers banjoist Oscar Hutchins (possibly "Hutchinson" from Ramseur, see Chapter Nine). Smokey hired Cub McGee on fiddle, along with Jimmy and Gene Anderson. Graves later worked at WWGP in Sanford, with Cub, guitarist Henry Luck, Johnny Burton on bass, and Jack Jon on steel guitar.

The station manager of WBBB was E. Z. Jones, who asked Glenn to remain at the station. Glenn, in a bold and unusual move, requested payment in exchange for his services:

> When me and Smokey Graves was gonna split up, E. Z. wanted me to stay. He says, "You're gettin' the majority of the mail, I want you to stay here, you can do well." And he was right. And I said, "Well, I'll stay. But I've played my last day on the radio to [just] advertise my show dates. If you want to pay me a salary, I'll stay." I seen I's gonna have to [draw a salary].

"Smokey" Graves on fiddle and Glenn (then Glen) Thompson on guitar, at the start of Glenn's tenure over WBBB Radio in Burlington, 1945. Southern Folklife Collection; courtesy Glenn Thompson.

> And that was the last time I ever played on the air for nothin'. They was gettin' all our music, our popularity, free of charge. All that we could do was to advertise our songbook for sale and the show date where we was gonna be, which was good and it worked fine. But still, I didn't think it was fair and I asked for money and I got money.

At that time, WBT and the other Charlotte broadcasters were the only stations within North Carolina to salary their talent. Other musicians had either accepted the fact that radio stations would not pay them, presold and then bought their own airtime, or became their own sponsors. Thompson was the first performer on WBBB to receive a salary, which was especially unusual for a regional station (Thompson and Weiss and Davis interview).

For the sum of $50 per week, Glenn stayed in Burlington. He named his new group the Dixie Playboys. Along with three of the Blue Ridge Entertainers—Stacy Fry on bass, Sleepy Johnson of Sanford on guitar, and Curley Garner on lead electric guitar and mandolin—Thompson hired Bill Purcell of Altamahaw, who played steel guitar. Fiddler Pee Wee Williams, from Summerfield, and guitarist Woody Greeson also worked with Thompson at WBBB.

For the three years Glenn Thompson and the Dixie Playboys were in Burlington, they broadcast a half-hour program, which started at 6:30 A.M. and later moved to 9:30 A.M. The band worked personals six nights a week, and made recordings that Thompson issued on his own record label. Glenn Thompson and the Dixie Playboys proved to be extremely popular with area listeners. To stay as long as they did at one station and to continue to book appearances and draw audiences was a strong comment on their appeal. This was due in part to Glenn's choice of material and the band's ability to interpret these songs. Rather than dance music, western swing, or honky-tonk, Thompson liked the slow, sadder songs. As he remarked: "I liked country, I wasn't a mountain music person. I was a Jimmie Rodgers fan. And about that time Ernest Tubb and Bob Wills was comin' along in there. But mine wasn't western swing."

While Glenn was at WBBB, he was winning a lot of Raleigh listeners away from WPTF. Thompson was summoned to Raleigh for an audition, but even though the listeners liked his music, Thompson proved too progressive for station manager Graham Poyner. "You've got to have a banjo and a fiddle," remarked Poyner. So Glenn stayed in Burlington.

But eventually new opportunities beckoned. In early 1949, Thompson moved for three months to Wilson, North Carolina, and then, in May, to WDVA-Danville, Virginia (*Danville Register*). Unlike Gurney Thomas, Glenn did well in Danville, and made history when in July he began the Virginia Barn Dance on Saturday nights (*Danville Register*, 6).

"Get your banjer, let's get gone" — Glenn Thompson

The Barn Dance proved to be an extremely popular event. Many well-known country and what was to be called rockabilly and rock 'n' roll acts appeared with Glenn, including Bill and Earl Bolick, aka the Blue Sky Boys, Jim Eanes, his old friends Jim Hall and Smokey Graves, Tommy Magness and Don Reno (who drew an unprecedented 1,575 people), and Danville's own Janis Martin. The three-and-a-half hour Barn Dance was held in a building on the Danville Fair grounds. WDVA and the Fair Association promoted the weekly happening and provided bus transportation to and from downtown Danville and the Fair Grounds. Parts of the 8–9:30 P.M. concert segment were broadcast locally, a half-hour of which could be heard for a time over the Mutual Radio Network. When the broadcast was over, a dance was held for the gathered multitudes. When the guest stars were especially well known and the weather cooperated, the broadcast moved outside to the grandstand area of the Fair Grounds (www.hillbilly-music.com).

In addition to the Virginia Barn Dance, Glenn and the Playboys performed at movie theaters in the wintertime and hauled a tent around in the summer. A good gauge of Thompson's popularity during this period was his sale of songbooks. Between 1947 and 1951, Glenn sold 110,000 copies of his publications. Seemingly, Thompson was unstoppable. Events that would have sidetracked a less-determined individual became opportunities for Glenn, as was proven when his whole band quit one night. "It just so happened that my band, the whole shebang went on strike," told Glenn.

They was gonna dictate to me how much money I was gonna pay 'em. And I was doin' well in Danville. So, they come to me fifteen minutes before I was supposed to go on the air on my barn dance, and I had over a thousand people sittin' out there, and they come to me, and said they wanted a raise. I said, "Well, I've been thinkin' about givin' you one." They said, "No, we want one now," told me how much. Now, the boys is all right, but they had a ringleader on it, so they all walked out. I went on the air by myself, just me and my guitar like I started. I told everybody there, "Now, if there's anybody came here especially to see any member of my band, and paid your money to see them, go to the gate, they'll give you your money back. But if you come to see me, I'm here and I'll be here till twelve o'clock tonight." And I hit my old theme and went ahead. Before the air show was over, musicians had come around, offerin' to help me.... Before I went off the air, I had a full band.... And the next day, Tommy Goad of Asheboro had called me wantin' a job.... And at that time I had a tent show, trucks and everything. So on Sunday afternoon after I played the barn dance on Saturday night, I had the tent on Sunday afternoon at another place and Sunday night at the same place. So, there I was, nobody but me, and that show comin' up. So, I called Tommy Goad in Asheboro. I said, "Tommy, you still want that job?" "Oh, yeah, yeah, when do you want me to start?" I said, "How quick can you get to Danville? I need you now." This is on Sunday mornin'. He says, "I'll be there as soon as I can put my banjer in the car." He thought that I had that big band of fine musicians. Got there, and I said, "Boy, it's about time for us to leave." I had one fella, which was a black-faced comedian, he drove my truck, and lookin' after puttin' up the tent. And I said, "Get your banjer, let's get gone."

Glenn Thompson, then sponsored by Service Distributing Company, appearing during the Eisenhower and Stevenson presidential campaign possibly at the Dixie Classic Fair. Left to right are unknown, Glenn Thompson, unknown, unknown, Paige Hepler (fiddle). Winston-Salem, Forsyth County, 1952–1956. Southern Folklife Collection, courtesy Glenn Thompson.

We started down the road, he says, "Where's the band?" I said, "You're it!" That old boy like to fainted! He said, "Lord have mercy!" I said, "Rusty will do some comedy, but it will be me and you playin' the music at the tent, an hour and a half." I said, "You know a lot of instrumentals, don't you?" I made a joke out of it, what the heck. Got there, that tent was packed full of people that Sunday afternoon. I went out on the stage, and I told the audience the same thing I did on Saturday night. And incidentally, on Saturday night, didn't a soul go and ask for their money back, and I've always been really proud…. And most of those people near Danville had heard the barn dance that Saturday night, and knew I was by myself. Me and Tommy went on that stage, I did an hour and a half show, and I think I done about as good a show as I ever did, cause I really put out. That night, the thing was runnin' over again, right in the same neighborhood, I did the same thing.

The [Louvin Brothers] were over in Greensboro on the station and they'd called me wantin' a job. On Monday mornin', I called Ira and Charlie Louvin, and told them, "You all still wantin' a job?" "Oh, yeah, yeah." "Well, how quick can you get there?" They said, "We can't come until Tuesday." I though, "Lord have mercy, I've got a Monday night to go through again." And I said, "That'll be fine." I told 'em on the phone what I'd pay 'em. It was $50 a week apiece, and ten percent of all the road shows I done was the deal I made to Charlie and Ira. What happened then was Ira calls me back. And he stumbled and stuttered a while. He said, "Glenn, we haven't got the money to come. Can you send us some money?" I said, "Sure!" I sent 'em the money, they come right on.

Charlie and Ira Louvin had left Knoxville in 1950 to be a part of the new barn dance program just begun by WBIG in Greensboro. After only a short time, it became apparent that Greensboro would not work out for the Louvins, and so they, along with their fiddler, Lexington native Robert Paige Hepler (July 20, 1922–April 25, 1983), joined Thompson's band in Danville.

But every show's success has its limits. By early 1952, bookings had fallen off, as had the audience for the Barn Dance. Jim Eanes was hosting a competing Saturday barn dance over at WBTM. Glenn felt it was time for a change (*Danville Register*, 9).

As luck would have it, Thompson had a standing offer to be sponsored by Service Distributing Corporation. The owner of the service station where Glenn had first worked when leaving the farm had built three stations into the chain. Glenn disbanded his group and headed back to North Carolina. He became a kind of goodwill ambassador for the gas stations, appearing over local radio stations from Fayetteville to Winston-Salem to Charlotte, with his airtime purchased by his benefactor.

As Glenn Thompson told me, television brought an end to his live performing. As the tube captured more and more of America's attention, Glenn's appearances got fewer and fewer. In the late 1950s, he worked dances at Lexington's Cow Palace on Saturday nights. He ran a barn dance for half of the 1960s in Burlington, and spent the first part of the 1970s working with Homer "Briarhopper" Drye on television and at his club in Raleigh. His days on stage were over.

ELEVEN

Bluegrass

"True banjo picking is not how much you put in it; it's the perfection that you put in there, what you know and what you can do with it. That's what makes a musician, the way he expresses a note, the way he gets on it or off it. I always tell people to learn the melody, then, if they want to go off into left field or right field, all right."

— L.W. Lambert

In the aftermath of World War II, the music of Piedmont North Carolina, along with Southern music in general, was undergoing another transformation. Mainstream country music, powered by WSM-Nashville, the Singing Cowboys of Hollywood, and the swing dance music of the Southwest, was becoming more singer and song centric. In the postwar 1940s, performers such as Hank Williams, Lefty Frizzell, and Ernest Tubb had replaced the ensembles of earlier times. During the same period, Bill Monroe and others of his ilk took the old fiddle and banjo string band, added a touch of blues and swing, raised the keys for singing, and kicked up the tempo into overdrive.

North Carolina has a reputation for being (next to Kentucky) *the* state for bluegrass music. Earl Scruggs, Jim Shumate, Curley Seckler, George and John Shuffler, Allen Shelton — the list goes on and on of those from the old North State that have had an impact on bluegrass history. Lester Flatt worked the Piedmont during the years of World War II. Bill and Charlie Monroe established their careers in North Carolina, and the radio stations featuring the Monroe Brothers, such as WPTF-Raleigh, WSJS-Winston-Salem, WBT-Charlotte, and WPAQ-Mount Airy, became major bluegrass broadcasters (See Chapter 9).

Along with full-timers like the Monroes, there were many musicians from the state who chose to stay at home and play on a semi-professional basis. These bands kept high-quality bluegrass in front of area audiences and provided a training ground for some of the best in the current generation of pickers and singers. One of these was banjoist L. W. Lambert.

L. W. Lambert, as he looked while working WPAQ Radio in Mount Airy, Surry County, April 1956. Courtesy L. W. Lambert.

Luin Wilford Lambert, Jr., was born on April 18, 1926, in the Wilkes County community of Summers, his mother's hometown, the oldest child and only son of L. W. Sr. (October 21, 1902–October 20, 1994) and Grace Luella Gregory Lambert (September 13, 1904–January 15, 1985). His father was from New Hope, North Carolina. "The first part of my childhood there was music all around me," recalls L. W.,

> because mother picked the banjo [in] what you call a "steady clawhammer" [in a down and up motion]. It was a beautiful rhythm. [She played] "Old Jimmy Sutton," she played a lot of the older tunes. She could read music, the shape notes. Her uncle, Andrew Gregory, taught singing schools in Wilkes County back in those days and she went with him all the time. Her daddy, William Gregory, picked a little, but I never did hear that. She never did play out, just for our entertainment. One of her sisters could pick a guitar; her name was Lena [born 1924], the baby sister. [My father] played the banjo, but he played it a different style, with two fingers [thumb and first finger], "Lonesome Road Blues" and "Old Joe Clark" and stuff like that. Some of his brothers tried to play a little bit, I never did know how good they were. He played the guitar and he could play the fiddle a little bit and the autoharp and the mandolin, about all of it.
>
> From the time I can remember, Dad kept a bunch of instruments layin' around house and they consisted of mostly an old beat-up guitar, an old five-string banjo that he made — he took bailin' wire to make the frets, and he killed an old cat and tanned the hide — an old autoharp and an old tater bug mandolin. Me and my sister [LaVaughn, born March 24, 1928] had access to those things. I learned to play a little on all of 'em and she did, too, right behind me. They never did force us.
>
> The neighbors would come in on Saturday night from the time I was ten year old just to listen to the family playin'. They'd be two or three other ones that could

play would come in and we'd set by lamplight and pick and sing all night long, especially in the wintertime. And I wouldn't take nothin' for that raisin'.

This routine eventually led to the formation of a family band. Their name was taken from a banjo case L. W.'s father had swapped for back in the 1930s:

> In '38, he traded an old saddle and a pistol for another banjo. And it was a good banjo. When LaVaughn and myself was nine and ten year old, he'd start going out playin' for chicken stews and for ice cream suppers and any kind of gathering like that. And we got a lot of exposure in a ten-mile radius. We'd play at tobacco barns where you'd have to set up with the tobacco and cure it. He picked the banjo and I picked the guitar and she played the mandolin. Thirty-eight was the first year the family band went up there to Union Grove and we called ourselves the Carolina Neighbors. There was a neighbor that played with us a lot, I had a cousin that picked the guitar with us by the name of Ed Lambert and I also had a second cousin by the name of Ella Ladd that was a good singer and she played the guitar. We'd been practicing and, of course, we was scared to death, us kids was.
>
> Panhandle Pete boarded with my aunt. He was playing at WAIR in Winston-Salem at that time. Cliff Carlisle and maybe Bill [Carlisle], too, was stayin' there. They were playin' and a bookin' schoolhouses out of WAIR. And they had with 'em Claude Boone and Pete — Howard Nash was his right name. And a weekend that they wasn't a-playin' somewhere, they would ride with my aunt Gertrude and my uncle Arville and stay two or three days up here. And we'd pick and sing the whole weekend. We learned a lot of songs from them. I was eleven year old and my sister was nine and they wanted dad to let them take us two kids back down there and put us on the radio. Today, you might a done that, but dad just couldn't think about lettin' us get away from home that young.
>
> Then, after we grew up and started dating, my sister and myself, we kindly got disinterested [in music] and there was a slack period for me.

After leaving school at the age of fifteen, L. W. worked various jobs. These included working at a glass factory in Statesville and for the state of North Carolina. In his late teens, after this period of musical inactivity, Lambert grew fascinated by the playing of Earl Scruggs, and returned to the banjo. "To me, Earl, even though he ain't but two year older than I am, he was THE influence on my banjo style." As L. W. tells it:

> I was playin' with two fingers, mostly [like his father]. [And] I could hear Snuffy Jenkins [on the radio]. The first that I changed over was in middle or the late '40's, and I heard Earl Scruggs off of the Hickory radio station [probably WHKY]. I sit down and wrote him a letter and drawed a picture and ask him to show me the style roll he was using. He never did answer my letter. And when I started rollin' it, I was rollin' it backwards from his style. And I rolled it like that through the late '40s on up till about 1950, I guess, until I got a chance to go see Earl. And it took me a long while to turn that roll around. But it was an advantage in later years because I could go back to either one of 'em I wanted.

While refining his banjo style, L. W. was also trying to upgrade his instrument. After going through several banjos, Lambert graduated to a Gibson RB-100 made in 1948.

I couldn't get the sound [I wanted]. I knew there was a [Gibson] Mastertone out there that I wanted somewhere, but I didn't have the money to get it. So I tried pie pans, I tried everything in the world in it to get that thing to sound like a Mastertone. And I finally come up on a circular saw that I took and had the teeth ground off and attached it to that rod at the back and it sound like a Mastertone! It would ring and it'd have a good ring to it. And finally I found a tone ring and put it in the thing. But everybody thought it was a Mastertone from listenin' to it.

With his interest in the banjo renewed, L. W. reformed the Carolina Neighbors with himself on the five-string. "After I got married" [in January of 1947], Lambert recollects:

everything kindly slowed down and changed for about a year or two. And then we went back and Dad wanted to quit and I took over the banjo; he didn't want to get out anymore. So we organized a little group and still went under the Carolina Neighbors and it consisted of myself on banjo, Harold Tomlin, my brother-in-law on mandolin, my sister LaVaughn Tomlin on guitar, and Zeb Speece on guitar. I believe that LaVaughn might have switched over on the bass. That was in '52.

The late Pee Wee Yokeley (ca. 1925–1960) from Winston-Salem joined on the fiddle and the band began to branch out from community playing and into schoolhouses and fiddlers' conventions throughout the area, including those at Union

Left to right: L. W. Lambert (banjo), Johnny Compton (fiddle), Harold Tomlin (mandolin) and La Vaughn Lambert Tomlin (guitar), known as the Carolina Neighbors. Courtesy L. W. Lambert.

Grove, North Carolina, and Galax, Virginia. They also began doing radio work, their first on-air job being Saturdays with WKBC in North Wilkesboro. The Stanley Brothers had been playing on WKBC and possibly former Stanley Bros bassist Ralph Pennington, who replaced Zeb Speece in the Neighbors, brought them to the station's attention. L. W.'s group also joined the cast of Dwight Barker's "barn dance" show (See Chapter 9). "Dwight Barker started a jamboree in Statesville," tells Lambert. "He first started at the radio station, then moved to Mulberry School [and later to the Playhouse Theater] around the summer of '50 or '51. While playing there, I met Jim Shumate. Jim played there a lot and he'd just come off the road with Bill Monroe not long before that."

Other pickers at the jamboree included Jason Lambert, Gar Bowers, Jack and Dwight Barker, and L. W.'s two brothers-in-law, Johnny Compton and Hoyt Herbert. According to L. W., "We was packing that little auditorium." During the time of the Statesville jamboree, the group was continuing to play on WKBC. The Neighbors also cut a 78-rpm record for the Blue Ridge label. Sister LaVaughn and Zeb Speece left the band around 1955, and were replaced by Curly Kilby on guitar and Ralph Pennington on bass. Shortly after that change of personnel, L. W. moved to WPAQ in Mount Airy. The band at this time consisted of L. W., Harold Tomlin on mandolin, Curly Kilby on guitar, Cub McGee on fiddle, and Elmer Bowers on bass. This group would soon split up following the death of Kilby at the age of 24.

Not long after Curly Kilby's passing, Lambert began playing with Johnny Compton at Mount Airy. Charlie Monroe also happened to be playing there and offered the two a job:

> In '55 ... Johnny Compton ... had just married my sister. Heck of a good guitar picker, he could pick a banjo, he was a heck of a mandolin player, fiddle player, high tenor singer and all. He wanted a job with Charlie Monroe. At that time, Charlie had moved into Mount Airy, to WPAQ, and was bookin' shows out of WPAQ. [Johnny] said, "Would you take a job with him pickin' the banjo?" I said, "No, I can't. I've just put a crop in." He said, "Ride with me over there, take the banjo and I'm gonna audition with him." So we rode over that mornin' and went to the hotel where Charlie and his wife was stayin' and went in. Charlie said, "Well, go get your instruments and I'll audition both of you right here in the hotel room." So we went and got 'em. And he didn't need the other instruments, but he needed a banjo picker. And he says, "I'll give you a job if you want." And I said, "Well, I can't take it." He said, "Well, I'll hire him on one of the other instruments if you will go." And I said, "I can't do it, but I will help you play a few shows if you need a fill-in." So I did some shows with Charlie, but, in the meantime, I had another brother-in-law, Hoyt Herbert. He married my other twin sister [Jurrell]. And he was workin' for Vance McClain as a mechanic down there. And I told Charlie, "I can't go with you, but I'll tell you what I'll do. I'll call my other brother-in-law and see if he wants to go." And he said, "Okay." So, [Johnny and Hoyt] they went to work for him and they worked while he was in Mount Airy and they went on to Winston, moved down there to WSJS, I think.

Along about that same time, Lambert met the Murphy Brothers, who would greatly affect his musical career. The Murphys had first organized their band, The Blue River Boys, in the 1940s. As the members were drafted into the Army in World

War II, the original group ended. The band got back together with L. W. on the banjo, and stayed together for about six years. This ensemble can be heard (with Joe Medford playing the banjo) on the Cattle Records LP, *Early Bluegrass Recordings of the Murphy Brothers and the Original Blue River Boys*. As L. W. remembers: "I had met some of the Murphy Brothers in '54, maybe before that. I met Fred and played some with him. Dewey and John was still in the service. One of them got out in '55, I think it was and we started doing some picking and sort of reorganized the [Blue River Boys] group."

Around the same time as he joined the Blue River Boys, Lambert also quit farming. "In '55," he remembers, "I seen I couldn't make it on the farm because the government wouldn't give me enough tobacco allotment." So in 1956 L. W. went into the tire recapping business in Statesville and stayed with that profession until 1964. At the beginning of this reformation by the Blue River Boys, Fred Murphy played with the group. However, Fred soon dropped out to join the ministry. By the time he left, both Dewey and John had returned from the service and had begun playing with Lambert on WPAQ. The line-up then had L. W. on the banjo, his brother-in-law Harold Tomlin on guitar, Pee Wee Yokeley on fiddle, Dewey Murphy on mandolin, and John Murphy on bass. After the Murphy Bros quit Mount Airy, the Blue River Boys gained the sponsorship of the local Farmer's Federation, representing the group through tours around the mountains north and west of Mount Airy. The departure of Dewey Murphy, who also joined the ministry, and the death of Pee Wee Yokeley at the age of 34, finally caused the band's disintegration around 1960.

The Blue River Boys on stage. Left to right are John Murphy on string bass, his brother Dewey Murphy on mandolin, Pee Wee Yokeley on fiddle, Harold Tomlin on guitar and L. W. Lambert on banjo. Location unknown. Circa 1956. Courtesy L. W. Lambert.

As L. W. became more involved in the tire business, his playing time was cut to a minimum. Lambert recollects:

> Through '60 or '61 I kept the name Blue River Boys. I tried to keep the name and the band alive by playing conventions. I started playing with a cousin of mine, Herb Lambert, and John Shuffler [bass, who worked with Lambert after leaving the Stanley Brothers] and some fellows in the Valdese area and a girl by the name of Betty Barrier [guitar] and her husband, Johnny [dobro]. But I done a lot of freelancing with first one group and [then] another.

L. W. played banjo with area musicians, including mandolinist Dewey Farmer (born August 6, 1942) and fiddler Tommy (Red) Malboeuf, and with Benny Martin and Don Reno when they worked in western North Carolina. Bill Monroe even offered him a job in 1961, but, Lambert says, "I had to turn that down 'cause I had too much at stake here."

In 1962, Lambert met Carroll Haire (guitar) and his brother Rector (bass), and they began playing on WKBC. Other members of the group during this period included Compton once again on mandolin, Otis Campbell on fiddle, and Harvey Baity on bass. "In the latter part of '63 and '64," L. W. says, "I did a television show in High Point [on WGHP] with a country musician by the name of Carl Davis and we had bluegrass in the morning show. Jim Shumate and myself carried the bluegrass end of the show for that year. Also, while we was doing that, I was still playing [at WKBC]."

By the mid–1960s, involved in a music store of his own, L. W. was encountering a number of musicians. One was to become a key member of the contemporary Blue River Boys. "Ray Cline was one of them and he'd been playing some country and rock and roll," Lambert says. In 1967, Cline, Willard Nestin, Darrell Barnhart, and G. H. Goforth joined L. W. to form a band. John Sipe, later of the Roustabouts in Charlotte, often helped them on fiddle, but this was still pretty much of a pickup group.

"In the latter part of '68," L. W. says, "I joined a group we called the Border Mountain Boys. It consisted of myself, Tommy Malboeuf, Cullen Galyean, Buck Arrington, Jim Holder and Winford Hunt [who replaced Galyean]. In the spring of '69 we went to Cherokee, North Carolina and played there the whole year. Then we played some in Virginia in the winter of '69 then went back to Cherokee in the summer of '70." This group also cut an album on the Homestead label just before illness forced Lambert to quit music for a while. As L. W. recollects:

> I didn't do too much picking in '70. Then in '71, Herb Lambert called me and he was playing with some boys and they didn't have a banjo picker and they wanted me to come and go as the Blue River Boys and see if we couldn't get out and play regular. In 1972, I told my wife, "I'm out of the music store now, and both of my daughters are married and I want to do what I want to do for a while. And I'm goin' to organize a group." So I decided that I would organize my own group back under the name of the Blue River Boys and go with that for a while.
>
> So I decided the first thing I'd do is hit fiddlers' conventions the first year. I hit 34 fiddlers' conventions one year and that was from as far north as I could find 'em,

Left to right: L. W. Lambert (banjo), "Buck" Arrington (electric bass), Jim Holder (mandolin), Cullen Gaylean (guitar) and Tommy Malboeuf (fiddle), when performing as the Border Mountain Boys. Location unknown. 1969. Courtesy L. W. Lambert.

> plum as far as Memphis, to Florida and everywhere. We played 34 fiddlers' conventions and out of the fiddlers' conventions alone we won $15,800 and some dollars.... We won 31 of the conventions that first year. The other three, we won either second or third. And we always took an average of three to four of the first instrument prizes on ever one of 'em. And that's what boosted us up in the money so. And that created a audience of ours, because a lot of 'em that was gonna go to the fiddlers' conventions would go to the festivals. So that brought us into the festivals more or less. We done that for about fifteen years … we played all over the country.

The rejuvenated Blue River Boys had Herb Lambert on mandolin, Ray Cline on lead guitar, Tommy Malboeuf on fiddle, Joe Greene on bass, and Elbert Arrington on guitar. Danny Campbell and Harold Murphy soon replaced Greene and Arrington, respectively, and, after two years, Malboeuf gave way to Terry Baucom on the fiddle. Tim Smith later replaced Baucom.

On May 17, 1980, L. W. Lambert and the Blue River Boys appeared at Lincoln Center in New York City on the same bill with Emmylou Harris, Norman Blake, and the Whites. Robert Palmer wrote in the *New York Times*, "To these ears the portion of the show devoted to L. W. Lambert and the Blue River Boys was the best. Mr. Lambert and his band worked together superbly as a unit, their instrumental solos were inspired and inventive … they played the finest bluegrass this listener has ever heard on a New York stage." The 1980 version of the band included Herb Green as lead vocalist and rhythm guitarist (who had replaced Harold Murphy); Herb Lambert on mandolin; Ray Cline on guitar; Danny Campbell on bass; and (who had replaced Tim Smith) Roger Ledford on fiddle. With Robin Warren as their final fiddler, the Blue River Boys eventually disbanded around 1985.

Today, L. W. lives on 160-acre farm in the western Piedmont. The father of two daughters, Phyllis and Melissa (the later named for Bill Monroe's offspring), with four grandchildren and three great-grandchildren, Lambert raises cattle, rebuilds antique Ford tractors, and still plays occasional music. "I don't think anybody ever learns it all," he says.

> As you grow older, you get more settled in your style, you get more confidence in what you can and can't do, but every time I pick up the banjo I can learn something new if I really try.
>
> I never have played full-time with any professional band — I never did want to. I have helped a lot of different musicians down through the years. I've filled in for a lot of them: Mac Wiseman [who offered L.W. a job back in the 1950s], Jim & Jesse, Charlie Monroe, Benny Martin, Don Reno and even Bill Anderson when he's come in here as just a two-man act.
>
> What I've found over the years, that if you'll stick straight to Scruggs or Monroe or Stanleys, you're gonna sell that audience twicet of what you can the Seldom Scene or somethin' like that. Now, the Seldom Scene has their own following. But the audience, I mean your average listener, can relate to Monroe or Flatt and Scruggs a lot better ... and especially when you go into the progressive type picking. And I did a little of that on one album one time and that's as far as I want to take it because I didn't want to get away from my roots of what I loved. And I've always found this, that you could go out here to an audience and play a good, straight five-string banjo and play the melody of that tune and you will get a lot bigger response than you will if you're playin' a lot of progressive stuff in it.... I've always said this, the most of 'em that plays real progressive and all that are playin' to other musicians.

APPENDIX

"Mountain Folk Music Is Being Recorded Here: Talent from Three States Recording at Studio in Old West End School Building"

That mountain ballad the old-fashioned gospel songs sung at the arbor camp meeting accompanied by the portable organ that is often carried many long and weary miles, the self-styled country fiddler, ye old-time musicians who made merry for the corn shuckin' and chicken stews at the tobacco barns, have their places in American music, is the opinion of the Okeh Record Company. This statement was made by a representative of the company who states that one desires records of music of this type, as dear to those living in the mountains or the rural districts, as the grand opera, jazz, popular or other types of music are to those living in the city or towns. He stated, too, that many persons living in the city find interest in this type of music peculiar to the mountain sections and are beginning to study its origin and background. The studio is in the Old West End school building.

Realizing the need for preserving this type of music the company has sent its rep-resentatives into the hills of North Carolina, Virginia, Tennessee and Kentucky to search for persons who could best sing or play the mountain music. Several groups were first taken to New York City for recordings and then the firm decided to secure the best possible recording equipment and send it to Winston-Salem to record a large number of groupings. Winston-Salem was selected for the studio because of its accessibility to talent of the three states. The outfit is now working on the records and will be in Winston-Salem for at least another week.

Tuesday morning the Neal Sisters, Ruth and Wanda, of Old Fort, sang a number of duets, accompanied by Jewel Davis, Burt Layne and Mack Williams of Chattanooga, Tenn., who played two violins and a guitar. Monday morning records were made of selections for the Aiken County String Band from Graniteville, S.C., and in the afternoon records were made by the Valdese Quartet of Valdese, N.C.

Article reprinted with permission of the *Winston-Salem Journal*.

The personnel in charge of the recording here consists of T. G. Rockwell, director of recording; Peter Decker, recording engineer; A. T. Taylor, electrical expert; P. C. Brockman, secretary and director of sales of James K. Polk, Inc., Atlanta, Ga., Richmond, Va. and Dallas, Texas, Southern distributors of Okeh records; Charles J. Rey, district sales manager in charge of Richmond office.

Bibliography

Books

Conway, Cecelia. *African Banjo Echoes in Appalachia*. Knoxville: The University of Tennessee Press, 1995.

Crews, C. Daniel. *Villages of the Lord: The Moravians Come to Carolina*. Winston-Salem: Moravian Archives, 1995.

Denny, Zeb R. *Farmer Yesterday and Today*. Welcome, NC: Wooten Publishing Company, 1981.

Epstein, Dena J. *Sinful Tunes and Spirituals*. Urbana: University of Illinois Press, 1977.

Escott, Colin. *Hank Williams: The Biography*. Boston: Little, Brown and Company, 1994.

Federal Writers Project. *Slave Narratives: Volume 14, Part 2*. St. Clair Shores, MI: Scholarly Press, 1941 and 1976.

Floyd, Tommy. Songbook #2. 1951.

Fowler, Gene, and Bill Crawford. *Border Radio*. Austin: Texas Monthly Press, 1987.

Gillespie, Gail, and Wayne Martin. *Raleigh Fiddlers' Convention*. Raleigh, NC: Pinecone, 1990.

Greene, Victor. *A Passion for Polka: Old-Time Ethnic Music in America*. Berkeley: University of California Press, 1992.

Hendley, Fisher. Untitled. Undated. Courtesy of the Folklife Section, North Carolina Arts Council.

Hinson, Marie L. *Marriage Records of Davidson County, North Carolina, Volume III*. Lexington: Genealogical Society of Davidson County, 1994 and 1995.

Iredell County Landmarks. Statesville: Iredell County American Revolution Bicentennial Commission, 1976, 1982.

Johnson, Guion Griffis. *Ante-Bellum North Carolina*. Chapel Hill: University of North Carolina Press, 1937.

Jones, Loyal. *Minstrel of the Appalachians: The Story of Bascom Lamar Lunsford;* Boone, NC: Appalachian Consortium Press, 1984.

Keever, Homer M. *Iredell: Piedmont County*. Statesville, NC: Iredell County Bicentennial Commission, 1976.

Knouse, Dr. Nola Reed, and C. Daniel Crews. *Moravian Music: An Introduction*. Winston-Salem, NC: Moravian Music Foundation, 1979.

Kreitner, Kenneth. *Discoursing Sweet Music*. Urbana: University of Illinois Press, 1990.

Local History from the Lexington Dispatch 1905–1907. Letter from J. L. Clemmons, Louisville, Kentucky, November 8, 1905.

Meade, Guthrie T., Jr, et al. *Country Music Sources: A Biblio-Discography of Commercially Recorded Traditional Music*. Chapel Hill: University of North Carolina Press, 2002.

Michaux, R. R. *Sketches of Life in North Carolina*. Culler: W.C. Phillips, 1894.

Neese, J. Everette. *The Dutch Settlement on Abbotts Creek: A History of Pilgrim Reformed United Church of Christ Lexington, North Carolina ca. 1753 to 1979*. Winston-Salem: Hunter Publishing, 1979.

Newton, Grace Murray, as a part of Elinor Samons Eulis. *Alamance County: The Legacy of Its People and Places*, 1984.

Randolph County Historical Society and the Randolph Arts Guild. *Randolph County 1779–1979*. Ed. Charlesanna L. Fox, Carolyn N. Hager and Dwight M. Holland. Asheboro: Winston-Salem, NC: Hunter Publishing, 1980.

Rorrer, Kinney. *Rambling Blues: The Life and Songs of Charlie Poole*. London: Old Time Music, 1982.

Rosenberg, Neil V. *Bluegrass*. Urbana: University of Illinois Press, 1985.

Smith, Richard. *Can't You Hear Me Callin': The Life of Bill Monroe, Father of Bluegrass*. New York: Da Capo Press, 2000.

Thayer, Stuart. *Annals of the American Circus*. Seattle, WA: Dauven & Thayer, 2000.

Tyson, Bryan. *The Institution of Slavery in the Southern States, Religiously and Morally Considered in Connection with Our Sectional Troubles*. Washington, DC: H. Polkinhorn, 1863.

Wiley, Calvin Henderson. *Alamance: Or, the Great and Final Experiment*. New York: Harper & Brothers, 1847. Electronic edition. Available online: http://docsouth.unc.edu/nc/wiley/wiley.html.

Wishon, Helen S. *Marriages of Yadkin County NC 1867–1901*. Self-published, 1998.

Wolfe, Charles. *A Good-Natured Riot*. Nashville: The Country Music Foundation Press and Vanderbilt University Press, 1999.

York, Brantley. *Autobiography*. Durham: Seeman Printery, 1910.

Articles, Dissertations, Papers

Ahrens, Pat J. "Crazy Water Crystals and Its Union With Pioneer String Band Performers," *Bluegrass Unlimited*, August 2001: 56–60.

Ahrens-Striblin, Pat J. "The Aristocratic Pigs: An Early Carolina String Band," *Old Time Country*, Winter 1990: 8.

Bastin, Bruce. "The Devil's Goin' to Get You." *North Carolina Folklore* 21, November 1973: 190.

Brewer, James Howard. "Legislation Designed to Control Slavery in Wilmington and Fayetteville." *North Carolina Historical Review* 30, April 1953: 160.

Cahan, Andy. "Manly Reece and the Birth of North Carolina Banjo." *North Carolina Banjo Collection*. Excerpted from "Adam Manly Reece: An Early Banjo Player of Grayson County, Virginia," University of North Carolina-Chapel Hill, 1987.

Carter, Tom. "Virgil Craven." Paper, University of North Carolina-Chapel Hill, March 1973.

Conway, Cecelia, and Tommy Thompson. "Talking Banjo," *Southern Exposure* Vol. II, No 1: 63-64.

Coulter, Della, and John Rumble. "The Piedmont Tradition" and "Charlotte Country: A Sixty-Year Tradition," in *The Charlotte Country Music Story*. Charlotte: NCAC Spirit Square Arts Center, 1985.

Craver, Mrs. Kathleen M. "A Social Center: The Old Country School," *Historical Gleanings* 1977: 125–6.

Crazy Barn Dance and Crazy Bands. Charlotte: WBT, ca. 1934. Courtesy Rachel Wiles.

Davis, Amy Noel. *"When You Coming Back?": The Local Country Music Opry Community*. Thesis, University of North Carolina-Chapel Hill, 1998.

Erbsen, Wayne. "Wiley & Zeke: The Morris Brothers," *Bluegrass Unlimited*, August 1980: 40+.

Ewing, Tom. "Mac Wiseman: Giving Something Back," *Bluegrass Unlimited*, April 1998: 4.

Godbey, Marty. "The Artistry and Accomplishments of Earl Scruggs," *Bluegrass Unlimited*, August 1996: 56–67.

Green, Archie. "Hillbilly Music: Source and Symbol," *Journal of American Folklore*, Vol. 78, No. 309, July-September 1965: 212–214.

Greene, Clarence H. "Mack Crow and Clay Everhart: Early Carolina Banjo Pickers," *Bluegrass Unlimited*, March 1986: 62–64.

Greene, Hugh. "The Michael String Band," *Homespun*, Vol. 9, No. 1, Spring 1982: 8, 37.

Grundy, Pamela. "'We Always Tried to Be Good People': Respectability, Crazy Water Crystals, and Hillbilly Music on the Air, 1933–1935," *The Journal of American History* March 1995: 1591–1620.

Hicks, Bill. "1970 [Union Grove] Fiddlers

Convention," *The north carolinANVIL*, Vol. 3, No. 149, April 4, 1970. Available online: http://members.tripod.com/~redclay ramblers/fmsb3.htm.

Hudson, Arthur Palmer. "Festival Review," *Southern Folklore Quarterly*, August 1948.

Kirkman, Will G. *The O.R.I. Band and Orchestra Journal*, Vol. 1, No. 1, August 1895.

Lornell, Christopher "Kip." "Banjos and Blues," in *Arts in Earnest*, ed. Daniel Patterson. Durham: Duke University Press, 1990.

Lornell, Christopher "Kip." "Pre-Blues Banjo and Fiddle," *Living Blues*, Autumn, 1974: 25–27.

Lornell, Christopher "Kip." *A Study of the Sociological Reasons Why Blacks Sing Blues: An Examination of the Secular Black Music Found in Two North Carolina Communities*. Thesis, University of North Carolina-Chapel Hill, 1976.

Monroe, Charlie. *Charlie Monroe's Souvenir Songbook*.

Nelson, Donald Lee. "'Walk Right in Belmont': The Wilmer Watts Story," *JEMF Quarterly*, Autumn 1973: 91–96.

Nuggets. Spring 1986. Various articles.

"Old Fiddlers' Contest During Reunion," *Confederate Veteran*, Vol. 24, 1916: 93.

Phillips, Bill. "Hoedown Meets Swing: The Swingbillies and the Tobacco Tags," in *Warren County Folklife Festival*. Henderson, NC: Brodie-Jones Printing: 3–4.

"Playin' the South," *Leader Magazine*, March 17, 1988.

Russell, Tony. "H. M. Barnes' Blue Ridge Ramblers," *Old Time Music*, Vol. 17, 1975: 11.

Russell, Tony. "Step Stones," *Old Time Music*, No. 40, Winter 1984: 11, 14.

Saunders, Walt, "Notes and Queries," *Bluegrass Unlimited*, January 1998: 20.

Shaw, Evelyn. "L. N. Shaw: A Harnett County Fiddler," *The Old-Time Herald*, Vol. 5, No. 2, Winter 1995-1996: 15.

Spottswood, Dick. "Happy Birthday, Wade!" *Bluegrass Unlimited*, June 1997: 53–55.

Thompson, Roy. "Beginnings." *75th Anniversary Old Time Fiddlers & Bluegrass Festival*.

Tribe, Ivan. "Charlie Monroe," *Bluegrass Unlimited*, October 1975: 12–19.

Wallace, Wesley. "Development of Broadcasting in North Carolina, 1922–1948."

Dissertation, University of North Carolina-Chapel Hill, 1962. Summary available online: http://www.unc.edu/~bsemonch/radio.html.

WBT.com. "History." Available online: http://www.wbt.com/history/history.cfm.

Wennonah Cotton Mills. Wennonah Story: 100th Anniversary, 1886–1986. Lexington, NC: Wennonah Cotton Mills, 1986.

Wennonah Cotton Mills. Wennonah Story: 75th Anniversary, 1886-1961. Lexington, NC: Wennonah Cotton Mills, 1961.

Whitaker, C. Z. *My Memories.* Self-published, 1946. Courtesy Francis Allred.

Wolfe, Charles, and Tony Russell. "The Asheville Session," *Old Time Music*, #31, Winter 1978/79: 5–12.

Womick, Chip. "Glenn Davis played the banjo and the crowd," *The Bulletin*, April 30, 1998: 1.

Woodside, Jane Xenia Harris. *The Womanless Wedding: An American Folk Drama.* Masters Thesis, University of North Carolina-Chapel Hill, 1987.

Worth, Lynn. "The Denton Dance Story," *The Old-Time Herald*, Vol. 6, No, 4, May-July 1998: 12–14.

Yates, Michael. "Cecil Sharp in America." *Musical Traditions Internet Magazine.* Available online: http://www.mustrad.org.uk/articles/shar_txt.htm.

Ye Olde Tyme Fiddlers' Convention program. 1907. Courtesy Francis Allred.

Birth and Death Certificates, Obituaries and Other Public Records

Davidson County Cemetery Records.

Davis, Marshall. Certificate of Death.

Everhart, Clayton. Designation of Beneficiary, August 26, 1957. Courtesy Ruth Coffey.

Everhart, Clayton. North Carolina Motor Vehicle License, not dated, 1928 and 1929. Courtesy Ruth Coffey.

Everhart, Clayton. Obituary. Courtesy Ruth Coffey.

Everhart, Clayton. Receipt for car payments, February 23, 1933. Courtesy Ruth Coffey.

Everhart, Clayton. Registration certificate, 1917. Courtesy Ruth Coffey.

Everhart, Clayton. Tax receipt, 1912. Courtesy Ruth Coffey.

Everhart, Jack. Parent's or Guardian's Agreement for Minor's Employment. Courtesy Ruth Coffey.

Forsyth County Death Records.

Forsyth County Marriage Records.

Gaither, William. Death Certificate.

Puett, Fate. Obituary. Courtesy Ruth Coffey.

Simmons, Matt. Military discharge papers.

United States Census, 1800-1930.

Wilson, Kathryn. Birth certificate. 1923.

Wilson, Odessa Mae. Birth certificate. 1926.

City Directories

Burlington City Directories.
Greensboro City Directories.
High Point City Directories.
Lenior City Directories.
Lexington City Directories.
Winston-Salem City Directories.

Interviews, Correspondence and Scrapbooks

All interviews conducted by the author unless otherwise noted.

Allen, Bill. Personal Interview. April 29, 1989.

Allred, Francis. Personal Interview. August 18, 1994.

Allred, John "Red." Personal Interview. April 29, 1995.

Arnold, Roy, and Glee Arnold. Personal Interview. February 15, 1991.

Beam, Larry. Personal Interview. January 13, 1991 and February 9, 1991.

Beck, Dave. Personal Interview. February 25, 1991.

Beck, Jeanne. Personal Interview. January 22, 1991.

Berrier, Leonard. Personal Interview. January 8, 1991.

Berrier, Olin. Interviewed by Bette Sowers, circa 1979.

Berrier, Olin, and Bessie Berrier. Interviewed by Donna Michael, circa 1979 and March 16, 1982.

Berrier, Olin, and Leonard Berrier. Interviewed by Paul Brown and Lynn Michael, January 29, 1989.

Boyd, Elgin, and Thelma Boyd. Personal Interview with Kirk Sutphin. May 14, 1994.

Brady, Kermit. Personal Interview with Charles Cheek and Larry Davis. August 22 and 29, 1996.

Brewer, J. Mason, letter to A.P. Hudson, April 2, 1961, Southern Folklife Collection, University of North Carolina-Chapel Hill.

Britt, J. G., Gene Britt, and Jerry Wayne Britt. Personal Interview with Lynn Michael. June 20, 1997.

Bruton, Hoyle. Personal Interview. March 13, 1991.

Bumgarner, Shelia to Bob Carlin. Email. September 11, 1997.

Christenberry, George. Personal Interview. October 3, 1996.

Christenberry, Mrs. Gilbert. Personal Interview with John Wood. September 30, 1996.

Clinard, Cliff. Personal Interview. November 18, 1994.

Coffey, Ruth. Personal Interview. May 27, 1991.

Cooper, Elmer, and Lawrence Cooper. Personal Interview. February 20, 1991.

Cooper, Matthew. Personal Interview. June 17, 1991.

Cranford, Wilburn. Personal Interview. October 6, 1994, and September 16, 2002.

Craven, Virgil. Interviewed by Tom Carter. March 1973.

Dunn, Elmer. Personal Interview. November 14, 1996.

Eubanks, Leonard. Personal Interview. February 20, 1995.

Everhart, Clayton. Personal Interview. July 15, 1991.

Everhart, Clayton. Dixie Furniture Company, letter of recommendation, August 22, 1925, courtesy Ruth Coffey.

Everhart, Clayton. Union Mirror Company, letter of recommendation, August 9, 1955. Courtesy Ruth Coffey.

Floyd, Tommy. Personal Interview. August 7 and September 10, 1997.

Fulp, Preston. Personal Interview. December 8, 1990.

Gillean, Janet. Personal Interview. August 16, 1991.

Greeson, Hubert "Woody." Personal Interview. March 7, 1997.

Hege, Phillip. Personal Interview. February 8, 1991.

Hill, Lawrence. Scrapbook. Courtesy Leroy Hill.

Hill, Leroy. Personal Interview. July 4 and October 2, 1997.

Holden, Elmer. Personal Interview. May 21, 1996.

Jones, Harvey. Interview with Ed Babel. August 10, 1977.

Lamb, Vernon. Personal Interview with John Wood. September 30, 1996.

Lohr, Jack. Personal Interview. June 19, 1991.

Lowe, Sam Jr. Personal Interview. February 15, 1997.

Lunsford, Bascom Lamar. Letter to Dr. Russell Grumman, University of North Carolina-Chapel Hill Extension Director, December 24, 1946. Southern Folklife Collection, University of North Carolina-Chapel Hill.

Maines, Dean. Personal Interview. February 22, 1991.

Mare, Frank. Telephone interview. September 15, 1997.

McAndrew, Peggy. Telephone interview. February 8, 1993, and January 5, 1994.

McCarn, David. Interviewed by Archie Green and Ed Kahn, in Stanley, North Carolina, 1961 and December 1, 1965.

Miller, Polk. Scrapbook. Valentine Museum. Richmond, Virginia.

Moffitt, Everett. Personal Interview. May 6, 1996.

Monroe, Charlie. Interview with Douglas B. Green, Country Music Foundation Oral History Project, September 1, 1972.

Morrison, Floyd. Personal Interview. December 4, 1997.

Oberstein, Eli. Letter to Gurney Thomas.

Olson, Fred. Personal Interview. September 11 and 18 and October 13, 1994.

Orrell, Cleve. Interview by Hugh Greene. September 30, 1974.

Osborne, Bud. Personal Interview. April 26, 1995.

Peace, Gurney. Personal Interview with Gary Lane. July 24, 1997.

Pegram, Dorothy. Personal Interview. November 29, 1994, and August 26, 1995.

Porter, Lester. Personal Interview. June 5, 1997.

Prevette, Andy. Personal Interview. February 7, 1991.

Prevette, John. Personal Interview. February 8, 1991.

Reid, Hilda. Personal Interview. May 16, 1991.

Reitzel, Joe. Personal Interview. March 5, 1997.

Robertson, Bob. Personal Interview with Alice Gerrard. April 24, 1989.

Satherley, Art. Ledgers. Southern Folklife Collection, University of North Carolina-Chapel Hill.

Saunders, Howard. Interviewed by Mac Whatley.

Scott, Tommy. Personal Interview. October 16, 1996.

Scotten, Wil. Personal Interview. March 6, 1991.

Smith, Amos and Ron Smith. Personal Interview. September 23, 1994.

Smith, Micki. Personal Interview. January 10, 1991.

Sutton, Kathryn. Personal Interview. August 5, 1997.

Thomas, Gurney. Personal Interview. September 25 and November 14, 1997, and September 16, 2002.

Thompson, Glenn. Interview with Steve Weiss and Amy Davis. May 16, 2001.

Thompson, Glenn. Personal Interview with Alice Gerrard and Wayne Martin. April 24 and 25, 1989.

Thornburg, Grace. Personal Interview. February 20, 1991.

Tussey, Holland. Personal Interview. March 6, 1991.

Tussey, John III. Interviewed by Glenn Tussey.

Walker, Mark, and Oberia Walker. Personal Interview. June 18, 1991.

Walker, Ray. Personal Interview. March 14, 1991.

Walker, Tommy, and Tommy Parker. Personal Interview. June 13, 1991.

White House Correspondents' Association to Al Hopkins. Undated. Courtesy Dot Moss.

Wilson, Frank. Letters to Edna Wilson.
Wilson, Totten. Marriage certificate.
Wilson vs. Wilson. Divorce decree.
Winslow, Worth. Personal Interview. June 17, 1991, and August 5, 1992.
Wolfe, Charles to Bob Carlin. Email. October 7, 1997.
Workman, R. Bryce. Letter to Steve Green, May 11, 1994. Southern Folklife Collection, University of North Carolina-Chapel Hill.

Newspapers

Alamance Gleaner. January 30, 1908.
Ansonian. February 11, 1908–February 25, 1908.
Argus. February 6, 1908–February 10, 1908.
Asheboro Courier-Tribune. January 9, 1908–March 1, 1976.
Burlington Daily Times-News. July 12, 1969.
Carolina Watchman. October 11, 1849–December 25, 1907.
Charlotte News. December 19, 1907–January 9, 1908.
Charlotte Observer. December 18, 1907–January 19, 1908.
Concord Times. January 6, 1908.
Cooleemee Journal. March 21, 1923.
Danville Register. May 7, 1949–February 23, 1952.
Davidson County News. July 1, 1897.
Davie Record. April 2, 1913–September 17, 1930.
Democrat. November 14, 1946.
Durham Morning Herald. March 21, 1948–April 10, 1988.
Erwin Chatter. October 1946.
Fayetteville Observer. August 25, 1841–September 1, 1841.
Gastonia Gazette. October 21, 1962.
Greensboro Daily News May 23, 1948–November 1979.
Greensboro Patriot. November 27, 1907–March 4, 1908.
Greensboro News and Record. December 11, 1907–July 30, 2002.
Henderson Daily Dispatch. September 26, 1990.
High Point Enterprise. June 24, 1887–June 23, 1985.
Lexington Dispatch. October 22, 1891–April 28, 1909.

Lexington North State. February 12, 1908.
Louisville Courier-Journal. November 9, 1939–November 15, 1939.
Mt Airy News. November 21, 1907–December 15, 1908.
North Carolinian. February 20, 1908.
Raleigh News and Observer. September 5, 1905–April 4, 1953.
Raleigh Register. February 10, 1815–July 19, 1822.
Raleigh Register, NC Gazette. August 20, 1841–November 1, 1848.
Raleigh Times. September 24, 1897.
Randolph Tribune. December 3, 1931–May 20, 1937.
Roanoke World News. September 1938–February 1939.
Salisbury Post. December 3, 1907–June 12, 2001.
Sanford Express. March 6, 1908–March 20, 1909.
Siler City Sylvanian.
Stanly Enterprise. February 28, 1907–February 27, 1908.
Statesville Landmark. December 20, 1907–April 13, 1909.
Tarborough Southerner. February 13, 1908–February, 20, 1908.
Twin City Sentinel. November 18, 1907–January 21, 1967.
Union Republican. November 14, 1907–May 28, 1908.
Webster's Weekly. January 16, 1908.
Western Carolinian. October 19, 1821.
Western Democrat, NC Whig. April 12, 1857.
Western Sentinel. November 1, 1907–August 28, 1925.
Winston-Salem Journal. May 10, 1904–April 10, 1966.
Yadkin Ripple. March 9, 1908.

Recordings, Liner Notes and Films

Bascom Lamar Lunsford: Ballads, Banjo Tunes, and Sacred Songs of Western North Carolina. Liner notes by Loyal Jones. Washington, D.C.: Smithsonian Folkways Recordings, 1996.
"The Blue Sky Boys on Farm and Fun Time."

Farm & Fun Time Favorites: Volume Two, Liner notes by Bill Bolick. Roanoke, VA: Copper Creek Records, 1994.

Brunswick Recording Logs. Southern Folklife Collection, University of North Carolina-Chapel Hill.

Charlie Monroe on the Noonday Jamboree—1944. Liner notes by David Freeman. Floyd, VA: County Records, 1974.

Conway, Cecelia and Cheyney Hales. Documentary of Dink Roberts, 1975.

Have You Forgotten? The Bailey Brothers. Lines notes by Rounder Collective, Gary Henderson and Walt Saunders. Cambridge, MA: Rounder Records.

The Hillbillies. Liner notes by Joe Wilson. Floyd, VA: County Records. 1973.

Music from South Turkey Creek. Liner notes by Loyal Jones. Cambridge, MA: Rounder Records, 1976.

Orange County Special. Liner notes by Bruce Bastin. Bexhill-on-Sea: Flyright Records, ca. 1972–1973.

The Red Fox Chasers. Liner notes by Richard Nevins. Floyd, VA: County Records, 1967.

Roy Hall and His Blue Ridge Entertainers. Liner notes by Ivan Tribe. Floyd, VA: County Records.

The Songs of Charlie Monroe and the Kentucky Pardners. Liner notes by Bill Vernon. Floyd, VA: County Records, 1974.

Songs of the Tobacco Tags. Southern Folklife Collection, University of North Carolina-Chapel Hill. Circa 1942.

The 37th Old Time Fiddler's Convention at Union Grove North Carolina. Liner notes by Mike Seeger. Washington, DC: Smithsonian Folkways Records, 1962.

Wiley, Zeke and Homer Wiley. Cambridge, MA: Rounder Records, 1973.

Willie Trice: Blue and Rag'd. Liner notes by Bruce Bastin. New York: Trix Records, 1973.

WPAQ: The Voice of the Blue Ridge Mountains. Cambridge, MA: Rounder Records, 1999.

Websites

Hillbilly-Music.com. Home of Old-Time Country Music. http://www.hillbilly-music.com.

wbt.com. News, Talk, Radio. http://www.wbt.com.

Index

Numbers in *italics* indicate photographs.